Tom and Gayen Wharton
Photography by Tom Till

COMPASS AMERICAN GUIDES
An imprint of Fodor's Travel Publications

Compass American Guides: Utah

Editors: Janet Lowe, Kristin Moehlmann Designer: Siobhan O'Hare
Compass Editorial Director: Paul Eisenberg Compass Creative Director: Fabrizio La Rocca
Compass Senior Editor: Kristin Moehlmann Production Editor: Linda K. Schmidt
Photo Editor and Archival Researcher: Melanie Marin
Map Design: Mark Stroud, Moon Street Cartography

Cover photo: Colorado River canyons, Dead Horse Point State Park by Tom Till

Sixth Edition
ISBN 1–4000–1416–6
ISSN 1553–1163

The details in this book are based on information supplied to us at press time, but changes occur
all the time, and the publisher cannot accept responsibility for facts that become outdated or for
inadvertent errors or omissions.

Compass American Guides, 1745 Broadway, New York NY 10019
PRINTED IN CHINA
10 9 8 7 6 5 4 3 2 1

To our parents, Max and Althea Bennett and Jack and Vi Wharton, who encouraged us to write and instilled in us their love of travel.

C O N T E N T S

Literary Extracts

Maps

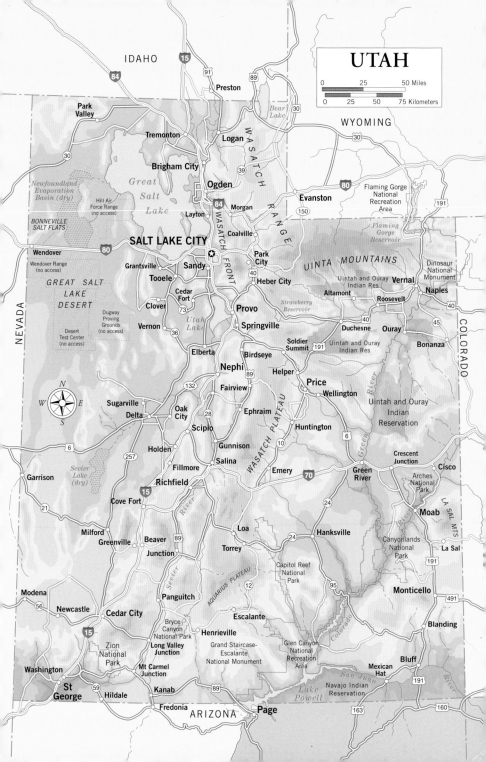

O V E R V I E W

■ **SALT LAKE CITY** *pages 89–131*
The Mormons arrived in the **Great Salt Lake Valley** in July 1847, and the very day of their arrival began building a settlement they called Deseret. The first town they founded, Salt Lake City, remains the centerpiece of the highly populated Wasatch Front, a 175-mile swath of land that lies at the base of the Wasatch Range and stretches from Provo north to Ogden. Both Utah's state capital and world headquarters of the Church of Jesus Christ of Latter-day Saints, Salt Lake City boasts fine museums, vibrant theaters, and sophisticated restaurants, in addition to the spectacular **Mormon Temple** and **Tabernacle** in **Temple Square.**

■ **WASATCH FRONT** *pages 132–157*
The **Wasatch Range** draws hikers to seven wilderness areas and, in winter, lures skiers with its world-famous ski resorts. South of Salt Lake City, **Provo** is home to **Brigham Young University.** North of Salt Lake City is **Ogden,** once the railroad hub and still the economic hub of northern Utah.

■ **NORTHEASTERN UTAH** *pages 158–179*
A favorite camping, hiking, and fishing destination, northeastern Utah is dominated by the wild and undeveloped **Uinta Mountains,** a forested range interspersed with four rivers and more than 1,000 lakes. At **Flaming Gorge National Recreation Area,** the **Green River** draws river rafters, while the reservoir is famed for its massive trout. In stark contrast to this alpine region is the **Uinta Basin,** today a desolate landscape of red, tan, and white rock—but 145 million years ago, a lush, verdant land where dinosaurs roamed.

■ **GREAT BASIN** *pages 180–204*
Lying in west-central Utah, stretching west toward Nevada from the Wasatch Front, the Great Basin encompasses the **Bonneville Salt Flats,** where many an automobile speed record has been set. Here too can be found the **Great Salt Lake** and its island mountains, including **Antelope Island.** The area's mining past is revealed in ghost towns with names such as Topaz, Gold Hill, and Mercur.

Spring flowers in Capitol Reef National Park: prickly pear cactuses and lupines.

■ **SOUTHERN UTAH** *pages 205–265*
From the badland topography of **Cedar Breaks National Monument** to the towering 3,000-foot canyon walls of **Zion National Park,** southern Utah is nothing short of spectacular. **Bryce Canyon National Park**—where the cliffs can turn white, orange, yellow, red, or purple, depending on the time of day—is actually a series of 14 amphitheaters extending 1,000 feet down a limestone plateau. **Kodachrome Basin State Park** is a scenic valley full of towering stone chimneys, while **Grand Staircase–Escalante National Monument** is red-rock country, with waterfalls, small arches, and an Ancestral Puebloan ruin. In **Cathedral Valley** at **Capitol Reef National Park,** huge monolithic sandstone remnants form jutting buttes that resemble Gothic churches in the desert. Awesome **Arches National Park,** with its salmon-colored **Delicate Arch** rock formation, and **Canyonlands National Park,** with its wind-carved, sandstone needles, defy the imagination.

INTRODUCTION

A PIONEERING PLACE

On the east bench of Salt Lake City, a weathered statue gazes silently at the valley below. A brown haze from automobiles and industrial stacks obscures the view slightly to the west, but the blue waters of the Great Salt Lake and the mighty peaks of the Oquirrh Mountains are still visible, as they were on July 24th, 1847, when Brigham Young first looked out from this spot, ending a perilous 1,300-mile journey by declaring, "This is the right place." Could even a wise and visionary man like Young have imagined what Salt Lake City—and, for that matter, all of Utah—would become?

Those who have made Utah their home—from the ancient Indians who built magnificent cliff dwellings in the southern canyons to the contemporary scientists who are mapping the human genome—have possessed the courageous spirit of true pioneers. This land brings out a conservative, independent streak in people: Utah's official motto is *Industry*; its state symbol is the beehive. Utahns take their work seriously.

Utah's earliest residents may not have known much about their homeland's geography and geology when they arrived, but they were quick studies. Largely by trial and error, the Native Americans, mountain men, explorers, and first settlers learned how to make a living from the land.

In the mid-19th century, newcomers from across the plains brought a distinctive, energetic spirit, which the independent mountain men, the Catholic explorer-priests, and even the Indians who preceded them might have respected. These Mormon pioneers sought the freedom to worship God in their own way, and dreamed of turning Utah into a modern-day Zion through hard work and community effort. The soldiers, miners, railroad workers, and other non-Mormon "gentiles" who came later may not have possessed the same religious beliefs, but certainly they were caught up in the pioneering spirit.

This book, to a great degree, is about all sorts of pioneers. It is based on the premise that residents and visitors cannot fully appreciate Utah's magnificent natural and cultural heritage without first understanding the spirit of the people who turned what many regarded as a wasteland into a thriving state.

Many know the story of Utah's most famous pioneer, Brigham Young, a man who knew the value of planning for the future. Young built Salt Lake City from almost nothing, laying it out in wide, square, well-organized blocks. He sent out Mormon settlers to remote corners of the unsettled West armed with little more than faith, a willingness to work hard, and a rare courage to face the unknown. He is, by most accounts, the archetypal Utah pioneer.

But Utah's pioneering spirit did not die with Brigham Young. Witness Maurice Abravanel, a Greek musician who came to Utah intent on building a world-renowned symphony and did not retire until his vision became reality. Or consider the team of University of Utah researchers and doctors who, for the first time, built an artificial heart and successfully implanted it in a living human being.

Evidence of this pioneering spirit can be seen everywhere in the Beehive State. Walk down the clean, wide streets of Salt Lake City, where dozens of new buildings rose in the latter part of the 20th century, where development prompted by the 2002 Winter Olympic Games has left its legacy, and where business executives and government leaders continue to plot the course of the state through the 21st century. Listen to a symphony, or attend a play, opera, ballet, or modern dance performance, and savor the enthusiasm of a community willing to support all kinds of artistic endeavors.

Then escape to the wild lands that lie in all directions from the Wasatch Front. Get a sense of the courage of explorer John Wesley Powell by taking a white-water raft trip through Cataract Canyon. Visit the site where the first transcontinental railroad was completed in 1869 to glean some feeling for the exciting day when West and East were joined for the first time. Hike through one of Utah's five national parks with a pack on your back to experience first-hand the incredibly rugged geography that the early explorers, settlers, and prospectors had to face and conquer. And as you wander through the High Uintas Wilderness Area, or follow the old Pony Express Trail across the western desert, or bounce up and down in the seat of an old Jeep through an obscure southern Utah canyon, imagine yourself as a mountain man, daring Pony Express rider, or grizzled prospector. The state's wild places still allow visitors to get a sense of what our forefathers faced in this desolate but wonderful land.

STORIES IN STONE

UTAH'S GEOLOGY

There are many ways to contemplate the geologic forces that have shaped Utah. Hike to the top of an alpine peak overlooking the Great Salt Lake Valley and look down on the sprawling metropolitan area. Drive across the desolate Bonneville Salt Flats and see mirages of floating mountains shimmer across the glistening, salt-encrusted surface. Take a raft trip through Cataract Canyon and listen to the roar of the rapids while you watch the colors and shapes of steep sandstone ledges change dramatically along the way. Then fly back over the same country and look out over the convoluted canyons, stately fins, windblown arches, and rock bridges formed by erosion. Wander down a remote, narrow canyon in Zion National Park and examine the texture of the sandstone closely. Feel the warm, red rock with your hands. Climb an almost vertical cliff. Lie on a hard, smooth rock surface, and study the countless hues.

Nowhere in the world, perhaps, have the elements of earth, wind, and water come together with such drama as they have in Utah, where underground forces have pushed massive mountain ranges and plateaus up more than a mile above sea level, and erosion continues to gouge them into spectacular pinnacles and canyons.

In most places around the world, water, soil, or vegetation covers the rock layers that tell the earth's history. Things are different in Utah, which the late Dr. William Lee Stokes—a University of Utah geologist and famous hunter of dinosaur bones—called the Bedrock State because the rocks over much of it are so well exposed. Only in the valleys of western Utah is the bedrock hidden by a cover of young sediments.

Much of Utah has a high desert climate. Little rain falls, and vegetation is sparse. As a result, rivers and streams cut directly into layers of rock, exposing them for study. Utah is one of the few states where all 13 periods of the geologic time scale are represented in the rock record—even the famed Grand Canyon in Arizona exposes only seven periods. Sedimentary layers of rock from every era have yielded thousands of fossils.

Certain areas in northeastern Utah are rich in fossils.

One need not be a geologist to appreciate the qualities that make Utah unique. Its physical features have dictated patterns of human settlement and economic development throughout its history and still shape its future.

Utah is divided into three major geologic provinces: the Colorado Plateau, the Basin and Range, and the Middle Rocky Mountains. Between them are transitional zones, in some places tens of miles wide, where features of both provinces occur. Each province extends into adjacent states, and each provides its own unique recreational opportunities and monumental vistas.

■ THE COLORADO PLATEAU

The Colorado Plateau is a highland province bordered on the north and east by the Rocky Mountains, on the south by the Sonoran Desert, and on the west by the Great Basin. It covers all of southeastern Utah and extends into adjacent areas in Colorado, New Mexico, and Arizona that are drained by the Colorado River. This sparsely vegetated landscape—a plateau itself filled with·plateaus, as well as mesas, sloping foothills, imposing vertical cliffs, deep canyons, and barren badlands— contains some of the world's most unusual scenery. "Here," wrote Dr. Stokes, "is a kingdom of rocks, an arena where the elemental forces of time and weather meet the raw stuff of the earth with nothing to soften or hide the scars of battle."

Most rocks exposed in the Utah part of the Colorado Plateau are sedimentary rocks deposited between 40 million and 250 million years ago, when the region was near sea level. Sandstones, often brightly colored, form some of the most dramatic outcrops. Some of these are fossilized sand dunes, while others are ancient beaches formed when seas advanced and retreated.

Fifteen or 20 million years ago, the Colorado Plateau and adjacent areas of western North America were pushed up far above sea level—a movement thought to be related to the forces that cause continental drift. This increase in elevation brought about new weather patterns, speeding up erosion. With little vegetation to absorb it, rain falling on the young plateau flowed from rivulets to gullies to rivers, carrying sand and detritus to the ocean. The softer shales eroded fastest, leaving the more resistant sandstones as cliffs and mesas. Following the path of least resistance, the Colorado River and its tributaries in time carved southern Utah into an elaborate maze of canyons and gorges. Visitors to Arches, Zion, Capitol Reef, and Canyonlands national parks can see the impressive sandstone cliffs formed by such erosion.

The classic geologic formation of Comb Ridge in extreme southeastern Utah.

Erosion has also created the extraordinary number of fins, arches, natural bridges, and reefs found on the Colorado Plateau. Water and ice cut, break, and wear down sandstone layers. Moving water carves the softer layers from between the harder layers. When a layer of harder rock is left standing by itself, it's called a fin. A good example is the Fiery Furnace in Arches National Park. Natural bridges are formed when water works its way completely through portions of a narrow rock fin.

Flowing water is not the only agent of erosion; standing water can have as great an effect. Sandstone consists of two parts: sand-sized grains of a mineral (often quartz) and a softer component, such as silica or calcium carbonate, that binds the grains (often weakly) into a framework. Water in pools and potholes can dissolve those binding minerals, loosening grains that are then carried away by wind or water. In winter, water freezing in the cracks between rocks expands and further pushes sandstone layers apart, causing wide gaps and freeing huge slabs from canyon walls. When a fin has been left standing alone for centuries, soil moisture, exposure to wind, and the freezing and thawing of ice can cause a hole to appear and slowly widen into an arch. A sandstone spire is created when a thin wall collapses and leaves behind a monolithic remnant.

Several scenic areas of the Colorado Plateau are the results of geologic uplifts. These appear as gigantic sandstone outcroppings, with the normally horizontal rock strata tilted almost vertically. Over time, erosion notches crack-like canyons into the upturned sandstone. These near-vertical ridges presented barriers to travel for many pioneers, who called them "reefs." The San Rafael Reef and Comb Ridge are examples.

The mountain ranges of the Colorado Plateau are also unusual. Geologists, who call them "laccoliths," describe them as volcanoes that never quite erupted. The La Sal, Abajo, and Henry mountains, as well as Navajo Mountain near Lake Powell, were formed by molten rock pushing up through and into the overlying sedimentary strata, raising it into a dome. In many cases, erosion, especially glaciation, has removed the upper rock layers, revealing their igneous inner cores. Of these ranges, only Navajo Mountain retains an intact outer shell of sedimentary rock.

All of Utah's five national parks are found on the Colorado Plateau, and visiting any will help you understand the forces that formed this unique and beautiful part of the world. Geologic guides are sold at all the park visitors centers, or you can read interpretive signs along the roads.

The Colorado Plateau also contains much of Utah's energy resources. Numerous Colorado Plateau fields still produce oil and gas, and mines here, now inactive, once yielded much of the uranium and radium produced in the United States. Nearly all of Utah's coal mines are on the Colorado Plateau, and huge reserves of coal, Utah's state rock, remain undeveloped.

■ THE BASIN AND RANGE PROVINCE

Western Utah is part of the Basin and Range province, a region of elongated mountain ranges separated by basins or valleys that extends from the Wasatch Range westward to the Sierra Nevada and north and south into Idaho and Arizona. Much of this province is occupied by the Great Basin: the huge, elevated depression in the western United States where water has no escape to the sea. Today, rainfall is sparse and the valleys of most of the area are no longer filled with water, but toward the end of the last ice age, perennial rivers fed many lakes in the basin. Lake Bonneville, Utah's prehistoric precursor to the Great Salt Lake, was the largest. This massive inland sea dominated the landscape; at its highest level, approximately 15,500 years ago, it measured more than 1,000 feet deep, 145 miles wide, and 346 miles long, covering much of northwest Utah and reaching into Idaho and Nevada.

The pounding waves of Lake Bonneville carved terraces and benches into the surrounding shores, and when the lake receded these ancient shorelines—there are four main ones, marking four main stages in the lake's fluctuating levels—became visible

Rock strata millions of years in the making are exposed at the confluence of the Green and Colorado rivers.

All of Utah's national parks are on the Colorado Plateau. This is Capitol Reef National Park.

on the mountainsides of this part of the state. Rivers flowing into the lake developed deltas at their mouths, which today stand out prominently in the mountains encircling Salt Lake City: Utah's State Capitol stands on one such delta, and the University of Utah is on another. The Great Salt Lake, the largest saltwater lake in the Western Hemisphere, is a mere remnant of the giant Lake Bonneville, as is Utah Lake, the state's largest freshwater lake, which drains into the Great Salt Lake by way of the Jordan River. Farther west are the 44,000-acre Bonneville Salt Flats, another remnant of Lake Bonneville's evaporation, and Utah's largest sand-dune field, the Little Sahara Recreation Area, on the east-central edge of the Great Basin.

The Great Salt Lake derives its salinity from its position on the floor of the Great Basin, where it receives all the dissolved minerals that rivers would normally carry to the sea. As lake water evaporates, the minerals become even more concentrated in the remaining water. Sodium chloride, or common salt, is only one of dozens of salts that saturate the Great Salt Lake and are extracted from its waters by large commercial operations.

The Great Salt Lake has several islands, some of which become peninsulas at low water levels. Antelope Island, the largest, is the site of a state park.

The granite of the Wasatch Range comes both polished and rough.

At about the same time that intrusions of magma were forming the laccolith mountains of the Colorado Plateau, large volumes of magma were erupting from volcanoes in western Utah. Some of this magma solidified to form masses of granitic rock, and, in association with these rocks, deposits of valuable minerals, such as gold, silver, and copper, were formed. The world's largest open-pit mine, Bingham Copper Mine, in the Oquirrh Range, has produced billions of dollars in ore—mostly copper, but also gold, silver, lead, and other minerals.

Farther south, the Tushar Mountains, remnants of extinct volcanoes, contain numerous mineral deposits. The Big Rock Candy Mountain, near Marysvale, was named for the distinctive multicolor pattern created by the mountain's various minerals. Iron Mountain and Iron County received their names from the ore deposits found there.

For tens of millions of years, the area that was to become the Great Basin was a broad highland. About 15 million years ago, the earth's crust here began to stretch in an east-west direction. As it stretched, it created faults, or long fractures, trending generally in a north-south direction. Along the faults, long blocks sank to form basins or valleys, while alternate blocks remained high and became ranges.

The stretching of the Basin and Range is a continuous process, and although it is overall a slow one, the movement on individual faults occurs as dramatic slippage of several feet at a time. These large, abrupt shifts cause earthquakes. Much of the stretching of the Basin and Range province is now concentrated near its eastern and western margins, with the eastern margin of faults forming a zone of frequent earthquakes that is part of the Intermountain Seismic Belt. Most of the earthquakes are small—many too small to be felt. In historic time, however, Utah's earthquakes have caused significant damage.

The state's most important earthquake fault, the Wasatch Fault, lies at the western base of the Wasatch Range and has not produced a major earthquake since the Mormon pioneers settled the area 150 years ago. Geologic studies of the Wasatch Fault—which is not actually a single fault, but a zone of faults 200 miles long—have shown that a very large earthquake occurs in this zone every few hundred years. A large earthquake here would wreak havoc. Utah's population center, Salt Lake City, built on the old Bonneville lake bed, would jiggle like gelatin in the event of a major tremor.

Nearly all of Utah's hot springs lie in this zone of earthquake activity, sometimes on one of the active faults. These springs occur where water that has circulated deep enough into the earth to be heated rises to the surface along a fault.

■ THE MIDDLE ROCKY MOUNTAIN PROVINCE

The Wasatch Range, which dominates north-central Utah, and the Uinta Mountains, which monopolize the skyline of northeastern Utah, both stand within the Utah portion of the Middle Rocky Mountains province. These mountain ranges receive much more precipitation than most of the rest of Utah, and rivers originating in them supply the water for the Wasatch Front—the well-populated band west of the Wasatch Range where Salt Lake City, Provo, and Ogden lie, and where most Utahns live.

The Wasatch Range is an assemblage of sedimentary, igneous, and metamorphic rocks, among them the oldest rocks in Utah—more than three billion years old. Each major canyon along the Wasatch Front exposes a different suite of rocks. Mines in Big and Little Cottonwood canyons and at Park City have been major producers of minerals, since the interaction of magma and rocks usually forms mineable ores.

The Uinta Mountains were pushed up to form an east-west range—unlike most major ranges in the continental United States, which run north to south. These mountains are composed primarily of old sedimentary rocks and have no important mineral deposits. Large oil and gas fields occur south of the Uinta Mountains in the Uinta Basin and north of the Uinta Mountains in an area of complex geologic structure known as the overthrust belt. In the "crossroads" region—the part of this belt where the Wasatch Range and the Uinta Mountains intersect, near Park City—the geology is extremely complex.

■ PREHISTORIC LIFE

Utah has been called "a King Tut's tomb of fossils"; its rocks hold fossils from every geologic age. Petrified wood can be found throughout the Colorado Plateau, and visitors to Escalante State Park can hike a trail that passes among the petrified logs of an ancient coniferous forest. Fossilized trilobites—extinct marine invertebrates—are common in the western desert regions of the Great Basin.

A boater at Lake Powell strolling on the shoreline might discover dinosaur tracks, just as miners in Price, in the heart of dinosaur country, have uncovered dinosaur footprints in the coal deposits. In the early part of the 20th century, tons of dinosaur fossils and surrounding rock were removed from the quarry at what became, in 1915, Dinosaur National Monument, and since the late 1920s, thousands of dinosaur bones have been taken from another prolific site, the Cleveland-Lloyd Dinosaur Quarry.

Why is Utah so full of dinosaur and other fossils? The Morrison Formation—a series of strata deposited at the height of the dinosaur age and found in the western states from the Dakotas to New Mexico—is found throughout eastern Utah, and erosion and the dry climate have combined to expose the strata to an unusual extent. Both Dinosaur National Monument, in northeastern Utah, and the Cleveland-Lloyd Dinosaur Quarry, near the town of Cleveland in central Utah, are in the Morrison Formation, and both have yielded some of the finest fossilized dinosaur skeletons found anywhere.

Andrew Carnegie, the famous capitalist and philanthropist, stirred dinosaur fever throughout the world with specimens from Utah. Carnegie had constructed a huge museum for the people of Pittsburgh, Pennsylvania, and was looking for items grand enough to fill it. "Someone slapped a picture of a Brontosaurus [today called Apatosaurus] from the monument on his desk," dinosaur hunter Dr. Stokes once recounted, "and his eyes lit up. He said, 'Get me one!'."

In fact, it was a Carnegie Museum paleontologist, Earl Douglass, who was responsible for the discovery of the dinosaur graveyard at Dinosaur National Monument. Dispatched to the west on a fossil-hunting mission, Douglass in August 1909 spotted eight vertebrae of an Apatosaurus sticking out of the sandstone at Split Mountain, near Vernal. It took years to excavate the whole skeleton, nearly 70 feet long, and reassemble it at the museum—and by the time removal of fossils from the quarry stopped in 1924, approximately 350 tons of material had been sent to Pittsburgh.

Apatosaurus was an herbivore, as were most of the dinosaurs whose bones have been found at Dinosaur National Monument. Stegosaurus is common, as are several types of sauropods, the largest animals ever to roam on land, and tiny Nanosaurus, a creature no larger than a chicken. The Dinosaur Quarry Visitor Center, a glass-walled building opened in 1958, preserves the ancient riverbed where these prehistoric animals were buried—it actually encloses the cliff face where the dinosaurs were found, so that visitors can view the bones exactly as they were when they were uncovered.

The Cleveland-Lloyd Dinosaur Quarry is a more remote and rustic site than Dinosaur National Monument. The area was once a bog where large plant-eating dinosaurs became trapped and eventually entombed, along with the carnivores that preyed on them. The meat-eating Allosaurus, the largest carnivore of the Jurassic period in North America, is the most common species found here. Stokesosaurus, a small meat-eater discovered here, was named for Stokes, who helped initiate the digging here as a geology student and later was in charge of excavations for a time.

Dinosaur National Monument and the Cleveland-Lloyd Dinosaur Quarry, designated a national natural landmark in 1966, are managed by different government agencies for somewhat different purposes. Dinosaur National Monument is under the aegis of the National Park Service; it was enlarged in 1938 from its original 80 acres to more than 200,000 acres, extending well into neighboring Colorado, and excavations continue in this expanded area, although they have ceased at the historic Carnegie quarry, which now serves as an educational tool. The Cleveland site, managed by the Bureau of Land Management, is an active quarry from which fossils are removed for research and study—anyone with a proper permit may dig for fossils at the Cleveland quarry.

The Dinosaur Garden at the Utah Field House of Natural History State Park in Vernal contains life-size replicas of the prehistoric creatures.

THE FIRST UTAHNS

The American Southwest, and Utah in particular, contains some of the country's most spectacular traces of Native American civilization. Many of these ruins, artifacts, and rock pictures were left by people of the vanished Ancestral Puebloan culture, more commonly known as the Anasazi, who occupied southern Utah and the Colorado Plateau about 700 to 2,000 years ago. The Fremont culture, which existed roughly 800 to 1,300 years ago, also left distinctive rock art. Other archaeological sites are those of the more recently arrived Shoshone, Ute, Navajo, and Paiute peoples. The human history of Utah, however, begins much earlier.

Paleo-Indians, who had probably arrived in the Americas via the Bering land bridge, were the first inhabitants of what is now known as Utah. They hunted and gathered throughout the area as early as 13,000 years ago. Their stone-tipped spears, used to fell large Ice Age fauna, have been discovered in caves along the shoreline of prehistoric Lake Bonneville. They probably hunted mammoth and giant bison and cached the meat in the frozen ground, supplementing their diet with seeds, nuts, and small rodents.

When the Wisconsin Glacier began to recede about 8,000 years ago, weather patterns changed. Six millennia or so later, great inland deserts were forming in the Southwest, causing many of the larger mammals to become extinct. Those who had depended on them for sustenance could no longer survive, and subsequent generations adapted by collecting wild seeds and nuts and trapping game such as elk, deer, mountain sheep, antelope, rabbits, and rodents.

Around A.D. 500, corn and other crops from Mexico were introduced into the North American Southwest. With a more dependable food source, the Indians could stay in one place and produce enough corn, squash, and beans to put away for the winter and for periods of drought; meanwhile, they developed effective implements for harvesting and storing, especially kiln-fired pottery and intricately woven baskets. Archaeologists classify these agricultural societies as the Ancestral Puebloan and Fremont cultures, roughly contemporaneous. The Ancestral Puebloans, in general, flourished on the Colorado Plateau south of the Colorado River, while the Fremont people lived north of the Colorado River and east of the Virgin River in the Great and the Uinta basins.

The state of Utah is named for the Ute Indians, whose name means "people of the mountains" in their own language. Here a Ute chief and his family pose for their portrait, ca. 1885.

■ THE ANCESTRAL PUEBLOANS

Since 1936 archaeologists have used the term Anasazi to refer to the ancient Native American cultures that populated the Southwest from about A.D. 1. The term *anasazi* is a Navajo word meaning "ancient enemies" or "ancestral enemies." This term has long been offensive to the Hopis and other contemporary Pueblo Indians who descended from the Anasazi. The Hopis instead use the word *hisatsinom,* which, simply translated, means "people of long ago" or "old ones" to describe their ancestors, and other modern Pueblo Indians have their own words for their ancestral people.

Toward the end of the 20th century, federal land management archaeologists and other scientists agreed upon a different designation for the ancient peoples, one that would eliminate the negative connotations of the Navajo word. Since that time the term Ancestral Puebloan has come to describe the people once known as Anasazi.

The earliest of the Ancestral Puebloans are known to archaeologists as the Basketmakers. They lived in pit houses—saucer-shaped dwellings that were half aboveground and half underground and were walled and roofed with a combination of logs and mud mortar. They apparently had frequent contact with other peoples, and their dramatic cultural advancement from A.D. 700 to 1300, designated as the Pueblo Period by archaeologists, shows them to have been extremely adaptable and dynamic. By around A.D. 700, the bow and arrow had replaced the less efficient spear and atlatl (wooden spear-thrower). Cotton weaving had been introduced, and dogs and turkeys had been domesticated.

Around A.D. 900, the Ancestral Puebloans began to build multi-story stone structures grouped around courtyards. Beneath the courtyards were underground chambers called kivas. The roofs—a wooden framework topped with mud—were level with the surrounding plaza; a hole in the center served as the entrance and as an exhaust for smoke. Each kiva had a place for a fire, ventilation to keep the fire going, and a small indentation in the floor called a *sipapu*. Because the modern Hopis—for whom the *sipapu* symbolizes the opening through which mankind entered the world—use the same kind of room for their ceremonies, archaeologists theorize that the purpose of the Ancestral Puebloan kiva was similar: a ceremonial chamber where men gathered to perform various rituals, and also a workshop where they would do the weaving. Women were not allowed, though judging by the evidence skeletons show of the effect grinding corn had on the women, they would have had very little time or energy left for either of these activities.

During the latter part of the Pueblo Period, dwellings were constructed in the protected alcoves of sandstone canyons. Built on cliffs high above the valley floor, most were reached by ladders or handholds and footholds chipped in the rock. Some were nestled back into large open caves in the rock walls of the canyon.

The rock art left by the Ancestral Puebloan people was typified by large triangular figures with stick arms and legs. Some figures carry bags or pouches and there

An Ancestral Puebloan kiva found with its original ladder—a rarity. This kiva is called a "perfect kiva" because its roof is still in place; the small hole is a sipapu.

are often series of wavy lines, dots, or spirals associated with the drawings. The images were either "petroglyphs," pecked into the rock, or "pictographs," rock paintings. Thousands of remnants of this civilization can be found throughout the Colorado Plateau. Among the Utah sites you can visit are Butler Wash, Grand Gulch Primitive Area, Sego Canyon, Nine-Mile Canyon, Natural Bridges and Hovenweep national monuments, Anasazi State Park, Canyonlands National Park, and Newspaper Rock. Edge of the Cedars State Park Museum in Blanding is one of the nation's foremost museums dedicated to the study of Ancestral Puebloan people. The museum displays a variety of pots, baskets, spear points, and sandals. Behind the museum you can visit an Ancestral Puebloan ruin. The Moab Information Center can direct you to dozens of rock art and/or dwelling sites on public lands throughout southeastern Utah. Some river and land tour outfitters in Blanding, Bluff, and Moab offer special expeditions to visit archaeological sites in the region.

■ THE FREMONT INDIANS

Much less is known about the Fremont Indians, who lived north of the Ancestral Puebloans, along the edge of the Great Basin and the Colorado Plateau. Such an extreme range of climate and geography prompted individual bands to adapt in different ways. Some lived as nomadic hunters and plant collectors. Others established villages and lived as farmers. But there are enough similarities in the artifacts they left to identify them as a common people. Among these are particular styles of basketry and leather moccasins (unlike the yucca-fiber sandals worn by the Ancestral Puebloans). Their pictographs, petroglyphs, and clay figurines generally show them with necklaces and a distinctive hair style. Also unique was the Fremont recipe for making pottery by mixing granular rock or sand with the wet clay.

There are fewer known Fremont village sites than Ancestral Puebloan sites. One reason for this is that the pit houses of the Fremont deteriorated faster than the stone and mortar of the later Ancestral Puebloans. The pit houses are hard for the layman to differentiate from the desert floor, although the granaries and rock graphics stand out clearly.

An excellent place to learn about these early settlers is Fremont Indian State Park, southwest of Richfield, where Five Finger Ridge Village was uncovered when Interstate 70 was built through Clear Creek Canyon in 1983. A museum displays artifacts collected at the village and shows how the Fremont hunted for game and

Hunting scenes on a prehistoric fresco in Nine-Mile Canyon.

This ancient reptile petroglyph is about 10 feet long and appears near other Fremont period rock-art panels.

wild plant foods and farmed in the canyon bottoms. Visitors can examine full-sized replicas of a pit house and granary and see the Fremont rock graphics along the Show Me Rock Art and Discovery trails.

Fremont Indian petroglyphs may also be viewed at Parowan Gap, 12 miles north of Parowan in Iron County, and in Nine-Mile Canyon, northwest of Price.

■ VISITING ARCHAEOLOGICAL SITES

As you visit ancient Native American sites, try to hear the echoes of the Ancestral Puebloans as they go about their daily chores. Women chatter as they grind corn, children chase domesticated turkeys. Young adults carefully beat the tops of rice grass, letting the seeds fall into their ornate baskets. While you try to recreate the centuries-old scene, please remember you are in someone's home, standing in someone's cemetery. Treat it with respect. Ruin walls are fragile; the mortar holding them together crumbles easily. Please do not walk or lean on them. By touching rock graphics, you can deposit skin oils that hasten deterioration of the pigments and rock surfaces.

If you are privileged enough to find a piece of pottery, a tiny corn cob, or other artifact, enjoy it with the appropriate awe due something hundreds or thousands of years old, but leave it in place. The beauty of these places is that pieces of the past can be seen. If any one artifact is taken or destroyed, the quality of the experience is diminished for visitors to come. Moreover, all prehistoric remains are protected by United States laws. Fines of up to $20,000 and/or imprisonment may be imposed on anyone removing or destroying these cultural resources on public lands. Rewards are offered for information leading to the arrest and conviction of anyone disturbing a site.

■ THE FATE OF THE ANCIENT ONES

What became of the Ancestral Puebloans and the Fremont? The years between 1100 and 1300 found Pueblo people grouping together in larger and larger villages. Pottery, basketweaving, jewelry, and other arts flourished. However, as resources began to be depleted, the Ancestral Puebloan people began to move south into Arizona and New Mexico. This movement reached a peak in the late 1200s and by 1300 it is believed that the Utah villages had been abandoned.

Ancestral Puebloan pots from the vicinity of Edge of the Cedars State Park.

Ancestral Puebloan dwellings in Road Canyon. More than 700 years ago, the Ancestral Puebloans vanished as mysteriously as they had appeared centuries before.

There is much speculation as to the sudden disappearance of this culture from the region. Several theories have been proposed, and no solid evidence has been produced to support one theory over another. By studying tree rings, scientists have documented that a severe drought took place in the Southwest from about 1276 to 1299. In addition, cutting timber for fuel and building material and clearing land for agriculture may have started a cycle of erosion, ending with a loss of fields due to gullying. With a diminished capacity to grow and store enough food, social disruptions undoubtedly took place. While no evidence of violence has been found in the cliff dwellings, their relative inaccessibility makes them seem like fortresses. Some Hopi people, meanwhile, believe a spiritual covenant prompted the migration of their ancestors. It is a mystery that scientists continue to study today.

■ THE LATER TRIBES

Today, Utah's Indians consist primarily of the Ute, Paiute, Shoshone, Goshute, and Navajo nations. Historically, these Indians were hunters and gatherers, with each group moving from place to place within particular boundaries. Small bands camped near water in cooler areas in the summer and moved to warmer areas in the winter. Each tribe consisted of many different bands, and the bands came together occasionally for seasonal celebrations.

The story of Utah's Indians, and of their domination and frequent betrayal at the hands of non-Indian settlers and politicians, parallels that of other tribes throughout the United States. The first Spanish explorers in the Southwest encouraged Utes to prey on Paiutes and Goshutes and bring them as slaves for trade. The settlers were generally accepted by the Indians in the beginning until the number of non-Indians increased, along with their demand for more land.

■ THE UTES

At the time of early European contact with Native Americans, there were 12 informal bands of Ute Indians occupying Utah and western Colorado. They moved through hunting and gathering territories seasonally. Men hunted deer, rabbits, antelope, and birds with bows and arrows, nets or spears. The women gathered seeds, nuts, berries, and roots and processed meats for winter storage. The Utes also enjoyed the abundance of fish from Utah Lake, using them for trade and winter sustenance. Horses acquired from the Spanish in 1680 facilitated their raids and trading, making the Utes respected warriors and tradesmen.

With the exception of the 1776 Dominguez-Escalante expedition, few explorers ventured into Ute territory. In 1847, however, the Mormon pioneers arrived in Utah, changing Ute life forever.

The first wave of Mormon settlers did little to disrupt the Utes, but as settlers moved south they began competing with the Utes for scarce natural resources. Pushed from their lands, the Utes began a series of raids against the Mormon settlements. The Walker War (1853–54) was the beginning of Ute displacement and of the "open hand, mailed fist" policy of Mormon leader Brigham Young. In other words, the Mormons would feed the Utes when possible but fight them when necessary.

(following pages) An Ancestral Puebloan cliff dwelling in Canyonlands National Park.

The government hoped to settle the Utes in one place where they could farm and subsist. The Ute people, however, used to consistent crop failures, believed that staying in one place meant certain starvation. They resisted settlement, and their recalcitrance eventually led to the Black Hawk War (1863–1868). By 1869, however, the Utes were worn down and starving and allowed themselves to be led to reservation lands in the inhospitable Uintah Valley. Government removal and relocation of various Ute bands created continuing problems. There was suspicion and jealousy over land and money, along with diminished opportunities for hunting. The bands also held differing beliefs about farming and religion. These problems were made worse in the late 1800s and early 1900s, when the government divided the reservations into parcels and opened the remainder to white settlers. From 1906 to 1908, 400 Utes fled to South Dakota.

Decades of change kept the Utes struggling for land and natural resources. The process has made them savvy and powerful politicians, however. Today the Northern Ute Tribe has more than 3,000 members and is an increasingly important force in local and state politics.

■ THE PAIUTES

The Southern Paiutes live in southwestern Utah, where they are known to have been since about A.D. 1100. The largest population settled near the Virgin and Muddy rivers; other Paiutes lived in the nearby arid desert. Both bands lived by hunting, gathering, and farming, sometimes using the rivers for irrigation.

Like other Utah Indians, the Paiutes had their first contact with white men with the Dominguez-Escalante expedition in 1776. Through the early 1800s, it became increasingly difficult for them to maintain their quiet, agricultural lifestyle as European trappers and explorers moved through the area. The newcomers' animals fed on Paiute grasses and crops, and Utes and Navajos traded the Paiute people, especially women and children, to the Europeans as slaves.

As it was for the Utes, however, the most dramatic impact to Paiute way of life came with the Mormon settlers. The Mormons situated themselves in prime locations along the rivers and in the valleys that had traditionally served the Paiutes as foraging and camping areas. Starvation and disease drastically reduced the Paiute population, beginning the tribe's long downward spiral. Although a reservation was established in 1891 near St. George, very little federal help came with it. A brief glimmer of hope appeared with the 1935 Indian Reorganization Act, which encouraged tribal self-government and the protection of Indian land rights. This beacon of light was brief, however, as during the 1950s the U.S. government included the Paiutes on a list of tribes that were to lose their official status. In 1965, 14 years after having filed for their lands, the Paiutes were awarded 27 cents per acre. Efforts toward reinstating their federal status as a tribe began in 1973, and in 1980 President Carter signed legislation that restored their federal recognition.

The Paiutes, still in southern Utah, continue to work toward economic development and stability.

■ THE SHOSHONES AND GOSHUTES

Utah's Shoshones, comprising the Northwestern Shoshones and the Goshute Shoshones, were only two of seven distinct Shoshone groups in the West. The Goshutes lived in the valleys and mountains west and southwest of the Great Salt Lake. The much larger group of Northwestern Shoshones resided in what is today Weber Valley, Cache Valley near the Bear River, and along the eastern and northern shores of the Great Salt Lake.

While the Goshutes and Shoshones withstood the onslaught of European immigrants longer than other American Indians, the changes that occurred were no less dramatic.

By 1862 Mormon pioneers had moved along the eastern shores of the Great Salt Lake and taken over Cache Valley. But after the discovery of gold in Montana and a rise in the number of California-bound settlers greatly increased the traffic through Shoshone territory, the Northwestern Shoshones decided to strike back. They raided Mormon cattle herds and attacked gold miners on their way to Montana. The Indian attacks ended abruptly on January 29, 1863, when volunteers from Camp Douglas in Salt Lake City assaulted the winter camp of the Indians. After a four-hour battle, 23 soldiers were dead, but more than 250 Shoshones, including 90 women and children, had been slaughtered. This battle is now known as the Bear River Massacre.

Later that year the Northwestern Shoshones signed a treaty bringing peace to the area. After the signing, however, government officials attempted to move the tribe to the newly established Fort Hall Indian Reservation in Idaho. After years of pressure, the Shoshones gave up their homelands in Utah and moved to Idaho.

The Goshutes suffered a similar fate. After the Mormon settlers claimed the area, the Pony Express and Overland Stage routes cut through Goshute country.

Mormon communities were established at Tooele, Grantsville, and Ibapha—all locations important to the Goshutes—and white ranchers and farmers occupied the best lands, usurping water and forage areas. In an effort to fight back, the Goshutes threatened settlers and killed livestock. These raids were successfully quashed by government soldiers, who attacked and killed many of the Goshutes in 1863. Survivors were forced to sign a treaty and end hostile activities. While the Goshutes were allowed to keep their land, the treaty did allow for construction of military posts, station houses, stage lines, and railways on it. Mines, mills, and ranches could be built and timber harvested. The Goshutes were originally compensated $1,000 a year for loss of game, but soon the federal government reneged on its treaty obligations. Finally, in the first decades of the 20th century, the government established two reservations for the Goshutes, one on the Utah-Nevada border and a smaller one in Skull Valley, near the Great Salt Lake. The Goshutes, small in number, live there today.

■ THE NAVAJOS

The extreme southeast corner of Utah is home to more than 260,000 Native Americans of the Navajo Nation. They call themselves *Dine* or "The People."

Scholars still disagree on how the Navajos came to be in the Southwest. Some argue that the Dine were entering into the Four Corners region even as the Ancestral Puebloans departed, in the 14th century. Most anthropologists do agree that the Navajos migrated from northern Canada and that by the 1500s they were populating northern New Mexico, a portion of southern Utah, and part of northern Arizona. There is no evidence in the Navajo oral tradition to support this theory, however. The Dine religion teaches that they traveled through three or four worlds and emerged into this one near the near southwestern Colorado or northwestern New Mexico.

The Spanish and Mexicans sometimes pursued the Navajo people, but it was white settlers, with the help of Kit Carson, who in 1848 forced the surrender of 8,000 Navajos. The captives were forced to walk from northeastern New Mexico to the Bosque Redondo, a desolate place on the Pecos River in eastern New Mexico—a journey of more than 300 miles. This event, known as the "Long Walk" is one of the darkest periods of Navajo history. This new reservation was nothing more than a prison. The brackish waters of the Pecos made the Navajos ill,

(opposite) Spires in Monument Valley Navajo Tribal Park.

and disease was rampant. The armyworm destroyed their crops. They endured these conditions for four years until the government relented and allowed the Navajo people to return to their homeland.

Today the Dine people in Utah reside on more than 1.1 million acres in the southeastern corner of the state. While a small percentage still raise sheep and grow crops, the arid environment limits these ventures. Rug weaving, jewelry-making, silversmithing, and other arts and crafts are important to the economy and tradition of the Navajo people. At the core of Navajo belief is the importance of strong family ties and the desire of family members to remain near one another. Like many other people, they struggle to make a living while staying near their homeland.

■ THE LAST STAND IN UTAH

The "last battle" between Indians and non-Indians on the United States frontier took place in 1923 outside of Blanding, Utah. Chief Posey and his band of Paiutes eluded a large posse by making a 15-foot jump in west Comb Wash, but Posey was wounded and died of blood poisoning; his band gave itself up two days later. The event brought the tribe's plight to the nation's attention and they were later given the White Mesa Indian Reservation, 12 miles north of Bluff.

The inevitable ending to the clash between the Indian and non-Indian cultures was a virtual elimination of the Indians' way of life. The Indians were forced to stay on reservations and become ranchers and farmers. Those who chose not to live on the reservations, where conditions were never very good, had to fit into a society that did not accept their culture. Most adopted non-Indian clothes and homes. Perhaps worst of all, the Indians were forced to abandon their religious beliefs and social customs. Children were sent away to school to learn "civilized" ways. The federal government ran the Intermountain Indian School, a large boarding school in Brigham City. The Mormon Church sponsored an Indian Placement Program where Indian children were placed in Mormon homes to be raised and educated.

■ VISITING NATIVE LANDS AND PEOPLE

Monument Valley, in the southeast corner of Utah, has been described as the "Eighth Wonder of the World," an enduring symbol of the West. Monument Valley is located on the Navajo Indian Reservation, which sprawls over vast areas of Utah, Arizona, and New Mexico. Like their neighbors, the Hopis, the Navajos

Bringing the "Posey War" to life for local residents meant incorporating a bit of melodrama and exaggeration into news articles.

PIUTE BAND DECLARES WAR ON WHITES IN BLANDING

The renegade Piute Indians are again on the rampage. The same gang which has on various occasions during the past ten years declared war against the whites and terrorized the towns of Blanding and Bluff, is again up to its old tricks. . . .

This weeks' fracas started Monday when two young bucks who had raided a sheep camp, were hauled into court. After their trial they escaped from the sheriff, and fled to the nearby hills, where they joined the main body of renegades. Armed posses immediately left in pursuit, and a running fight ensued. . . .

The posses are determined to capture the entire band, and it is altogether likely a clash will occur sometime today. . . . That a government airplane may be used in rounding up the outlaw Piutes is a possibility. . . . It will be equipped with machine guns and bombs. . . . The most disquieting feature is the fact that Old Posey, the most dangerous of all Piutes, is in charge of the band. . . .

The Piutes cut the telephone line between Blanding and Bluff, but not until after the Bluff people had been warned of the situation and told to guard the trails and passes of the San Juan River to prevent the Indians escape to the Navajo Reservation.

Reinforced posses numbering about fifty men, left Blanding yesterday to join in the fight, prepared for a long siege. . . . It is thought that Old Posey will fight the whites to the last ditch, and there is little hope for a surrender.

—Moab *Times Independent*, March 22, 1923

have been able to retain much of their ancestral land and maintain much of their old way of life. Round mud and log hogans, the Navajo winter homes, are scattered throughout the reservation.

Fine examples of Indian jewelry and blankets can be seen and purchased from stores like Hatch Trading Post, on the way to Hovenweep National Monument, or historic Goulding's Trading Post in the heart of Monument Valley. Once in a while a few individuals will set up a stand by the side of the road to sell their wares. Expect to pay high prices for the jewelry and blankets. These articles take a long time to produce and are priced as works of art.

GOULDING'S TRADING POST

Goulding's Trading Post is tucked against the red cliffs of Navajoland in Monument Valley and has become something of a legend in the West. The trading post had humble beginnings. Harry Goulding, an adventurous settler, wandered into the stunning landscape of Monument Valley in 1921 and knew he wanted to call this place home. At the time, the land belonged to the Paiutes, but when the government relocated the tribe to northern climes, the deep orange landscape, populated with spires and monoliths, became public domain. Harry and his wife purchased 640 acres at the base of Tsay-Kiss Mesa ("Big Rock Door Mesa") for the price of $320. They lived in a tent and set up a makeshift counter, which became their first trading post.

Over the years the two made friends with the Navajos, who occupied the rest of the land. In 1928, Harry and his wife, "Mike"—Harry couldn't spell her real name,

Leone—built a two-story rock house. The second floor became their living quarters, while the first floor housed the trading post. Soon visitors started arriving and a cabin was needed to house them. By 1938 there were three buildings on the site.

Goulding's Trading Post, ca. 1950.

Hollywood had discovered Monument Valley as a film location in 1925 and again in 1930, but the setting hadn't begun to reach its potential. Harry and Mike recognized that more films, and greater publicity, would mean more visitors to the area and more tourist dollars for themselves and for the Navajo Indians. When Harry heard a western film was going to be shot on location somewhere in Arizona, he and Mike journeyed to Hollywood to persuade film producers to look at Monument Valley. Their persistence paid off, and they were granted an appointment with movie director John Ford. His first movie shot in southern Utah was *Stagecoach,* with John Wayne. Wayne took credit for introducing the director to the colorful region, and Ford himself said he discovered it while out driving around, but locals know that it was Harry and Mike Goulding who put Monument Valley on the big screen for the world to enjoy.

Naturally, Goulding's Lodge and Trading Post grew over the years. The original trading post is now a museum packed with Western and movie memorabilia. The cabins for visitors evolved into a lodge that has become an outpost for travelers who want to enjoy a classic Western experience in Navajoland.

—Janet Lowe

In the Mystery Valley section of Monument Valley Navajo Tribal Park are several hundred Ancestral Puebloan dwellings, most of them small and unnamed. Guides are needed to locate them.

The Four Corners Monument, where Utah, Colorado, New Mexico, and Arizona share a common point, is also an excellent place to purchase Navajo arts and crafts such as rugs, jewelry, sand paintings, and other traditional arts. The White Mesa Ute Council holds a ceremonial Bear Dance in September; also in September is the Native American Fair and Rodeo in Bluff. In Cedar City in June, the local Indian community sponsors the Paiute Restoration Gathering, with a parade, dances, traditional games, native food, and a beauty pageant.

Utes from Fort Duchesne, on the Uintah and Ouray Indian Reservation, hold a Ute Indian Powwow every summer, with tribes from all over the West in attendance. Rodeo action, craft displays, and food booths entertain the crowds. Other Indian powwows, dances, and rodeos are held throughout the year. Information on dates and times is available at the headquarters of the Ute Indian Reservation in Fort Duchesne, near Roosevelt. The Uintah and Ouray Indian Reservation covers nearly one million acres scattered across the East Tavaputs Plateau. Non-members are asked to keep to the main roads on the reservation and purchase permits for most activities, such as camping, hunting, boating, or fishing.

Many of the towns and sites you'll see throughout the state of Utah will bring you into contact with contemporary Native Americans, especially in southeastern Utah on and near the Navajo reservation. The best advice for etiquette when visiting reservations or encountering American Indian people is to treat them the way you would expect to be treated in your own neighborhood. While some Native Americans are open to being photographed, it is common courtesy to ask permission before you do so. Special rules may apply if you are visiting during formal ceremonies.

The Indians of Utah have a rich heritage. Their history is told in the markings on the rocks and in their dwelling places. It is told through the legends and traditions of those who came after—the Hopis, Utes, Paiutes, Goshutes, Shoshones, and Navajos. In a state that claims so many diverse natural wonders, the added dimension of a proud native people is a bonus. As those who travel Utah come to love the beauty of its canyons, mesas, mountains, and deserts, they must learn to appreciate the beliefs of the first Americans. The idea that mankind must live in harmony with the earth and protect it from harm is gaining more and more acceptance.

While in Utah you can learn more about Native American cultures, ancestral and contemporary, by visiting the Museum of Natural History in Salt Lake City, the Edge of the Cedars State Park Museum in Blanding, and the Utah Field House of Natural History State Park in Vernal. Crow Canyon Archaeological Center, on the Utah-Colorado border near Hovenweep National Monument, offers educational programs and field trips that give you hands-on experience with archaeology. Canyonlands Field Institute in Moab offers educational programs for youth and adults on Southwest archaeology, modern Indian tribes, pioneer history, wildlife, and geology.

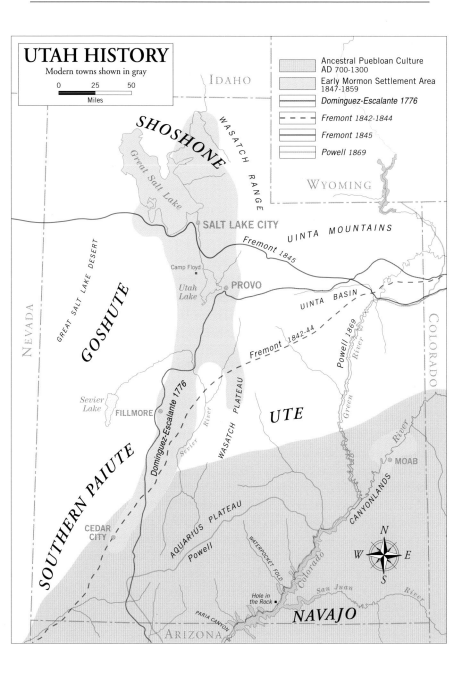

UTAH HISTORY
Modern towns shown in gray

0   25   50
Miles

Ancestral Puebloan Culture
AD 700-1300

Early Mormon Settlement Area
1847-1859

Dominguez-Escalante 1776

Fremont 1842-1844

Fremont 1845

Powell 1869

IDAHO

WYOMING

NEVADA

COLORADO

ARIZONA

SHOSHONE

WASATCH RANGE

Great Salt Lake

SALT LAKE CITY

UINTA MOUNTAINS

Fremont 1845

GREAT SALT LAKE DESERT

Camp Floyd

GOSHUTE

Utah Lake

PROVO

UINTA BASIN

Fremont 1842-44

Powell 1869

Green River

Sevier Lake

FILLMORE

Dominguez-Escalante 1776

Sevier River

WASATCH PLATEAU

UTE

MOAB

River

SOUTHERN PAIUTE

AQUARIUS PLATEAU

Powell

WATERPOCKET FOLD

CANYONLANDS

Colorado River

CEDAR CITY

N
W   E
S

Hole in the Rock

PARIA CANYON

NAVAJO

San Juan River

THE EARLY EXPLORERS

Utah is a vast territory just waiting for adventurers. Great expanses of alpine forest remain wild and natural. Red-rock canyons, forbidding-looking deserts, pristine mountains, and gleaming white salt flats stretch far into the horizon.

Peering over the edge of deep canyons or gazing over tortured landscape and rivers filled with perilous rapids gives you a hint of the courage and determination of the early explorers—Escalante, Dominguez, Bridger, Smith, and Powell—as they made their way across the land that is now Utah.

■ THE SPANISH EXPLORERS

By the early 1500s, the native people of what is now the American Southwest had settled into villages and were growing crops and learning through other Indians about raiding, war, immigration, and trade. Neither unified nor reliably peaceful, they nonetheless had an established, functional culture. Strangers had wandered into their midst and they had adapted to the changes, even adopting new construction and pottery techniques as a result.

The arrival of the Spaniards, however, ushered in a disturbing new era for the Indians. After Columbus landed on American shores, Spain claimed the western half of the continent and sent explorers far and wide to conquer and Christianize the natives.

Curiously, the first Spaniards to arrive in the Southwest did so quite accidentally. As Alvar Nunez Cabeza de Vaca was sailing toward Mexico in 1528, a storm pushed his party onto the shores of Texas, from which point the small group made its way overland to Mexico. His reports back to the mother country fueled rumors of a wealthy civilization north of Mexico—a myth perpetuated when Franciscan padre Marcos de Niza, in 1538, claimed to have seen "a city bigger than Mexico City." The natives, he said, called this city Cibola, and it was "the greatest and best of discoveries." Most likely it was nothing more than a Native American pueblo village, but de Niza must have seen it from afar, presumably at sunset, when it glowed with a golden hue, and assumed he was seeing the famed cities of gold.

Spanish Viceroy Mendoza, believing de Niza's colorful reports, authorized an elaborate expedition into the interior of North America. The party, headed by Francisco Vásquez de Coronado, was made up of 300 Spanish explorers (including

THE DOMINGUEZ-ESCALANTE JOURNAL, 1776

Nov. 7: We went very early to inspect the canyon and the ford. . . . In order to lead the animals down the side of the canyon mentioned it was necessary to cut steps in a rock with axes for the distance of three varas or a little less [8 feet]. The rest of the way the animals were able to get down, although without pack or rider. We went down to the canyon and having traveled a mile we descended to the river . . . until we reached the widest part of its current where the ford appeared to be. One of the men waded in and found it good, not having to swim at any place. We followed him on horseback a little lower down, and when half way across, two horses which went ahead lost their footing and swam a short distance. We waited, although in some peril, until the first wader returned from the other side to guide us and then we crossed with ease, the horses on which we crossed not having to swim at all. We notified the rest of our companions . . . that with lassoes and ropes they should let the pack saddles and other effects down a not very high cliff to the bend of the ford, and they should bring the animals by the route over which we had come. They did so and about five o'clock in the afternoon they finished crossing the river, praising God our Lord and firing off a few muskets as sign of the great joy which we all felt at having overcome so great a difficulty and which had cost us so much labor and delay.

Father Escalante Discovers Utah Valley *(1950), by E. Keith Eddington.*

at least three women), six Franciscans, 1,500 horses and pack animals, and a thousand Indian "allies." In search of precious metals and wealthy cities, they entered what is now New Mexico and Arizona.

Coronado's travels dramatically disrupted the lives of the native people. Not only did the group introduce European infectious diseases such as smallpox and measles, they also brought guns. Zuni Indians, whose villages were conquered and whose people were burned at the stake, spoke of "coats of iron and warbonnets of metal . . . and weapons . . . that spit fire and made thunder."

Of course, Coronado never found the city of gold. In fact, Spanish exploration into the interior of southwest North America ended for several decades after 1543. It was late in the 16th century when rumors of wealth resurfaced and Spain resumed exploration. And it was not until the late 18th century that Spanish explorers finally made their way into present-day Utah. Their purpose was to find an overland trade route from Santa Fe, New Mexico, to their newly established missions in California. An expedition headed by Fray Francisco Atanasio Dominguez and Fray Silvestre Velez de Escalante entered the territory near what is now Jensen, Utah—20 miles from the Utah-Colorado border—on September 11, 1776.

Moving westward, the Dominguez-Escalante expedition arrived on the eastern shores of Utah Lake on September 23. They were very likely the first white men to set eyes upon this verdant valley. Indeed, their written record reported that Utah Valley was "so spacious, with such good land in beautiful proportions that in it alone a province like New Mexico could be established . . . and supplied with every kind of cattle and grain." Local Indians informed them that the lake connected with another one to the north, one that stretched for many leagues. The waters of this lake, according to the Indians, were noxious and salty, so that "anyone getting a part of his body wet in that water instantly felt a severe itching."

The expedition was plagued with difficulty. As the padres continued their journey to the southwest, they found themselves with very little food. On October 5, their Indian guide abandoned them after a quarrel with other members of the party. Catastrophe struck again only three days later, when the group was surprised by a heavy snowstorm and frigid temperatures. On October 8, Dominguez and Escalante made the decision to abandon the expedition and return to Santa Fe. When the remaining members of party found themselves divided and unable to agree on a route, the fathers decided to "determine the will of God" by drawing slips of paper from a hat. One paper said "Monterey," their original goal in California; the other said "Cosnina," a settlement in New Mexico. Cosnina was drawn and the explorers turned south.

Only a priest could have faith enough to survive the grueling journey across Utah's rugged terrain. Escalante described a canyon on the Diamond Fork River of Spanish Fork Canyon, southeast of Provo, as a place where "there were many dangerous defiles and slides, with no other trail than the one we went opening all along, and over the sierra's corrugated ruggedness which all over here made us change direction and wind about excessively at every step." Visitors to the canyon today travel on pavement to view the same rugged mountains that so vexed the Spanish fathers.

Today, hikers in Paria Canyon near the Utah-Arizona border carry maps and water and enjoy the spectacular red-rock scenery. In 1776, however, the tall, vertical canyon walls stifled the Spanish explorers in their search for a way to ford the Colorado River. They had been warned by the Indians not to continue south to the Colorado because of the impassable sandstone terrain, but they distrusted this advice, and for 10 days struggled to find their way through trackless mesas and across massive gorges, suffering from hunger and thirst. Horses were killed to feed the starving party. Finally they reached the only point for 50 miles upstream and 150 miles downstream where a horse could reach the water, but the river was too wide and too deep for safe crossing. "We found nothing but insuperable obstacles for getting to the ford without retracing much terrain," wrote Escalante. The fathers, camping and resting in the deep canyons, called their camp in Paria Canyon *Salsipuedes* ("Get Out if You Can"). On November 7, 1776, they at last forded the Colorado about three miles north of the Utah-Arizona border.

Escalante described the climb out of the canyon as having "extremely difficult stretches and most dangerous ledges." They made the arduous climb and camped that night above the present-day swimming beach at Wahweap, on Lake Powell, the artificial lake created by the damming of the Colorado. The "Crossing of the Fathers," the point where the explorers forded the river, is now submerged under water.

Dominguez and Escalante did not succeed in finding a northern route to California, and the Indians did not convert to Christianity. Nonetheless, the expedition did open Utah to further exploration, and the expedition's map-maker, Don

Bernardo Miera y Pacheco, charted Utah's first maps. Modern travelers who read Escalante's journal and visit the rugged country of the Colorado Plateau, the Uintas, and the Wasatch Front can only marvel at the exploits of these brave men. How different might Utah have been if the fathers had succeeded! The Utes (or *Lagunas*, as the Spanish fathers called them) on the shores of Utah Lake grew to like the missionaries so much that they begged them to return. Dominguez and Escalante promised to send missionaries, but their superiors in Mexico chose not to. Almost a hundred years would pass before another church, that of Jesus Christ of Latter-day Saints, would arrive in their land. Even though the early explorers described the land as "the most pleasing, beautiful, and fertile site in all New Spain," Utah's colonization was left to the Mormons. If Dominguez and Escalante had succeeded, Provo might be the home of Catholic priests instead of Mormon bishops.

■ MOUNTAIN MEN

Long before Dominguez and Escalante arrived in the Great Basin in 1776, Russian explorers had discovered Alaska and found it rich with sea otters—a discovery that fostered the development of a lively worldwide fur trade. The frenzy of hunting rapidly depleted the supply of sea otters, however, and, with the emphasis on overland expeditions, the focus of the fur trade quickly shifted to the beaver.

The money to be made from beaver pelts drew trappers and traders to the West in astonishing numbers. Soon the Columbia and Missouri rivers were trapped out and adventurous entrepreneurs pushed into the "land of the Yutas." In March of 1822 William Henry Ashley placed an ad in a St. Louis newspaper asking to "engage one hundred young men to ascend the Missouri River to its source, there to be employed for one, two or three years." Among the young, enthusiastic men were Jedediah S. Smith and James Bridger.

■ JIM BRIDGER, 1804–1881

Jim Bridger—hunter, trapper, trader, Indian fighter, and guide—was one of the original "Ashley Men" and one of Utah's greatest frontiersmen. Stanley Vestal wrote about Bridger in his book, *Jim Bridger, Mountain Man:*

> He could read and recognize signs made by any critter on four legs or
> on two, readily determining the sex, age, gait, and often the purpose

LOOKING THE PART

The mountain man was almost Indian-colored from exposure to the weather. His hair hung upon his shoulders. He was bearded. Next to his skin he wore a red flannel loincloth. His outer clothes were of buckskin, fringed at all the seams. The jacket sometimes reached to the knee over tight, wrinkled leggings. His feet were covered by moccasins made of deer or buffalo leather. Around his waist was a leather belt into which he thrust his flintlock pistols, his knife for skinning or scalping, and his shingling hatchet. Over one shoulder hung his bullet pouch and over the other his powder horn. To their baldrics were attached his bullet mould, ball screw, wiper and an awl for working leather. When he moved he shimmered with fringe and rang and clacked with accoutrements of metal and wood. The most important of these were his traps, of which he carried five or six, and his firearm with its slender separate crutch of hardwood.

—Paul Horgan, *Great River: The Rio Grande in North American History,* 1954

of any animal whose trail he picked up. He could at once identify the tribe of any Indian whose moccasin tracks crossed his trail, and was so familiar with his own horse and those of his companions that he could usually recognize the tracks of any horse in the *caballada*. He could estimate accurately by the warmth of the ashes of a dead campfire how long it had been since those who had built it had departed. If a track were in sand, he could tell by the amount of sand that had crumbled into it how long before it had been made. In grass he could tell whether or not the tracks had been made before or after dewfall, before or after a shower.

In 1823 Bridger and other trappers and traders were assembled for the winter near what is now Cove, in northern Utah. During this encampment, a lively dispute erupted regarding the course of the Bear River south of the valley. Bridger was chosen to explore the river and resolve the dispute. It was this journey that took him to the Great Salt Lake, which he believed to be the Pacific Ocean because of its salty taste. While Bridger is often recognized as the man who discovered this great "Inland Sea," some authorities suggest that mountain man Etienne Provost actually saw the lake a few weeks prior to Bridger's sighting.

■ JEDEDIAH SMITH

Perhaps the most remarkable of the Ashley brigade was Jedediah Smith. Beginning his life as a mountain man in 1822, at the age of 23, Smith was among the first to cross west over the Continental Divide. He opened South Pass in Wyoming to the great route of Western migration. He traveled the length of Utah from north to south before any other non-Indian. He used the maps and journals of Spanish explorers to blaze the trail connecting California to the rest of the continent. Crossing the Great Basin, he proved once and for all the nonexistence of the legendary Buenaventura River, which was said to link the Great Salt Lake to the ocean. He was the first non-Indian to cross the Sierra Nevada and follow the California and Oregon coasts to the Columbia River.

In May 1826, in the company of Silas Gobel and Robert Evans, Smith was returning from an expedition in California to rendezvous with the Ashley brigade in Utah. They entered Utah on June 20, at a point just north of present-day Great Basin National Park in Nevada. Here they found the Great Salt Lake Desert, "a country completely barren and destitute of game," Smith wrote in his journal—a literate and colorful chronicle of his adventurous life that, published later, turned him into a legend.

> We frequently traveled without water, sometimes for two days over sandy deserts where there was no sign of vegetation. When we found water in some of the rocky hills, we generally found some Indians who appeared the most miserable of the human race, having nothing to subsist on (nor any clothing) except grass-seed, grasshopper, etc. With our best exertion, we pushed forward walking as we had been for a long time over the soft sand. That kind of traveling is very tiresome to men in good health who can eat when they choose and drink as often as they desire. To us, worn down with hunger and fatigue and burning with thirst increased by the blazing sands, it was almost insupportable.

During the day, the men buried themselves in the sand to escape the heat. At night, they pushed on through what is now the Dugway Proving Grounds (designated as a government bombing range and nerve-gas testing area because of its isolation and desolation). The men ate the horses and mules as the animals died along the way.

Jim Bridger, mountain man. Bridger was so adept at following a trail it was said that he could do it even in the dark of night, by getting off his horse and feeling the ground with his hands.

On June 25, Robert Evans could go no farther. Smith and Gobel left him under a small juniper tree and headed for the distant mountains in search of water. They found it three miles away at the foot of the Stansbury Mountains. The men plunged in and drank their fill. Jedediah took five quarts back to Evans, who was barely alive. The three rested for a day and moved on.

Two days later, they saw the Great Salt Lake, but pushed onward toward their rendezvous with Ashley and the other mountain men at the southern shore of Bear Lake. Because they had been thought to be dead, their presence caused quite a commotion. Ashley fired a cannon, the first wheeled vehicle to cross South Pass, to salute the returning heroes.

Smith continued his exploration of the American West through the Mojave Desert and into Oregon until he was 32 years old. In 1831 he was killed by Comanches as he guided a wagon on the Santa Fe Trail.

■ THE RENDEZVOUS

It didn't take long for Ashley to realize that the rugged country and rocky rivers were not ideal for transporting supplies and furs. He developed a new approach, with a system of pack trains that made an annual rendezvous at a designated spot. Thus began the tradition of the mountain-man rendezvous, which for many trappers became the most important link with the outside world: a chance to stock up on civilized goods and the premier social event of their long, lonely year.

By 1840, the fashionable men of New York, London, and Paris had abandoned their beaver hats for silk, and the mountain men had moved on and found other uses for their skills. The romance and excitement of the mountain lifestyle lives on, however, in annual rendezvous held throughout Utah. At these events, visitors can walk from one teepee to the next, watching men or women in buckskins or furs work on Indian beadwork or stir up Dutch-oven meals. There are skilled gunsmiths, tanners, leatherworkers, and hat makers. The cracking black-powder muskets echo in the distance, while Indian drums and chanting beckon visitors toward a dancing circle.

Many mountain men left both their legends and their names behind in Utah. Bridger Creek and Bridger Lake are both named for Jim Bridger; Provo is named in honor of Etienne Provost. Smiths Fork, which drains into Wyoming, is named for Jedediah Smith. The city of Ogden honors the memory of Peter Skene Ogden. Similarly, the trapper custom of hiding or "caching" their furs until rendezvous time gave Cache County its name.

■ JOHN WESLEY POWELL

It is all but impossible to run a Utah river and not hear of the exploits of John Wesley Powell, who in 1869 became the first man to explore the Green and Colorado rivers. Modern-day guides often read from his journal around the campfire and tell of the one-armed man— a Civil War veteran, he lost his right forearm at the Battle of Shiloh—who ran the river sitting in an armchair, lashed onto the bow deck of a flatboat.

Every river runner who floats through Lodore, Desolation, Westwater, Cataract, and other Utah canyons sees the same wild rivers that Powell did, and most of these visitors experience the same heart-thumping excitement the major wrote about in his journals.

> Now the river turns abruptly around a point to the right and the waters plunge swiftly down among great rocks. . . . I stand up on the deck of my boat to seek a way among the wave-beaten rocks. All untried as we are with such waters, the moments are filled with intense anxiety. Soon our boats reach the swift current; and a stroke or two, now on this side, now on that, and we thread the narrow passage with exhilarating velocity, mounting the high waves, whose foaming crests dash over us, and plunging into the troughs, until we reach the quiet water below. Then comes a feeling of great relief. Our first rapid is run.

Powell had become interested in botany and geology at an early age. He studied at Wheaton and Oberlin colleges, and after the war became a professor of geology at Illinois Wesleyan University. Not content with the confines of a classroom, however, Powell began a series of expeditions into the Rocky Mountains in 1867. After two years of field work, he became convinced that he could explore the canyons of the Colorado River and its tributary, the Green River. He set out on his most famous expedition on May 24, 1869, with four wooden boats. Starting at Green River, Wyoming, he covered 900 miles of the Green and Colorado rivers, floating the length of Utah into the Grand Canyon of Arizona.

Each year hundreds of river rafters and kayakers travel the same route as Powell, passing through whitewater and canyons he first explored. The experience is ever-changing. In the spring, snow melt from the mountains spills into the rivers, and they become raging torrents, whipping the rafts downriver with frightening speed.

Later in the summer boulders loom above the rapids, exposed by the lower water levels. Powell's description of whitewater is as accurate today as it was in the 1800s: "Today we have an exciting ride. The river rolls down the canyon at a wonderful rate and, with no rocks in the way, we make almost railroad speed. Here and there the water rushes into a narrow gorge; the rocks on the side roll it into the center in great waves, and the boats go leaping and bounding over these like things of life."

While Powell is most often remembered for his daring expeditions through remote canyons and rapids, he can also be credited with significant contributions to planning the use of Western lands. He argued that systems that worked in the water-rich East did not apply to the arid West, where water rights had to go along with land deeds. Engineers needed to create reservoirs so that precious water could be managed for recreation, agriculture, and flood prevention. Powell also called for forest preservation, land-use studies, and the setting aside of public land for the use of all citizens.

Along with photographer John Hillers, Powell also contributed to documentation of the Ute and Paiute Indian tribes. Photos and notes taken on an 1871 expedition created a body of knowledge about a disappearing people and way of life. In 1873 the U.S. government appointed Powell special commissioner to help establish reservations for Indian tribes in Utah and eastern Nevada. He told his superiors that the Indians, numbering only 5,500 in the territory, were on the verge of extinction. The government adopted his suggestions for reservation sites, but unfortunately dismissed his vision of a reservation as a school of industry, where instructors taught trades, skills, and English to help the Indians prosper in the modern world. With America not yet ready to accept responsibility for Indian welfare, the Indians were simply herded onto the reservations and largely ignored. Powell later joined the Smithsonian Institution, where he continued his work with the Indians as director of the Bureau of Ethnology.

When Powell became the second director of the United States Geological Survey, in 1881, he went to work establishing both an irrigation survey for the West and a department of science to help the government make intelligent decisions about its future handling of the environment and the Indians. Many of his ideas were not implemented until after his death in 1902—but his part in the development of land-use management came to fruition with the setting aside of public lands, the harnessing of the Colorado River, and the establishment of a bureau of forestry and a federal agency for the encouragement of science.

John Wesley Powell conversing with an Indian who was probably one of his guides.

GRAND VIEW POINT, AS SEEN BY AN EARLY VISITOR TO WHAT IS NOW CANYONLANDS NATIONAL PARK

What a world of grandeur is spread before us! Below is the canyon through which the Colorado runs. We can trace its route for miles, and at points catch glimpses of the river. From the northwest comes the Green in a narrow winding gorge. From the northeast comes the Grand, through a canyon that seems bottomless from where we stand. Away to the west are lines of cliff and ledges of rock—not such ledges as the reader may have seen where the quarryman splits his blocks, but ledges from which the gods might quarry mountains that, rolled out on the plain below, would stand a lofty range; and not such cliffs as the reader may have seen where the swallow builds its nest, but cliffs where the soaring eagle is lost to view ere he reaches the summit. ... Wherever we look there is but a wilderness of rocks—deep gorges where the rivers are lost below cliffs and towers and pinnacles, and ten thousand strangely carved forms in every direction, and beyond them mountains blending with the clouds.

—John Wesley Powell, *Diary of Colorado River Explorations,* 1869

Powell's travels and studies of Indian philosophy taught him that mankind needs to remain in balance with the land. His geological training helped him realize that the Colorado Plateau and River, along with the river's tributaries, are part of an equilibrium of precipitation, evaporation, and erosion. He preached that civilization must fit within the system or run out of water.

In spite of the construction of the Flaming Gorge and Glen Canyon dams on the Colorado and Green rivers, these waterways are constantly changing in character, swelling in wet years and withering in dry ones. Adventurous travelers to Utah can join an expedition on Powell's rivers with one of dozens of outfitters, many of whom have headquarters in Moab or Green River.

To get a feel for John Wesley Powell's exploits without getting wet, visit the **John Wesley Powell River History Museum** in Green River, Utah. A multimedia show examines the history of river running in the state, beginning with John Wesley Powell's adventure. Exhibits include the Utah River Runners Hall of Fame and several of the earliest boats used by river runners, including a replica of Powell's *Emma Dean. 885 East Main Street, Green River; 435-564-3427.*

Powell sets out on his second expedition down the Green and Colorado rivers, May 1871.

THE MORMON PIONEERS

Understanding the nuances of Utah's culture without knowing anything about the Church of Jesus Christ of Latter-day Saints would be as difficult as understanding Italian culture with no knowledge of Roman Catholicism.

Travelers in Utah cannot fail to sense the Mormon presence and heritage. It is evident in the gleaming white temples found in cities like Manti and St. George. It is preserved in historical sites and museums. It is woven into the fabric of the state's laws, politics, and cultural activities. Many names on the state's road map—Brigham City, Moroni, Nephi, Lehi, and Heber City—reflect Utah's Mormon origins. The Mormons have played, and continue to play, a tremendous and often misunderstood role. This is their story.

■ THE FOUNDING OF THE MORMON CHURCH

Persecution either destroys or unifies a people. Seventeen years of persecution gave the Mormons the strength to leave the civilized world east of the Missouri River and cross the Great Plains and Rocky Mountains in order to practice their faith. Under adverse conditions they took a dry and inhospitable wilderness avoided by other immigrants and made it "blossom like a rose."

The history of the Mormon Church begins with Joseph Smith. As a young man in the Finger Lakes region of western New York, Smith questioned the many Christian religions competing for converts and prayed for an answer as to which church to join. In the spring of 1820, when he was 14 years old, Mormons believe, God and Jesus appeared to Smith in a vision and told him to join none of them—that the existing churches were all wrong. In September 1823, in a series of visions, an angel named Moroni appeared to tell Smith that God had work for him to do. The angel is said to have shown Smith where he could uncover a set of gold plates containing the history of two of the 10 tribes of Israel that, around 600 B.C., had fled Jerusalem before it was destroyed by the Babylonians.

The plates told of the tribes' escape to the Western Hemisphere, where they established a new civilization. Eventually they divided into two warring camps, the Nephites and the Lamanites. The plates recorded the ultimate victory of the

The angel Moroni delivering the plates of the Book of Mormon *to Joseph Smith, in an 1886 lithograph based on a painting by the Danish-born Mormon artist C.C.A. Christensen.*

Lamanites, whom the Mormons believe to be the ancestors of the American Indians. Moroni was himself one of the characters in this history. He was the son of Mormon, the prophet who had inscribed the story on the plates, and he was the last surviving member of the Nephites. It was Moroni who had received the plates from his father and buried them, in A.D. 421, in a hill near Smith's home.

Moroni visited Smith once a year for four years, and then, on September 22, 1827, allowed him to take possession of the plates along with some magic stones buried with them that would be used to translate the inscriptions on them from their ancient language into English. That work began on April 7, 1829, when a local schoolteacher, Oliver Cowdery, came to Smith's door to assist. In an eight-week burst of inspiration, reading with the help of the "seer" stones, Smith dictated and Cowdery transcribed the nearly 600-page manuscript. When translation was finished, two other men were allowed to witness the existence of the plates before Moroni took them back.

Hand-setting of type to print the *Book of Mormon* began in August 1829, and in the spring of 1830, shortly after it was published, the Church of Jesus Christ of Latter-day Saints (LDS) was founded in Fayette, New York. Members of the faith hold the *Book of Mormon* to be divinely inspired, a supplement to the Old and New Testaments (its subtitle is Another Gospel of Jesus Christ). They call themselves Latter-day Saints, a reference to Paul's New Testament prophecy that the true believers in the last days of the world would be called saints. They believe that Joseph Smith restored the true Christian church to the earth, one that predated the division into Catholic, Eastern Orthodox, and Protestant churches. Contemporary visitors to Salt Lake City find the angel Moroni depicted in gold atop the Mormon Temple, blowing his horn to announce the restoration.

■ PERSECUTION

Persecution of the Mormons began almost immediately. Members of the new church were active missionaries, and their zeal and fervor were not appreciated by other citizens or religious leaders. They quietly practiced polygamy. It wasn't long before Smith and his followers were forced to move from New York to Kirtland, Ohio, and then to Independence, Missouri, both places that Smith had designated as gathering places. By 1837, nearly 2,000 church members were in Kirtland, but by 1838 tensions between Mormons and non-Mormons forced them to move to Missouri. They fared little better there, however. With approximately 10,000 Mormons now in Missouri, non-Mormons began to fear the new group's domination. During the winter of 1838–39, the situation became so inflamed that the Missouri governor issued an order for the Mormons to leave the state or be exterminated.

After leaving Missouri, the Mormons founded the city of Nauvoo, Illinois, in 1839. It soon had a population of 12,000, making it the second-largest city in that state. Smith and the city council were permitted by the state to raise a militia, levy taxes, and make laws, and once again provoked concern in the surrounding non-Mormon communities. The prosperity of this near city-state brought jealousy; meanwhile, the Mormons soon irritated both political parties in Illinois by voting for neither one.

While the Illinois Legislature considered repeal of Nauvoo's charter, mobs descended on outlying Mormon farms, killing and mutilating the inhabitants and burning their houses and crops. Joseph Smith decided it was time to move again and sent scouts to look for a suitable place. Meanwhile, on May 17, 1844, he declared himself a candidate for the presidency of the United States. His stated intention was to spread "the dominion of the Kingdom of God" throughout the country.

Smith's political ambitions were cut short when he and his brother Hyrum were arrested after members of the Mormon city council smashed a printing press they believed was being used to print anti-church libel. Joseph and his brother were taken to await trial in a jail in Carthage, the county seat 15 miles to the east. On the night of June 27, 1844, a mob stormed the jail and killed them both.

■ Exodus to Utah

Brigham Young became the second leader of the LDS Church. He had grown up near Joseph Smith's New York home and was baptized into the church in 1832. At the time of Smith's death, Young was president of the ruling body of the church, the Council of the Twelve. (Since that time, the leader of the Council of the Twelve has assumed the church presidency upon the death of an existing president.)

Descriptions of Brigham Young vary with writers' views of Mormonism. Some describe him in glowing terms, others with suspicion and contempt. In *Giants of the Old West,* published in 1930, Frederick R. Bechdolt wrote that the first impression one received was of heavy strength: "There was no fineness in his lines. Throughout, there was a certain homely indomitability. His face was large and fair;

the blue eyes keen. A brown beard ringed his strong jaw; his upper lip was shaven, revealing the coarse, firm mouth. He would have passed for a well-to-do farmer or a British drover. He was, by trade, a carpenter. By destiny he had become leader of a people."

After Smith's death, the Mormons continued to have problems with their non-Mormon neighbors. Anti-Mormon looting, arson, and riot repeatedly tore through Nauvoo and the surrounding countryside. Fearing further mob action, Young sent scouts to search for sites for possible resettlement. Church leaders studied maps of explorers and mountain men. In 1845, the Mormon newspaper, the *Nauvoo Neighbor*, published accounts from the journals of the explorer John C. Frémont, and his description of the Great Salt Lake Valley proved convincing. Late in 1845, after the state of Illinois repealed Nauvoo's city charter and the violence increased, Young announced that it was time to leave. In February of 1846, the Mormons moved out of Illinois, headed beyond the Rockies.

This exodus was the beginning of one of the largest, most carefully planned, and successful migrations in North American history. Before it was over, tens of thousands of Mormons would have crossed oceans, mountains, and plains to establish their "Zion" in Utah. As Young wrote to President James Polk in June 1846, a "combination of fortuitous, illegal and unconstitutional circumstances have placed us in our present situation, on a journey which we design shall end in a location west of the Rocky Mountains, and within the basin of the Great Salt Lake, or Bear River valley, . . . believing that to be a point where a good living will require hard labor, and consequently will be coveted by no other people."

For their safety, Young organized the emigrants with military precision, in groups of hundreds, fifties, and tens, each with a captain. En route, those who blazed the trail built bridges and set up ferries to cross rivers and established permanent campsites as way stations for those who were to follow. The first leg of the trip, from Nauvoo to the Missouri River, about 265 miles, took the first emigrants four months to cover. It ended in the vicinity of present-day Council Bluffs, Iowa, which the Mormons called Kanesville, and, on the other side of the river, near Omaha, Nebraska, at present-day Florence, in a camp they called Winter Quarters.

The original plan had been to press on to the Great Basin without interruption. But in Council Bluffs the need for greater preparation and for hard cash prompted postponement. Young had hoped that the U.S. government might provide assistance for the Mormons' migration. Although church leaders had a right to be bitter

Mormon Battalion veterans at their 50-year reunion, Salt Lake City, 1897.

about the lack of support the United States had given them in the past, a proposal by President Polk that the Mormons supply 500 men to help fight the war against Mexico, declared in May 1846, was seen as an opportunity to prove their patriotism and earn some money for the resettlement. The Mormon Battalion, about 500 strong, departed in July for a 2,000-mile march to San Diego, California.

The winter of 1846–47 was a severe one. Approximately 4,000 Mormons spent it at Winter Quarters, and many of them died. In the spring, on April 5, 1847, Brigham Young and an advance party of 143 men, three women, and two children set out on the second leg of the trip westward—a distance of more than 1,000 miles. On July 22, the main body of this group came through Emigration Canyon and looked out over the Great Salt Lake Valley, a place described by two early Mormon pioneers, George Washington Brimhall and Gilbert Belnap, as "a vast desert whose dry and parched soil seemed to bid defiance to the husbandryman." But the sight that day prompted Thomas Bullock to shout "hurra, hurra, hurra, there's my home at last." The next morning the pioneers were up by 7 for the final push into the valley; by afternoon they were plowing, planting, and diverting

Mormon immigrants coming through Echo Canyon east of Salt Lake City, ca. 1868–1880.

streams for irrigation, even before they began building their homes. Brigham Young himself, sick with mountain fever and traveling with a small group bringing up the rear, arrived on July 24. As he reached the summit of Big Mountain, the Mormon leader raised himself from his wagon bed and reportedly announced "This is the right place."

When the Mormons began the transformation of Utah, it still belonged to Mexico, but the land was ceded to the United States the following year. The Mormons named the land they settled the State of Deseret, a word from the *Book of Mormon* meaning "honeybee." Thus the bee and hive, signifying industry and community, became symbols of Utah, and both are depicted on the Utah state flag. Young's emphasis on these qualities made the new territory prosper.

■ ESTABLISHING ZION

Brigham Young proved to be a master planner with a vision for what the Mormon Zion should look like. Although more pioneers continued to arrive throughout the spring and fall of 1847—about 1,650 spent the first winter here—by August Young had already returned to Winter Quarters to prepare the main body of the church for a trek westward in 1848. While there, he dashed off a letter to the general membership exhorting Latter-day Saints throughout the world to gather in Winter Quarters to prepare for the trip to Great Salt Lake City. Mormon history records that 3,000 to 4,000 people came each year from 1848 through 1852, and that thousands per year began migrating from abroad after that. By the time of Young's death in 1877, there were approximately 125,000 settlers in the Salt Lake Valley. New communities had been established not only throughout Utah, but also in areas now part of the surrounding states.

The settlers faced innumerable hardships. In the spring of 1848, a late frost hurt much of the bean, corn, and wheat crop. Then came crickets "by the thousands of tons." The pioneers tried fruitlessly to beat them off the crops and were finally rescued by hungry seagulls who flew in to gobble the crickets up. This "miracle of the gulls" is a cherished part of Mormon folklore, and the seagull is the state bird. The state flower, the sego lily, also helped the pioneers survive their first year. Its nourishing, edible bulb was eaten when there was little else.

This hand-colored 1840s woodcut shows Brigham Young at the Great Salt Lake.

BRIGHAM YOUNG AND THE QUESTION ON EVERYBODY'S MIND

Ladies who come into my office very frequently say, "I wonder if it would hurt his feelings if I were to ask him how many wives he has?" Let me say to all creation that I would as lief they should ask me that question as any other; but I would rather see them anxious to learn about the Gospel. Having wives is a secondary consideration; it is within the pale of duty, and consequently, it is all right. But to preach the Gospel, save the children of men, build up the kingdom of God, produce righteousness in the midst of the people; govern and control ourselves and our families and all we have influence over; make us of one heart and one mind . . . is our business, no matter how many wives a man has got, that makes no difference here or there. I want to say, and I wish you to publish it, that I would as soon be asked how many wives I have got as any other question, just as soon; but I would rather see something else in their minds, instead of all the same thinking, "How many wives have you; or I wonder whom he slept with last night." I can tell those who are curious on this point. I slept with all that slept, and we slept on one universal bed—the bosom of our mother earth, and we slept together. "Did you have anybody in bed with you?" "Yes." "Who was it?" It was my wife, it was not your wife, nor your daughter nor sister, unless she was my wife, and that too legally. I can say that to all creation, and every honest man can say the same; but it is not all who are professed Christians who can say it.

—Brigham Young, speaking in Ogden, 1871, from the *Journal of Discourses*, Volume 14:156, 1852–1885

Great Salt Lake City was surveyed and divided into blocks and lots. Streets between the blocks were laid out to be wide enough so that a wagon with a team of oxen could turn around. Church leaders initially divided up the land among all married males, although widows and divorced women who were heads of households could receive an allotment. Each was required to work the land or lose the right to own it; they were also barred from selling off parts of their lots. Furthermore, they were required to give 10 percent of their income for the good of

Brigham Young, Salt Lake City founder and upholder of the Mormon faith.

the church, a practice called tithing that endures to this day. An extensive welfare system was established, whereby large storehouses were built to house excess crops that could be distributed to church members according to their needs—another arrangement that still exists in much the same form today.

Polygamy remained one of the main tenets of the Latter-day Saints' faith. Church members believed that the only way to achieve the highest reward in heaven was to have more than one wife. Polygamy had been practiced in secret since Joseph Smith received a revelation affirming it as a divine requirement (possibly as early as 1831, although the revelation was not published until 1843). But on August 29, 1852, Brigham Young, at a conference of Mormon missionaries, announced that "the doctrine of plural marriage" was an official tenet of the church. Young himself approached his duty with trepidation (he admitted that he "desired the grave" when Smith first revealed it to him), but he certainly fulfilled it: he is generally credited with having had 27 wives, and it may have been as many as 56. As was the case with other Mormons, many of these marriages, or "sealings," were purely contractual, a way to provide women and their children with a means of financial support. (In fact, several of his wives had been the wives of Joseph Smith; Young married them after Smith's murder in 1844.) With 16 of his wives Young had 57 children.

All Mormon men were (and are) expected to serve as missionaries for a period of time, usually two years, and Deseret was to be the gathering place for their new converts. In 1849, the Perpetual Emigrating Fund Company was established to collect voluntary donations to help the poor among them travel to the Salt Lake Valley. Those taking advantage of the funds were expected to pay back the amount borrowed as soon as possible, so that others could come. But even after the Midwestern Mormons had largely made their way west, newcomers continued to arrive, including tens of thousands sent to Utah by missionaries in England and Scandinavia. When organized funding became insufficient, Brigham Young came up with a unique solution.

"We cannot purchase wagons and teams as in years past," he told the faithful. "I am consequently thrown back on my old plan and that is to make handcarts and let the emigrants foot it. They can come just as quick, if not quicker, and much cheaper—can start earlier and escape the prevailing sickness which annually lays so many of our brethren in the dust."

A Mormon family in the Salt Lake Valley, ca. 1869.

Between 1856 and 1860, the first of almost a dozen handcart "companies" set out from Iowa toward Utah, pulling their belonging behind them in handcarts. All told, 2,962 immigrants walked to Utah in this fashion, with surprisingly few fatalities. Only the two largest parties, the Willie and Martin companies, suffered disaster. They had left the East too late in the year and then were hit with unusually early winter storms that stranded them on the Wyoming plains. Brigham Young sent rescuers, including Mormon leader George D. Grant, who was one of the first Mormons to reach them. According to William Smart in *Old Utah Trails*, Grant wrote that he found "between five and six hundred men, women and children, worn down by drawing handcarts through snow and mud; fainting by the wayside; falling, chilled by the cold, their feet bleeding and some of them bare to the snow and frost. The sight is almost too much for the stoutest of us."

As the survivors were brought into the Great Salt Lake Valley, Brigham Young cut short a church meeting in progress and sent the churchgoers to ready their homes for the new immigrants. "Prayer is good," he told the faithful, "but when baked potatoes and pudding and milk are needed, prayer will not supply their place."

(following pages) A handcart company walking westward, as depicted by one of its members, C.C.A.Christensen, in 1900, four decades after he made the journey in 1857.

As the Mormon population grew—only in the 1890s did the church begin to encourage converts to remain in their home towns—so did its capital, between the Wasatch Mountains and the Great Salt Lake. Civil engineering projects initiated by Young and the Mormon pioneers still impress visitors to Salt Lake City. The broad, tree-lined streets are laid out in a grid pattern, and clear water for irrigation runs down the gutters today. All street numbers are counted from the Base and Meridian marker at the corner of Temple Square, making it easier to find one's way around in Salt Lake City than in other large cities lacking such urban planning.

Brigham Young built Temple Square in the heart of the city. He had picked the site for the temple the day after his arrival in the Salt Lake Valley, although construction did not begin until 1853 and took 40 years. Because sacraments like marriage had to be performed in the temple to make them eternal, Mormons were obliged to make pilgrimages to the Salt Lake City temple for many years, until others could be built in other Utah towns.

Another major feature of Temple Square is the famed Mormon Tabernacle, home to the world-famous Mormon Tabernacle Choir. An egg-shaped dome set above a series of stone buttresses, the building is remarkable, especially when one considers the primitive conditions under which it was constructed. Because nails were scarce, the building was put together with wooden pins and rawhide.

Young's city home, called the Beehive House because of the sculpted beehive on its roof, was just east of Temple Square, where it still stands today. Here Young entertained visitors and passing dignitaries. One of his wives lived here with her children; more of his families lived next door in the Lion House. Another family lived on the outskirts of the city in his farm home. The Beehive House also held a store, where all of his wives and children had accounts.

■ END OF ISOLATION

The Great Salt Lake Valley's isolation had been advantageous for the church leaders of the young State of Deseret, but isolation could not last forever. In fact, Salt Lake City was becoming an important stopover on the trail linking the East and West coasts.

The outside world first intruded in 1849, when throngs of miners en route to the gold fields of California stopped in the valley to buy supplies for their journey. Mark Twain passed through during the Comstock silver boom of the 1860s. In *Roughing It,* he recorded sentiments shared by many immigrants during this early

A Famous Newsman Interviews a Newsmaker

On July 13, 1859, Horace Greeley, the most famous newspaperman of his time, interviewed Brigham Young for the New York Tribune. *Greeley questioned Young on various beliefs of the new religion, then zoomed in on the topic he knew would interest his readers most. At the end of the interview, published on August 20, 1859, he appended some comments on the Mormon leaders.*

H.G.—With regard, then, to the grave question on which your doctrine and practices are avowedly at war with those of the Christian world—that of a plurality of wives—is the system of your Church acceptable to the majority of its women?

B.Y.—They could not be more averse to it than I was when it was first revealed to us as the Divine Will. I think they generally accept it, as I do, as the will of God.

H.G.—How general is polygamy among you?

B.Y.—I could not say. Some of those present [heads of the Church] have each but one wife; others have more: each determines what is his individual duty.

H.G.—What is the largest number of wives belonging to any one man?

B.Y.—I have fifteen; I know no one who has more but some of those sealed to me are old ladies whom I regard rather as mothers than wives, but whom I have taken home to cherish and support.

Such is, as nearly as I can recollect, the substance of nearly two hours' conversation. . . . He spoke readily, not always with grammatical accuracy, but with no appearance of hesitation or reserve, and with no apparent desire to conceal anything, nor did he repel any of my questions as impertinent. He was very plainly dressed in thin summer clothing, and with no air of sanctimony or fanaticism. In appearance, he is a portly, frank, good-natured, rather thick-set man of fifty-five, seeming to enjoy life, and to be in no particular hurry to get to heaven. His associates are plain men, evidently born and reared to a life of labor, and looking as little like crafty hypocrites or swindlers as any body of men I ever met. The absence of cant or shuffle from their manner was marked and general, yet, I think I may fairly say that their Mormonism has not impoverished them—that they were generally poor men when they embraced it, and are now in very comfortable circumstances—as men averaging three and four wives apiece certainly need to be.

—Horace Greeley, *New York Tribune,* August 20, 1859

A Celebrated Explorer Encounters a New Culture

In 1860, Richard F. Burton, the famed British explorer, spent 24 days in Salt Lake City on a journey across the American West to California. Burton, one of the first European men to visit many Muslim cities (and eventually the translator of several sexually explicit Arabian and Indian classics), was not shocked by polygamy. His record of the trip is an excellent early account of Mormonism.

To the unprejudiced traveller it appears that polygamy is the rule where population is required, and where the great social evil has not had time to develop itself. In Paris or London the institution would, like slavery, die a natural death; in Arabia and in the wilds of the Rocky Mountains it maintains a strong hold upon the affections of mankind. . . . The other motive for polygamy in Utah is economy. Servants are rare and costly; it is cheaper and more comfortable to marry them. Many converts are attracted by the prospect of becoming wives, especially from places where, like Clifton, there are sixty-four females to thirty-six males. The old maid is, as she ought to be, an unknown entity. Life in the wilds of Western America is a course of severe toil: a single woman cannot perform the manifold duties of housekeeping, cooking, scrubbing, washing, darning, child-bearing, and nursing a family. A division of labor is necessary, and she finds it by acquiring a sisterhood. . . .

The Mormon household has been described by its enemies as a hell of hatred, envy, and malice—a den of murder and suicide. The same has been said of the Moslem harem. Both, I believe, suffer from the assertions of prejudice or ignorance. The temper of the new is so far superior to that of the old country, that, incredible as the statement may appear, rival wives do dwell together in amity; and do quote the proverb "the more the merrier." . . . They know that nine-tenths of the miseries of the poor in large cities arise from early and imprudent marriages, and they would rather be the fiftieth "sealing" of Dives than the toilsome single wife of Lazarus.

—Richard F. Burton, *The City of the Saints,* 1862

period: "The high prices charged for trifles were eloquent of high freights and bewildering distances of freightages. In the east, in those days, the smallest moneyed denomination was a penny and it represented the smallest purchasable quantity of any commodity. But, in Salt Lake there did not seem to be any money in circulation smaller than a quarter, or any smaller quantity purchasable of any commodity than twenty-five cents' worth."

In 1849, the Mormons drafted a constitution for a provisional State of Deseret, elected Brigham Young governor, elected a legislature, and sent a delegate to Congress to petition for statehood. Instead, Congress the next year passed a proposal by Henry Clay to admit California as a state and New Mexico and Utah as territories. Utah Territory embraced the present states of Nevada and Utah, and its capital was Fillmore. Brigham Young was its first territorial governor. Because Congress could not abide the religious connotations of the name "Deseret," the territory was named after the Ute Indians, but the Mormons persisted in calling it the "State of Deseret."

Tensions during this period of American history were high. There were rumblings that the South was about to secede from the Union. Compounding this crisis was the fact that in Utah Territory, the Mormons insisted on governing themselves, and in a manner very different from the way the rest of the United States was governed, with religious leaders wielding political power. Furthermore, the Mormon practice of polygamy was controversial: in Washington, it was deemed an assault on morality.

In 1856, the Republican National Convention platform labeled polygamy and slavery "twin relics of barbarism." Authorities in Washington were eager to focus public attention on something other than the constant strife over slavery, so it was perhaps a surprise only to the Mormons when President James Buchanan, in 1857, revoked Brigham Young's governorship over the territory and appointed a new governor, sending him to the Salt Lake Valley with an army escort to put down any insurrection that might arise. As Young's daughter Clarissa Young Spencer reported in her memoir, *Brigham Young at Home*, on July 24, 1857, "An army of twenty-five hundred from the States was marching toward the Territory, the Government had canceled the mail contracts, and numerous far-fetched rumors concerning the Mormons were being circulated in the East."

This kind of persecution was familiar to the Mormons, who were intent on staying in Utah and prepared to fight the U.S. government and burn Salt Lake City if the army threatened occupation. After Capt. Stewart Van Vliet called on Young in September to purchase supplies for these troops, the officer reported that "The governor informed me that there was an abundance of everything I required for the troops but that none would be sold to us." When Van Vliet replied that the Mormons might prevent the army from entering Utah that year but that next season the U.S. would send enough troops to overcome all opposition, Young boldly stated: "We are aware that such will be the case, but when the troops arrive they will find Utah a desert. Every house will be burned to the ground, every tree cut down and every field laid waste."

The infamous Mountain Meadows Massacre occurred while the Mormons were preparing for what would come to be called the Utah War. In August and September of 1857, a wagon train of 140 non-Mormon immigrants, mostly from Arkansas, passed through Utah Territory on their way to California. The wagon train was rich with livestock and had picked up a few defecting Mormons en route (at a time when defectors were hunted down). Rumors flew that the Arkansans had quarreled with local Paiute Indians, given them poisoned beef, and poisoned their springs. Some said that members of the wagon train had boasted about plans to attack the Mormons. For these reasons, and with the memory of past persecutions fresh in their minds, a group of Mormon men under President Isaac Haight and Bishop John D. Lee disguised themselves as Indians and convinced several hundred Paiutes to join them in attacking the immigrants. When the direct attack failed and the Indians would not finish the job, the Mormons took off their disguises, waved a flag of truce, and offered the men, women, and children a chance to put down their arms and walk away from the wagons. When the frightened immigrants complied, the men under Haight and Lee fell upon them and within five minutes the entire group, except for a number of children believed too young to talk, was massacred. The participants swore themselves to secrecy, but the story leaked out and evidence was discovered by a wagon train that happened upon the site. When the federal government pressed the church to accept responsibility for the massacre, Haight was excommunicated, but it wasn't until 1876 that Lee was tried and convicted. In 1877, he was shot by a firing squad.

But while the U.S. army, under the command of Col. Albert Sydney Johnston, was camped for the winter near Fort Bridger, Wyoming, the political mood in Washington changed. Captain Van Vliet had delivered Brigham Young's message to President Buchanan. A scandal involving army contracts and the spending of

This idealized portrait of a pioneer family contrasts sharply with the harsh conditions faced by original settlers.

millions of dollars with questionable results was exposed, and the press started calling the whole Utah affair "Buchanan's Blunder." Through another intermediary, Brigham Young agreed to admit the army into the territory as long as it neither molested the people nor settled there permanently. Assuring the Mormons they would not be disturbed, Johnston marched his men through Salt Lake Valley and on to the west side of Utah Lake, where he established Camp Floyd near what is the present-day hamlet of Fairfield.

The army and camp followers soon discovered Great Salt Lake City, and the Mormon capital soon discovered the soldiers' tendencies toward alcohol, theft, and violence. The capital's main thoroughfare became known as Whisky Street. Yet at the same time, the army presence did benefit the Mormon community: farmers could sell surplus foodstuffs and livestock to the army at high prices, and cheap manufactured good were available in Utah for the first time.

Although Johnston's army left Utah at the outbreak of the Civil War in 1861 (the colonel went on to distinguish himself as a commander for the South), government pressure on the Mormons did not end. In 1862, the Mormons drew up a third constitution for a "State of Deseret," elected a legislature, and elected Brigham Young as governor. The federal government viewed this as an act of rebellion and retaliated by passing the Morrill Act, which prohibited plural marriage, and sending Col. Patrick Edward Connor to Utah with 300 volunteers from California and Nevada vowing to "subdue the obstreperous Mormons though all Hell yawned." Connor marched his men into the Great Salt Lake Valley and built Fort Douglas on a bench overlooking the city.

The Mormons caused Connor no trouble, but the influence of the army certainly troubled the Latter-day Saints. Connor set out deliberately to undermine the Mormon Church's totalitarianism by encouraging his men to prospect for minerals, a practice the Mormons frowned upon, because it would distract the settlers from farming and because any strike would encourage an influx of non-Mormons into the territory. He organized the territory's first mining district, in 1863, and wrote its mining code, earning the title "the father of Utah mining." Silver was found in nearby Park City; copper in the Oquirrh Mountains. As the Mormons feared, the mining success brought more "outsiders" pouring into Utah, diluting its once homogeneous culture.

The Pony Express, which carried mail from Missouri to California beginning in April 1860; the transcontinental telegraph, which replaced it in October 1861; and the transcontinental railroad, which was completed at Promontory in 1869, signaled the end of Utah's isolation. Although the communication and transport improvements allowed church leaders better contact with members scattered throughout the large territory, the church nonetheless worried that gentile, or non-Mormon, traders would come to economically enslave the Mormons and undermine the principles of cooperation and communal life they had worked hard to ingrain in their society.

■ GROWTH OF ZION

The new railroad facilitated the expansion of Utah's mining industry. Boomtowns sprang up along the Wasatch and Oquirrh mountains. The coal-rich areas of Carbon and Emery counties were exploited. Cattle and sheep ranching prospered. But Mormons were exhorted to trade with Mormon merchants rather than with gentiles.

Brigham Young envisioned his new society as completely self-sufficient economically. He frowned upon the export of his people's money, goods, and crops in payment for merchandise. Pioneer lore details experiments undertaken to fulfill the church president's wishes. Mulberry trees and silkworms, for example, were imported to produce silk for ladies' fine garments. Perhaps the best-known experiment was the establishment of a cotton mission in sunny St. George, where cotton and silk were produced until the advent of the railroad.

Drawing on examples of existing cooperative tanneries and mills, the Mormons formed the Zion's Co-operative Mercantile Institution (ZCMI) in Salt Lake City in 1868, setting off a cooperative movement that lasted well beyond the 1880s and gave rise to a network of cooperative stores as new Mormon colonies came into being. Mormon leaders believed that only by extensive settlement could Deseret remain in church hands. There was to be no room for outsiders in the promised land of Zion. Meanwhile, Mormon pioneers spread to all corners of the territory and into lands now part of Nevada, Idaho, Arizona, Wyoming, Colorado, New Mexico, and California.

As new immigrants arrived, they were organized into groups and assigned land to develop into self-sufficient communities. Those dispatched to settle remote parts of Deseret were guided by experienced settlers, who were often called upon to leave the farms that they had established earlier. These moves often tested the faith of church members who had spent long, hard hours working to make their land prosper, only to be asked to leave and begin someplace else. Much of Utah is dry land and requires irrigation for successful farming. Only faith in their leaders and the Mormon belief that good works on earth promised salvation induced these pioneers to start over again.

In his journal, Parley P. Pratt, a Mormon leader who was among the 1847 pioneers, described the feelings of many of the earliest settlers: "My family and myself, in common with many of the camp, suffered much for food. . . . I had ploughed and subdued land to the amount of near forty acres, and had cultivated the same in grain and vegetables. In this labor every woman and child in my family . . . had joined to help me. . . . Myself and some of them were compelled to go with bare feet for several months, reserving our Indian moccasins for extra occasions. We toiled hard and lived on a few greens and on thistle and other roots. We had sometimes a little flour and some cheese, and sometimes we were able to procure from our neighbors a little sour skimmed milk or buttermilk." But he would write his brother in England, "All is quiet—stillness. No elections, no police reports, no murders, no wars, in our little world. . . . It is the dream of the poets actually fulfilled."

One of the most inspirational stories about the Utah pioneers' faith and perseverance was the Hole-in-the-Rock expedition of 1879–1880, when 200-plus men, women, and children took 82 wagons and hundreds of head of livestock to colonize the most remote corner of the state. The most difficult part of the journey came at the Hole-in-the-Rock, a narrow slit in the rim of Glen Canyon that had to be blasted through to widen it enough to allow the wagons to pass—a disheartening, six-week-long task. On the other side was a precipitous descent to the Colorado River, 2,000 feet below, which the settlers ferried across. Still more rugged terrain awaited them before they reached the end of their six-month journey. In *Old Utah Trails,* William B. Smart wrote of Mons Larson and his 23-year-old wife, Olivia, who reached the top of a mesa in a blizzard. "On the climb up,

A passage had to be cut through solid rock so that the wagons of the Hole-in-the-Rock expedition could proceed.

MAKING THE DESERT BLOSSOM

It was the necessity of irrigation that largely determined the shape and look of Mormon country. The task of digging and maintaining the irrigation canals was too great for a single family, thus dictating a communal pattern of settlement instead of the individualistic pattern that characterized the fertile Midwest. On the other hand, there was no capital available in the early days to construct massive reclamation works such as have been built in the West in this century. Each community was on its own in supplying labor and machinery, so the systems were relatively small and simple.

You see these irrigation systems everywhere in Mormon country, some of them little changed in a hundred years. The first settlers, anxious to get some land under cultivation, diverted small streams onto the floodplains. Later, more extensive diversion works and longer canals brought water to the higher land. When the highline canals were completed, the lower ditches were sometimes abandoned but sometimes not. As a result, the Mormon landscape is marked by parallel canals, each with its own thicket of trees and shrubs resembling the hedgerows of Europe.

—Edward A. Geary,
Goodbye to Poplarhaven: Recollections of a Utah Boyhood, 1985

Olivia had carried a two-and-one-half-year-old under one arm and a one-and-one-half-year-old child under the other, just as she had carried them down the Hole. The children's feet had been frost-bitten in the bitter cold, and the parents spent most of the night doctoring them. The next day, February 21, lying in the wagon seat while her husband struggled to pitch a tent against the raging blizzard, Olivia delivered her third child, a healthy boy."

■ ENTRANCE TO THE UNION

After the Civil War, the issue of polygamy elicited increasing criticism of the Mormons, even in Utah, where the anti-Mormon Liberal Party was established in 1870 and its mouthpiece, the non-Mormon *Salt Lake Tribune*, began to print as a counterpoint to the Mormon-owned *Deseret News*. In 1882, Congress passed the Edmunds Act, allowing the federal government to fine and imprison polygamists, many of whom hid their plural wives and children when federal marshals came to town. By the end of 1885, to escape persecution, hundreds of Mormons were

pouring into the Mexican state of Chihuahua; although the Mexican government had also outlawed the practice, it did not actively prosecute polygamists.

Brigham Young died in 1877, with controversy still whirling around him, and many wondered if Mormonism would die with him. The succeeding church president, John Taylor, died in hiding in 1887. That same year, the Edmunds-Tucker Act dealt a severe blow to the Mormons by disincorporating the LDS Church, confiscating all of its property, abolishing the Perpetual Emigrating Fund, and mandating a federally appointed government for Utah. No one in Utah could vote, hold elective office, or serve on a jury until he had taken an oath that he was not a polygamist. The law also abolished female suffrage in the territory, where women had had the right to vote since 1870.

In September of 1890, the new church president, Wilford Woodruff, published a manifesto in the *Deseret News* describing revelations from the Lord directing him to ask his followers to cease practicing polygamy. "The Lord showed me by vision and revelation exactly what would take place if we did not stop this practice," he wrote. "If we had not stopped throughout the land of Zion, confusion would have come upon the whole Church, and we should have been compelled to stop the practice."

This significant change made life easier for the Mormons. After publicly abandoning the practice of polygamy, they were allowed to vote and hold public office. They formed the Mormon People's Party and, in a gesture of reconciliation in 1889, offered four places on their Salt Lake City ticket to prominent gentiles. As a result of the infusion of gentiles into politics, the territorial legislature established public schools in 1890, further separating church and state. A year later, to demonstrate a desire to keep religious leaders from governing, the LDS leaders asked members to join the Democratic or Republican parties instead.

In 1895, a constitutional convention of Mormon and non-Mormon delegates met in Salt Lake City to frame a constitution for Utah Territory's seventh attempt at statehood. Those attending officially outlawed polygamy, though polygamous marriages already in existence were allowed to continue. They also gave women the right to vote—only the second territory and state to do so (Wyoming was the first)—a quarter of a century before the 19th amendment gave the same right to women nationwide. On January 4, 1896, President Grover Cleveland proclaimed Utah the 45th state in the Union.

When Utah became a state, the Salt Lake Temple was swathed in a huge 45-star flag, public buildings were draped with bunting, and these Utah women celebrated with patriotic style.

■ THE MORMONS TODAY

Being Utahn no longer means being Mormon. The influence of the Church of Jesus Christ of Latter-day Saints is everywhere in Utah, but other creeds are found as well. Mormons are in the majority in most rural communities and many suburban neighborhoods. The religious population of the urban areas is much more diverse (though still 50 percent Mormon).

State politics is influenced by the conservative opinions of the church. Most Mormons tend to vote Republican, though there have been and are many Democratic state officials, including governors and congressmen. Most candidates are sensitive to Mormon thought and avoid being labeled as "liberal."

The Mormon Church owns KSL Radio and Television, as well as the state's second-largest newspaper, the *Deseret News,* which expresses the Mormon viewpoint, along with differing opinions. The church also owns radio and television stations in other parts of the country. Deseret Book is an LDS-owned bookstore where Mormon as well as non-Mormon publications are sold.

The Mormon Church maintains many landholdings in Utah and around the world. In downtown Salt Lake City, 35 acres, including Temple Square and part of what was once Main Street, are still owned by the church. The city has benefited from this in many ways. For instance, the land where Salt Lake County's convention center, the Salt Palace, sits is loaned to the city for $1 a year. (These and other church businesses do not have nonprofit status, and are handled separately from the religious affairs of the church.)

The heart of the church has always been Temple Square. Although the Mormon Tabernacle Choir continues to broadcast from the Tabernacle, a new, 21,000-seat Conference Center was constructed north of Temple Square and opened in 2000. The twice-yearly general conferences of the church, which had long outgrown the Tabernacle, are now held here. In 2003, some five to seven million people visited Temple Square to see the headquarters of the LDS Church. Authorities estimate that two-thirds of this number were not church members.

The Church of Jesus Christ of Latter-day Saints, likewise, is no longer confined to Utah. Of the 11,721,548 church members worldwide at the end of 2002, 5,410,544 lived in the United States and the rest abroad. The church has an

The Mormon Temple and nearby Tabernacle are the most sacred places for members of the Church of Jesus Christ of Latter-day Saints.

ambitious program to build new temples throughout the world, so Mormons no longer have to come to Salt Lake City for sacraments. As of June 2004, the church had 119 temples, including brand-new ones in Copenhagen and New York City, with 10 more announced or under construction.

As of 2002, approximately 61,600 Mormon missionaries were living in 165 different countries and territories. Missionaries are mainly young men between the ages of 19 and 26, who are expected to spend two years as missionaries, but young women have been allowed to become missionaries, too, and their numbers are growing. Married couples are volunteering more and more to do mission work as well. Women and married couples may serve from one to one-and-a-half years.

Mormon boys are expected to start saving for their missions early, as it is primarily the family's responsibility to finance the mission. Money spent supporting a missionary is not tax deductible. The missionaries are given intense language training, if necessary, and sent out in pairs. Several sets of missionaries may work in the same area. They must adhere to strict moral guidelines while in the field. Dating, and even holding hands, is not allowed. Many a Mormon woman, however, will wait for her missionary and keep in touch by mail and telephone while his two-year commitment is fulfilled.

Visitors to Utah often notice the abundance of children in the state. The church's teaching that children are blessings and that family life is essential has helped give the state the youngest average population in the nation. The church also teaches that alcoholic beverages, caffeine, and tobacco are harmful to the body, and discourages their use by Mormons. This has resulted in a state population statistically healthier than the rest of the country, as well as some unusual liquor laws. The state has slowly been working on changing these laws, however, to attract more tourists.

Though punishable by law and excommunication, the practice of polygamy still exists in a few isolated places in Utah. It benefited from an official don't-ask-don't-tell stance and was not actively prosecuted, however, until 2001, when a polygamist with five wives revealed his marital status on talk shows and was consequently tried and convicted of bigamy and sentenced to five year in prison. Several fundamentalist groups have broken with the established church over the polygamy issue, and also over the idea of communal property.

With its emphasis on family life and clean living, the Mormon Church has enabled a prosperous and vital state to evolve. As it holds on to these values into the future, Utah will remain a great and beautiful place to live.

SALT LAKE CITY

Salt Lake City is the heart of a metropolitan area of more than a million people spread through the Salt Lake Valley. It has served as a hub of the Intermountain West ever since the Mormons founded it in 1847. For more than a hundred years, people from Wyoming, Idaho, Nevada, Utah, Montana, and Colorado have traveled to Salt Lake City to shop, work, worship, make transport connections, and simply enjoy themselves. Wrote one of the writers of the 1941 Work Projects Administration's *Utah: A Guide to the State:*

> From the time of its settlement, an air of the incredible has attended Salt Lake City. . . . Travelers have forever been coming to see for themselves "the New Jerusalem," "the Utah Zion," "the City of the Saints." In all but a handful of the books written on Utah and the Mormons during the first 30 years of the city's existence, the Mormon capital *was* Utah, a way of thinking not yet entirely disposed of.

Naturally, many a citizen of the more sparsely populated southern and eastern portions of Utah has grumbled that Salt Lake City residents think the state ends at the city's southern boundary. It is, of course, the state's capital. Utah's major television and radio stations and two of its three major newspapers operate here. It is also the world headquarters of the Church of Jesus Christ of Latter-day Saints, whose annual spring and fall conferences draw thousands from all over the world and whose Temple Square is easily Utah's top tourist attraction.

Salt Lake City is the state's cultural center as well. People flock into the valley to enjoy performances by the Utah Symphony, the Pioneer Theatre Company, Ballet West, the Utah Opera Company, the Ririe-Woodbury Dance Company, the Salt Lake Acting Company, the Repertory Dance Theatre, and the Mormon Tabernacle Choir. Eleven major ski areas are located within a 90-mile drive of the airport, and the state's two most popular professional sports teams—the Utah Jazz of the National Basketball Association and the baseball-playing Salt Lake Stingers of the Pacific Coast League —play in the valley. The state's largest university, the

(following pages) A winter's night in downtown Salt Lake City, after all the skaters at the Gallivan Center's outdoor ice rink have gone home.

venerable University of Utah, sits on the city's eastern foothills. (Its arch rival both in athletics and academics, the 29,900-student Mormon-owned Brigham Young University, is located less than 50 miles south in Provo.) The huge Salt Palace convention complex, the Delta Center sports arena, a large and continually expanding international airport, many of Utah's largest shopping centers, and its most important federal, state, and local government offices are found in Salt Lake City.

■ SALT LAKE CITY, OLD AND NEW

Modern-day Salt Lake City still reflects the vision of Brigham Young, the Mormon prophet who brought the small band of 143 men, three women, two children, 70 wagons, one boat, one cannon, 93 horses, 52 mules, 66 oxen, and 19 cows into the Salt Lake Valley in 1847.

Visitors to Salt Lake City can see the result of his early urban planning: first-timers usually comment on the width of the streets. After brief exploration, they marvel at the ease with which addresses are found. Most streets run north-south or east-west, and are numbered according to their direction and distance from the southeastern corner of Temple Square. Thus, the first street to the south of Temple Square is First South. Ninth East is nine blocks east of that corner. Nearly every Utah city is laid out in much the same manner.

When the U.S. government sent Capt. Howard Stansbury to survey the Great Salt Lake in 1849, the city was already developing into an important urban area. "A city has been laid out upon a magnificent scale, being nearly four miles in length and three in breadth," wrote Captain Stansbury. "Through the city itself flows an unfailing stream of pure, sweet water, which by an ingenious mode of irrigation, is made to traverse each side of every street, spreading life, verdure and beauty over what was heretofore a barren waste."

Though officially part of the United States, for many years Salt Lake City operated largely as a kind of theocracy under Brigham Young. Greater cultural and religious diversity arrived in later years, starting with the California gold rush of 1849, when many non-Mormons (referred to as "gentiles" by the Latter-day Saints) passed through the area. During the Civil War, soldiers were stationed in the city. The joining of the transcontinental railroad 80 miles to the north in 1869, and the promise of silver, gold, and lead in the nearby mountains, brought more gentiles.

At times, the clash between the Mormons and non-Mormons became intense. In fact, many of the rivalries between the factions exist today, though they are cer-

Modern-day Salt Lake City reaches skyward.

tainly less evident than in the 1890s. At the time, the Mormons dominated the northern part of the city, which contained Temple Square, Brigham Young's homes and offices, stores, and other buildings. Non-Mormon business leaders, such as Samuel Newhouse, Albert Fisher, and the Auerbachs, built major buildings at the southern end of the city's business district—the Auerbach Department Store; the 11-story Newhouse Hotel; the New Grand Hotel; the Salt Lake Stock and Mining Exchange, built in 1908 to house the exchange, which had been founded in 1888; and the building constructed in 1909 to house the Commercial Club, which was founded in 1902 to attract outside business to Utah.

Salt Lake City's present character began to take shape around the turn of the 20th century. Buildings such as the Gothic Cathedral of the Madeleine and the State Capitol were completed within the next few decades. Residents of the new neighborhoods—the Avenues, Capitol Hill, Liberty Park, and Sugar House—rode trolley cars into the city. During the Great Depression, buses gradually replaced the trolleys and construction slowed.

GARFIELD BEACH.
REACHED ONLY BY THE UNION PACIFIC RY.

AMERICAN NATIONAL BANK
INTERIOR & EXTERIOR VIEW.

PROGRESS BUILDING.

HOTEL ONTARIO.

SALT LAKE

PUBLIC BUILDINGS.

1 The Temple.
2 The Tabernacle.
3 Assembly Hall.
4 City Hall.
5 Capitol Building.
6 Post Office.
7 Unit Repositos.
8 Court House.
9 Fire Department.
10 Hospital of the Holy Cross.
11 Insane(st) Home.
12 Masonic Temple.
13 Odd Fellows Hall.

HOTELS.

14 The Collin   S. G. Giving, Prop't.
15 The Grunin
16 Hotel Knutsford.

RAILROADS.

17 U. P. Passenger Station.
18 U. P. Freight Depot.
19 U. P. Shops.
20 Rio Grande Western Passenger Station.
21 Rio Grande Western Freight Depot.
22 Rio Grande Western Shops.
23 Utah & Nevada Passenger Station.
24 Utah Central.
25 Utah Central Freight Depot.

SCHOOLS.

26 Rowland Hall.
27 Salt Lake Collegiate Institute.
28 Salt Lake Academy and Theatrical Hall.
29 Salt Lake Seminary.
30 St. Mary's Seminary.
31 Deseret University.
32 Deaf and Dumb Institute.
33 All Hallow's College.

During the late 19th century, before the days of aerial photography, there was the hand-drawn panoramic map. This one, by Henry Wellge, shows Salt Lake City in 1891.

Like many urban areas across the country, Salt Lake City seemed threatened in the 1960s when new malls and shopping centers opened in the suburbs, and the city retail district began to decline. That's when city leaders launched the Salt Palace, a downtown convention complex, to anchor an urban renewal effort designed to bring people back into the heart of the city. The Mormon Church invested $40 million to develop a downtown shopping mall, the ZCMI Center, named for Zion's Co-operative Mercantile Institution, which was founded in 1868 and claims to be the oldest department store in the United States. (The store still anchors the mall but it has since been sold and is now known as Meier & Frank; the mall, however, retains the ZCMI name.) Shortly thereafter, the Crossroads Plaza mall was built directly across the street from the ZCMI Center, effectively concentrating most of the retail trade on both sides of Main Street between South Temple and First South. A city-wide beautification project was completed at about the same time.

The concentration of businesses at the north end of town did cause problems in the old "non-Mormon" district to the south. Famous old department stores such as Auerbachs and the Paris Company went out of business, and the Newhouse Hotel was razed. So the city council began to revitalize this area next—first by restoring the Richardsonian Romanesque City and County Building, and then by constructing a combination of open spaces and new office buildings in the southern portion of downtown. Many of the older buildings located just south of the Salt Palace were spruced up to become part of a restaurant-entertainment district.

In the early 1990s the glittering Delta Center opened, revitalizing the western part of Salt Lake City. Development accelerated later in the decade, when Utah won its bid to host the 2002 Winter Olympics. Among the improvements were new hotels, an expanded and redesigned freeway system, and light-rail mass transit, which provided efficient travel from downtown to the University of Utah and through the Salt Lake Valley. In the post-Olympic era, the city has added such state-of-the-art attractions as the Clark Planetarium and the modernistic Salt Lake City Main Library, which both opened in 2003.

Despite their modern veneer, however, Salt Lakers still keep a warm spot in their hearts for the past. The state's biggest event remains the Days of '47 celebration, commemorating the day (July 24, 1847) when Brigham Young and the Mormon pioneers arrived in the Salt Lake Valley. On that day, one of the largest parades in the United States marches through downtown Salt Lake City, preceded earlier in the week by a youth parade, an all-horse parade, a rodeo, and other events. The celebration draws hundreds of thousands.

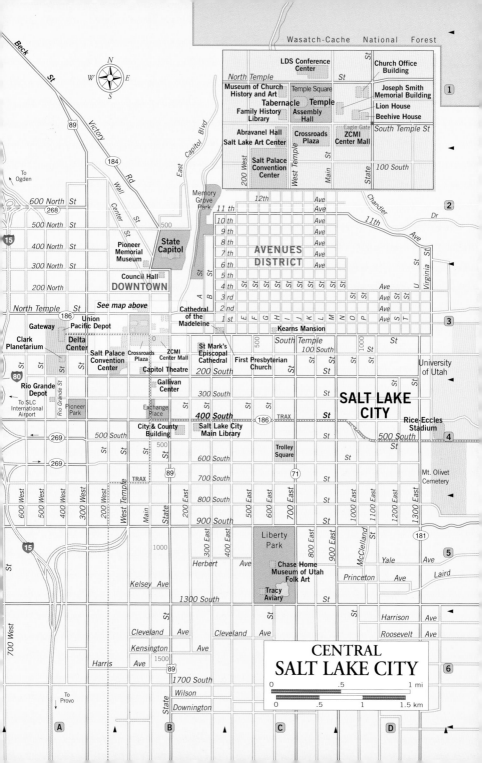

CENTRAL SALT LAKE CITY

Wasatch-Cache National Forest

To Ogden

To SLC International Airport

To Provo

Inset map (top)

LDS Conference Center
North Temple St
Church Office Building
Museum of Church History and Art
Temple Square
Temple
Joseph Smith Memorial Building
Tabernacle
Assembly Hall
Lion House
Family History Library
Beehive House
South Temple St
Abravanel Hall
Salt Lake Art Center
Crossroads Plaza
ZCMI Center Mall
Eagle Gate
Salt Palace Convention Center
200 West
West Temple
Main
State
100 South

Main map

Beck St

Victory Rd
Wall St
Center St
East Capitol Blvd

Memory Grove Park

600 North St
500 North St
400 North St
300 North St
200 North

Pioneer Memorial Museum
State Capitol
Council Hall
DOWNTOWN

See map above

North Temple St

11th Ave
10th Ave
9th Ave
8th Ave
7th Ave
6th Ave
5th Ave
4th Ave
3rd Ave
2nd Ave
1st Ave

12th Ave

AVENUES DISTRICT

11th Ave
Chandler Dr
Virginia St

Gateway
Union Pacific Depot
Clark Planetarium
Delta Center
Salt Palace Convention Center
Crossroads Plaza
ZCMI Center Mall
Capitol Theatre
Gallivan Center
Exchange Place
City & County Building

Cathedral of the Madeleine
Kearns Mansion
St Mark's Episcopal Cathedral
First Presbyterian Church

South Temple
100 South

SALT LAKE CITY

University of Utah
Rice-Eccles Stadium

Rio Grande Depot
Pioneer Park

200 South
300 South
400 South
500 South
600 South
700 South
800 South
900 South

Salt Lake City Main Library
Trolley Square
TRAX

Mt. Olivet Cemetery

600 West
500 West
400 West
300 West
200 West
West Temple
Main St
State St
200 East
300 East
400 East
500 East
600 East
700 East
800 East
900 East
1000 East
1100 East
1200 East
1300 East

700 West

Liberty Park
Chase Home Museum of Utah Folk Art
Tracy Aviary

Herbert Ave
Kelsey Ave
1300 South

McClelland St
Yale Ave
Laird Ave
Princeton Ave

Cleveland Ave
Kensington Ave
Harris Ave
1500
1700 South
Wilson
Downington

Harrison Ave
Roosevelt Ave

Scale

0   .5   1 mi
0   .5   1   1.5 km

■ TEMPLE SQUARE *map page 97, C-1*

In much the same way that Trafalgar, Red, and St. Peter's squares reflect the personalities and histories of their respective cities, so Temple Square embodies the essence of Salt Lake City. Drawing five to seven million visitors a year, the 10-acre walled complex of gardens, statuary, and historic buildings fashioned in the last half of the 19th century by Brigham Young and the Mormon pioneers is Utah's premier tourist attraction. The largest crowds come during the Christmas season, when hundreds of thousands of twinkling lights decorate the square for the holidays, illuminating trees, bushes, and buildings. A life-sized nativity scene, concerts, Christmas movies, and slide shows add to the festive atmosphere.

With the exception of the temple itself, all buildings on Temple Square are open to the public. More than 1,100 volunteer guides, hosts, and hostesses—350 of whom speak at least one language other than English, and some of whom use sign language—are on hand to take visitors around and explain the history of Temple Square and the origins of Mormonism. Those wishing to take the tour, which departs every 15 minutes (or more frequently) year-round, gather at the flagpole in the center of the square.

The square's two modern visitors centers—one on the northwest side and the other on the southeast—house exhibits relating to the history, beliefs, and programs of the church. A 53-minute film, *Legacy,* about the Mormon trek westward, is shown regularly throughout the day at the **North Visitors Center.** The centerpiece of this building is a large white marble statue of Jesus Christ, a reproduction of *The Christus,* created in the 19th century by Danish master Bertel Thorvaldsen, whose original graces the Church of Our Lady in Copenhagen, Denmark. Temple Square is open from 9 A.M. to 9 P.M. daily. *For information about activities and tours, call 801-240-1245; for recorded information, 800-537-9703.*

■ SALT LAKE TEMPLE

The majestic focal point of the square, the Salt Lake Temple is a cathedral-like building with six spires that took 40 years to complete. Designed by architect Truman O. Angell and begun in 1853, this is the most famous of more than 100 such structures maintained throughout the world by the Latter-day Saints. Don't expect to see the interior of the temple when you visit—entry is restricted to

The Salt Lake Temple, with statues of Joseph Smith and his brother, Hyrum, in the foreground.

Latter-day Saints, and even they must have written "recommends," or passes, from their bishops assuring that they are active members in good standing. (The South Visitors Center displays an exhibit giving non-Mormons a vicarious tour of the temple.) Mormon temples are not used for Sunday worship services, which take place instead in thousands of local chapels or meetinghouses. They are used on weekdays for sacred "ordinances," or special ceremonies such as baptisms for the dead (for those who lived before the church was founded) and marriages—you will most likely see a bride on the steps of the temple, posing for her wedding pictures.

The walls of the temple, 9 feet thick at the base and tapering to 6 feet at the top, are made of granite blocks. The granite was quarried in Little Cottonwood Canyon, about 20 miles away. Until 1873, teams of oxen pulled the wagons loaded with the gargantuan blocks from the quarry to the construction site. Thereafter, the granite was shipped via a new railroad. Perhaps the most distinctive feature of the temple is a 12-foot-5½-inch-tall statue of the Angel Moroni on the middle spire on the structure's east side. Mormons believe that it was Moroni who buried the plates engraved with the *Book of Mormon* on a hill in western New York and later appeared to Mormon founder Joseph Smith to show him where they could be found. The statue is constructed of hammered copper covered with glistening gold leaf. Its installation utilized a unique suspension system to keep it sturdy but flexible. Leverage action in the system allows the statue to withstand wind storms of up to 90 miles per hour.

■ MORMON TABERNACLE

Next to the temple, the most famous building on the square is the egg-shaped, silver-domed Mormon Tabernacle, built between 1863 and 1867 as a house of worship and a place of assembly that could accommodate the church's general conferences. Seating between 5,000 and 6,000 people, the building is 250 feet long, 150 feet wide, and 80 feet high, and sits on 44 cut sandstone buttresses. It was designed by architects Truman Angell and William Folsom; Henry Grow, a Pennsylvania convert who was a bridge builder, was responsible for the roof. Because Brigham Young wanted a design that would not obstruct anyone's view, Grow used a system of latticed wooden arches secured with wooden dowels and rawhide to make a seamless structure spanning the entire width of the building without intermediate supports. The balcony surrounding the room and its supporting pillars were added three years later to increase seating capacity.

The Mormon Temple in Salt Lake City took 40 years to complete.

Originally, the roof was covered with 400,000 wood shingles, which were replaced with metal in 1900 and aluminum in 1947. The Tabernacle is both a national historic landmark and a historic civil engineering landmark.

Noted for its fine acoustics, the building houses the giant **Tabernacle Organ** and the world-renowned **Mormon Tabernacle Choir.** The original organ was designed by Joseph Ridges, an English carpenter, and constructed before the coming of the railroad. Ridges had lumber for the wooden pipes transported 300 miles, from the southern part of the territory, by a team of oxen. Wind to operate the organ was originally furnished by four men pumping bellows. The organ was rebuilt and enlarged several times, most recently in 1948 by the Aeolian-Skinner Organ Company of Boston. In its present configuration, the 11,623-pipe instrument—with pipes ranging from five-eighths of an inch to 32 feet tall—is far different from the 1,600-pipe organ designed by Ridges. After the pipes were cleaned and a new console installed in 1988, the president and tonal director of Schoenstein and Co. of San Francisco, Jack Bethards, wrote in *The American Organist* that the organ had a signature sound: "By this I mean an organ that is instantly recognizable, one with individual character. Creating a unique sound while staying well within the bounds of good taste and tradition is the work of genius. Achieving these things in an eclectic instrument is a miracle."

The Mormon Tabernacle on Temple Square.

The Mormon Tabernacle Choir formed a few weeks after the pioneers' arrival in the Salt Lake Valley and originally sang in a quaint "bowery" constructed of adobe blocks, with poles supporting a roof of leaves and branches to hold back the warm August sun. Now it is a 360-voice ensemble known for the weekly network radio and television broadcast, *Music and the Spoken Word,* which first aired in 1929; top-selling and award-winning recordings (five gold albums and a Grammy); and worldwide concert tours. Choir members are volunteers between 25 and 60 years of age and spend about five hours per week rehearsing and performing—some traveling 100 miles to do so.

Hearing the choir and organ in live performance is an experience not to be missed in Salt Lake City. When the choir is in town, the public can attend rehearsals at 8:00 P.M. each Thursday, as well as the Sunday radio broadcast at 9:30 A.M. (doors close at 9:15 A.M.). In addition, half-hour organ recitals (without the choir) are held Mondays through Saturdays at noon and Sundays at 2 P.M. All of these performances are free.

■ OTHER TEMPLE SQUARE ATTRACTIONS

Next door to the Tabernacle is the four-gabled **Assembly Hall,** which has its own, much smaller organ, and seats about 1,200. It was completed in 1880 using granite left over from the construction of the temple. It dominates the southwestern portion of Temple Square and serves, along with the Tabernacle and the Conference Center, as one of the venues for the Temple Square Concert Series—mostly free concerts by local and international artists presented on Fridays and Saturdays at 7:30 P.M. The building is also used for funerals, lectures, other musical programs, and summertime non-denominational services. *For recorded concert information, call 801-240-3318.*

The **Seagull Monument** in front of the Assembly Hall honors the birds that Mormons believe were sent by God to stop a massive infestation of crickets that threatened to destroy crops planted by the pioneers. Nearby is the bronze **Handcart Monument,** which honors the pioneers who made the journey to the Salt Lake Valley pulling their earthly goods in wooden carts.

■ OUTSIDE THE WALLS OF TEMPLE SQUARE

Because Utah's large Mormon population no longer fit into the Tabernacle, the church built the **LDS Conference Center,** 40 times the Tabernacle's size, just to the north of Temple Square. Dedicated in 2000, the building has a 21,000-seat auditorium, a 900-seat theater, and a 4-acre roof landscaped with trees, native Utah grasses and wildflowers, and a stream. The building accommodates the church's twice-annual general conferences, which take place in April and October and draw tens of thousands of the faithful from all over the world for a weekend of sermons and spiritual renewal—occasions that are broadcast to millions more worldwide and can be accessed via the Internet as well. During the conferences, the Mormon Tabernacle Choir performs here. Tours are of the center are given daily. *801-240-0075.*

The **Museum of Church History and Art** contains exhibits illustrating the history of the Latter-day Saints, as well as early Utah history. Artifacts range from pages of the original *Book of Mormon* manuscript to a reproduction of the dentated wooden odometer pioneers devised in 1847 to gauge their progress on the trail westward. There are also paintings, sculptures, and photographs by Mormon artists from early through modern times—including some by artists sent to Paris to study impressionism in order to apply what they learned to beautifying church property—and a large collection of Southwest Indian artifacts. On the plaza outside is the diminutive Deuel Log Home, one of only two surviving homes built in the Salt Lake Valley in 1847. *45 North West Temple; 801-240-3310.*

The **Family History Library**, better known as the church genealogical library, is the largest library of its kind in the world. Visitors come from all over the world to search out their family roots here—the library is open to non-Mormons and there is no charge to use it or to attend the many classes on genealogical research given here. Finding one's ancestors has always been important to the Mormons, who hold a proxy "baptism for the dead" for people who lived before the founding of the church. What's on the shelves here is only a small part of the library's resources. Most of its holdings are stored in tunnels carved into the granite near the mouth of Little Cottonwood Canyon. *35 North West Temple; 801-240-3702.*

The 28-story **Church Office Building** is the headquarters of the Mormon Church. On the 26th floor are two observation decks from which tourists can get a 280-degree view of the city and the surrounding mountains. It's a view well worth taking in. *50 East North Temple; 801-240-2190.*

The **Joseph Smith Memorial Building,** containing more church offices, was formerly the Hotel Utah, built in 1911 in an ornate French Renaissance style. The FamilySearch Center, an adjunct of the Family History Library equipped with computers and volunteers who help visitors start their genealogical research, is located here, as is a theater showing a 65-minute film, *The Testaments.* The old Hotel Utah lobby is stunning, and on the 10th floor are two restaurants with a view over Temple Square—The Garden, a casual place for lunch or dinner; and The Roof, more formal, serving a dinner buffet. *For the FamilySearch Center, 801-240-4085; the film, 801-240-4383; the restaurants, 801-539-1911; 15 East South Temple.*

A stone lion guards the entrance to the **Lion House,** farther east on South Temple. The house, built in 1856, was once a sort of apartment complex for Brigham Young's wives and children. According to Clarissa Young Spencer (Young's 51st child, who wrote about life with father in *Brigham Young at Home*), about 12 families usually lived in the house, which had three floors and 10 gables running the length of the roof on either side. "On the upper floor were twenty bedrooms, where the childless wives and the older boys and girls slept. Each bedroom had its own picturesque dormer window. . . . The middle floor held the apartments of the wives with small children and the parlor or 'prayer room'. . . . The basement floor was perhaps the most interesting of all. On the west side was the large dining room, where some fifty members of the family sat

(top) The Beehive House, home of Brigham Young, as it is today. Next door to it is the Lion House (bottom), seen here as it was when it was the home of some of Young's wives and children. Today it houses a cafeteria that is open to the public.

Do You Know Who Your Ancestors Are?

Chances are, the Mormons do. As anyone who has dabbled even a little in genealogy knows, the Church of Jesus Christ of Latter-day Saints possesses the world's largest genealogical library. At latest count, this gold mine consisted of more than 2.4 million rolls of microfilm, almost 745,000 microfiches, and more than 310,000 books and periodicals. What is not on the shelves of the Family History Library building in the center of Salt Lake City is stored in vaults hollowed out of a mountain 25 miles southeast of downtown. Whether your ancestors—Mormon or not—came to the New World before George Washington was born, were among the multitude that streamed through Ellis Island beginning in 1892, or never bothered to leave home—wherever that was—it's probable that details of their births, deaths, marriages, and other milestones are on file in Utah.

That this comparatively small group of people should have collected such a massive amount of information has to do with their religion, of course, and its emphasis on the importance of family. The Mormons believe that husband and wife are married or "sealed" together not till death do them part, but for all eternity, and not just the two of them alone, but also their children, those who come after them, and those who went before. They also believe in baptism for the dead, a belief that obligates them to identify their ancestors—who may have lived without the opportunity of hearing the gospel of Jesus Christ—and baptize them by proxy. The deceased may accept or reject the baptism: what's important is offering them the chance of salvation that the time and place of their birth may have denied them. In fact, the Mormons believe that this opportunity should be extended not only to their own dearly departed, but also to yours and in fact to everyone who ever lived.

Documenting every soul ever to alight on Planet Earth is a mind-boggling task if ever there was one, yet the church set about to do just that with the establishment of the Genealogical Society of Utah (GSU) in 1894. At first, the work proceeded the old-fashioned way, as church members copied family Bibles and traipsed through cemeteries reading headstones. Church missionaries, who visited town and parish clerks and arranged to have records copied and sent back to Utah, accomplished much. But real headway awaited the birth of an appropriate technology: microfilming. When the GSU (now known as the church's Family History Department) acquired its first microfilm camera in 1938, the world's most far-reaching record-gathering program was launched.

Initially, because of World War II, efforts focused on domestic projects, such as filming more than 50,000 pages of handwritten family histories in New York and every genealogical record of value in 83 North Carolina counties. When filming began in earnest after the war, the focus was Great Britain, Scandinavia, and other countries that had supplied most of the church's early converts.

Soon, it became clear that the work was useful not only to the Mormons. In the early 1950s, for instance, filming preserved Mexican census records found "covered with dust, and soiled with droppings from pigeons." Eventually, the church was filming throughout the world, with priority given to records threatened with deterioration or destruction. In many cases, given the program's reputation, civic leaders approached the church rather than vice-versa. Hungary's national archivist requested microfilming to preserve records during the revolution of 1956, and the Polish national archivist later did the same. In the 1970s Missouri agreed to have 17 million pages of state records microfilmed—a way to preserve them at church, not taxpayer, expense.

Inside the Granite Mountain Records Vault row upon row of 15-foot-tall metal cabinets hold drawer upon drawer of microfilm rolls.

The tunnels of the Granite Mountain Records Vault, where most of the Family History Library's genealogical records are preserved.

By 1959, storage was becoming a problem. That year workers began drilling six huge tunnels into the solid rock at Little Cottonwood Canyon, the same place where the granite used to construct the Salt Lake Temple had been quarried. In 1963, the Granite Mountain Records Vault, roomy enough to hold the equivalent of 25 million 300-page books, opened its doors. Today, you might say that much of the history of the human race is stored here. Filming has been done in all 50 states and in

110 countries, territories, and possessions, and in 2004, some 200 cameras were still shooting in 45 countries, adding to the cache. (Not only that, but with the church making converts in societies where written records are a recent development, microfilming has been supplemented by the taping of oral genealogies.)

Still, this is only part of the story, because what good would those documents be if no one knew what was in them? For the Mormons, answering that question implied more than creating a catalog of what was stored where. It also meant extracting individual names from those records, so that proxy baptisms and other rites could be performed for them. This extraction was initially accomplished by transcribing names longhand or typing them onto index cards. Later, as the church—an early adopter of appropriate technologies by any measure—automated the process, the names were fed into successive generations of data-entry systems. Today, thanks to the computer and millions of hours of largely volunteer labor on the part of tens of thousands of LDS faithful, the names of nearly 800 million of our forebears are rolling around cyberspace in searchable databases.

The good news is that you don't have to be a Mormon to tap into this mother lode, nor even go to Utah. You can begin locally, at a Family History Center, one of the more than 3,700 branches of the Family History Library that began to open in 1964 and now exist in 88 countries (call 800-346-6044 to find one). Or you can begin at the library's FamilySearch Internet site (www.familysearch.org), which debuted in 1999. The latter provides access to the library catalog and to various databases, including the International Genealogical Index, the largest.

Logging on to FamilySearch or visiting a center may not provide you with all you need to know, but it can narrow your search considerably—for instance, to the essential information that passenger lists for ships docking in New Orleans in the year you think your ancestor arrived are in FHL US/CAN films 200158–200160. For a small fee, you can then have those films sent from Salt Lake City, to be consulted at the Family History Center—and if you don't hit paydirt with those, you can order additional materials and continue the search.

But waiting for the mail can try your patience, which explains why so many people head for Salt Lake City to join the estimated 2,000 patrons who walk through the Family History Library doors each day. It's not exactly an off-the-beaten-track destination, but considering who you might meet there, it's definitely worth the trip.

—Kristin Moehlmann

down to every meal." The only part of the house open to the general public today is the dining room, which is now a cafeteria called The Pantry. *63 East South Temple; 801-363-5466.*

Visitors can tour the **Beehive House,** next door to the Lion House and built in 1854. This was Brigham Young's primary residence, where he "had his sleeping room and always ate his breakfast," according to Clarissa, who wrote that the Beehive House was "the home of my mother and her family exclusively." Clarissa's mother was Lucy Decker, Young's first plural (or second) wife, whom he married in 1842 and by whom he fathered seven children. The beehive, a symbol representing industry, appears as a decorative motif throughout the house. *Corner of South Temple and State; 801-240-2671.*

Spanning State Street beyond the Beehive House is the **Eagle Gate,** which once marked the entrance to Brigham Young's farm.

■ OTHER FAITHS

It would be too much to say that non-Mormons have always gotten along with the dominant Mormons in Salt Lake City. People who move to Utah from other parts of the United States often complain that government and culture in the state are dominated by the LDS Church. Still, Buddhists, Jews, Catholics, Methodists, Baptists, and members of most other major Christian denominations can be found in Salt Lake City. Many thrive on their minority status. Although Mormons do dominate state and local elected offices, the city's first woman mayor—Dee Dee Corradini, who took office in 1992—was a non-Mormon.

Early Mormon pioneers and the Catholic Church interacted cautiously, and only when necessary. Bernice Maher Mooney, in *The Story of the Cathedral of the Madeleine,* discusses the "reciprocal effort at peaceful association" between Lawrence Scanlon, the first Catholic bishop of Salt Lake City, and high Mormon officials: "In 1879, Apostle Erastus Snow, leader of the Latter-day Saints at St. George, invited Bishop Scanlon to offer High Mass in the Mormon Tabernacle there. The bishop did so on September 25, 1879. The Tabernacle Choir, conducted by John M. MacFarlane who had become friends with Bishop Scanlon, obtained the music for the Kyrie, Gloria, and Credo and practiced diligently for some weeks."

The spirit of cooperation between the Mormons and the Catholics continues to this day. In the early 1990s, many Mormons contributed to the $9.7 million restoration of the interior of the historic and architecturally significant **Cathedral of the Madeleine,** which Utah's Catholics regard as the heart of their diocese. Bishop Scanlon purchased the cathedral property for $37,000 in 1890. The exterior of the building was finished in 1909, but the ornate interior was not completed until 1926. The cathedral possesses some of the most beautiful stained-glass windows in North America, created in 1906 by Zettler Studios of Munich, Germany. *331 East South Temple; 801-328-8941.*

St. Mark's Episcopal Cathedral (100 South Street), begun in 1871, is Utah's oldest non-Mormon church. The red sandstone exterior of the **First Presbyterian Church** (347 East South Temple, at C Street), completed in 1906, makes it stand out as one of the most impressive structures on South Temple.

■ Exploring the City

■ South Temple Mansions *map page 97, C-3*
Some of the most impressive mansions in the state can be viewed along South Temple. These include the **Enos A. Wall Mansion,** which now serves as the headquarters for the LDS Business College, and the **Kearns Mansion** (603 East South Temple; 801-538-1005), constructed in 1902 by Thomas Kearns, an early mining baron who became a U.S. senator in 1901 and bought the state's largest daily newspaper, the *Salt Lake Tribune,* the same year. His elegant 28-room house now serves as the official residence of Utah's governor, but it's open for tours on Tuesday and Thursday afternoons from April through mid-December.

■ Utah State Capitol *map page 97, B-2*
The ornately decorated Capitol overlooks Salt Lake City from a hill atop State Street. Constructed of granite and capped by a copper dome, the Renaissance Revival building was completed in 1915 at a cost of $2,739,538. It houses the state legislature, governor's office, and Supreme Court; the inside of the rotunda is decorated with scenes from Utah's history painted by Work Projects Administration artists during the Depression. In the basement are displays of Utah's history and industry. Although the building is certainly worth exploring, it unfortunately closed down in July 2004 for restoration and earthquake proofing; it is scheduled to reopen for the legislative session of January 2008. *350 North Main Street; 801-538-3000.*

MARK TWAIN'S SALT LAKE CITY

Next day we strolled about everywhere through the broad, straight, level streets, and enjoyed the pleasant strangeness of a city of fifteen thousand inhabitants with no loafers perceptible in it; and no visible drunkards or noisy people; a limpid stream rippling and dancing through every street in place of a filthy gutter; block after block of trim dwellings, built of "frame" and sunburned brick—a great thriving orchard and garden behind every one of them, apparently—branches from the street stream winding and sparkling among the garden beds and fruit trees—and a grand general air of neatness, repair, thrift and comfort, around and about and over the whole. And everywhere were workshops, factories, and all manner of industries; and intent faces and busy hands were to be seen wherever one looked; and in one's ears was the ceaseless clink of hammers, the buzz of trade and the contented hum of drums and fly-wheels.

Salt Lake City was healthy—an extremely healthy city. They declared that there was only one physician in the place and he was arrested every week regularly and held to answer under the vagrant act for having "no visible means of support." They always give you a good substantial article of truth in Salt Lake, and good measure and good weight, too. Very often, if you wished to weigh one of their airiest little commonplace statements you would want the hay scales.

It is a luscious country for thrilling evening stories about assassinations of intractable Gentiles. I cannot easily conceive of anything more cosy than the night in Salt Lake which we spent in a Gentile den, smoking pipes and listening to tales of how Burton galloped in among the pleading and defenseless "Morrisites" and shot them down, men and women, like so many dogs. And how Bill Hickman, a Destroying Angel, shot Drown and Arnold dead for bringing suit against him for a debt. And how Porter Rockwell did this and that dreadful thing. And how heedless people often come to Utah and make remarks about Brigham, or polygamy, or some other sacred matter, and the very next morning at daylight such parties are sure to be found lying up some back alley, contentedly waiting for the hearse.

—Mark Twain, *Roughing It,* 1872

■ OTHER ATTRACTIONS

Council Hall *map page 97, B-3*
This historic building once served as city and territorial government offices. It was moved to the hilltop in 1960, where it now serves as the home of the **Utah Travel Council**. It is an excellent place to pick up tourist literature for the entire state. *Just south of the State Capitol; 801-538-1030 or 800-200-1160.*

Pioneer Memorial Museum *map page 97, B-2/3*
Southwest of the State Capitol you will find one of the West's most complete collections of authentic 19th-century pioneer memorabilia. The museum holds dolls, clocks, Brigham Young's personal effects, pioneer fashions, paintings, grand pianos hauled across the plains on wagons, a carriage house, and a children's playroom— all providing glimpses of early life in Salt Lake City. The Daughters of Utah Pioneers, who operate the facility, are diligently seeking stories and histories concerning the people who settled Utah. The many portraits are of pioneers who arrived in Utah from 1847 through 1869. *300 North Main; 801-538-1050.*

Salt Lake Convention and Visitors Bureau *map page 97, A/B-3*
In the Salt Palace Convention Center, this is another good place to pick up tourist information and current details about cultural activities. *90 South West Temple; 801-521-2822 or 800-541-4955.*

Clark Planetarium *map page 97, A-3*
The large, state-of-the-art Clark Planetarium, which opened in 2003 at the Gateway shopping center, features both the Hansen Star Theatre, which presents a bill of current astronomical shows, and the IMAX 3-D Theatre, which presents astronomical shows as well as touring IMAX productions in its specialized format. Hands-on science exhibits and the planetarium's Wonders of the Universe science store share the building. *110 South 400 West; 801-456-7827.*

Utah State Historical Society Museum *map page 97, A-3*
The 1910 **Rio Grande Depot** is the home of the Utah State Historical Society's museum and research library. The museum hosts rotating exhibits on Utah history, and the library provides a fascinating glimpse into the past for those with time to spend rummaging through old books and magazines. (If you work up an appetite, try the Rio Grande Mexican restaurant at the northern end of the building.) *300 South Rio Grande Street; 801-533-5755.*

Shopping

The **Gateway** is Salt Lake's newest shopping experience, with two stories of shopping, entertainment, and dining covering 30 acres. An open-air shopping center, its businesses are accessed from the sidewalk. The main entrance to the whole, however, is via the Grand Hall of the Union Pacific Depot, which served as the city's railroad transportation center from 1909 into the 1970s. *Between 50 North and 200 South Streets and between 400 West and 500 West Streets; 801-456-0000.*

Two indoor malls face each other on Main Street. **Crossroads Plaza** (50 South Main Street; 801-321-8745) has 100-plus stores, including Nordstrom and Mervyn's department stores. Across from it, **ZCMI Center Mall** (35 South Main Street; 801-531-1799) has Meier & Frank, a direct descendant of the Zion's Cooperative Mercantile Institution, which Brigham Young helped found in 1868 as a way to encourage home manufacturing and self-sufficiency among the Mormons and keep the larger world at bay. Only the facade on Main Street remains of the original building, erected in 1876; note its "Holiness to the Lord" motto.

Historic **Trolley Square** provides the most interesting shopping atmosphere. This upscale complex of chic boutiques, restaurants, and movie theaters occupies buildings that once housed the city's trolley cars and buses; it is patterned after other industrial conversions, such as San Francisco's Ghirardelli Square. Take time to explore the winding brick hallways and one-of-a-kind antiques found in this charming center. *550 South 700 East; 801-521-9877.*

Salt Lake City Main Library *map page 97, B-4*

Ground was broken for the city's new Main Library in October 2000 and the grand opening took place in February 2003. The building quickly became one of Utah's top tourist attractions, clocking three million visitors in its first year. Designed by Moshe Safdie and Associates, the building is fronted by a curving, six-story "walkable" wall that looks much like the shell of the Roman Colosseum. Glass is the predominant material in this open, light-filled structure, which is scattered with artwork throughout and topped by a roof garden of trees, grasses, and flowers. The library has a collection of more than 500,000 books and other items. Volunteers give tours daily. *210 East 400 South; 801-524-8200.*

The Daughters of Utah Pioneers run this museum, which has three floors and a basement filled with the personal and household goods pioneer families held dear or couldn't do without.

City and County Building   *map page 97, B-4*

Just down the street from the library is the seat of city government, where you can either tour the building or wander around its parklike grounds. Built in the Richardsonian Romanesque style, with 5-foot-thick sandstone walls, the building is solid and stately, the antithesis of its neighbor. Dedicated in 1894, it initially housed both city and county offices; it also housed Utah's state government from 1896 to 1916, when the State Capitol was completed. The building was extensively renovated in the late 1980s, during which time more than 400 "shock absorbers" were installed underneath it; the retrofit was intended to protect the building from earthquakes up to 7 on the Richter scale. Tours of the building take place on Tuesdays and Saturdays. *451 South State Street; tour information: 801-533-0858.*

■ **PARKS AND NATURAL AREAS**

Liberty Park   *map page 97, C-5*

One of the oldest recreation areas in Salt Lake City, Liberty Park is the city's answer to New York's Central Park. The venerable green space, four blocks long and two blocks wide, has served as a gathering place since Isaac Chase built a mill here in 1852. Free flour from the mill saved many families during the two-year famine of 1856–1857. The millstones and irons used at the mill—which still stands at Liberty Park—were brought across the plains by teams of oxen. A small amusement park, a modern children's playground, and landscaped gardens stand between the mill and Chase's yellow adobe brick home, which was constructed in 1853 and is now the **Chase Home Museum of Utah Folk Arts** (801-533-5760), exhibiting contemporary works by Utah artists. For the most part, though, Liberty Park serves as a quiet, shaded retreat for city dwellers, who come to stroll through the manicured grounds or paddle canoes on the boating pond. Many Salt Lakers learned to play tennis in the large public complex on the west end of the park, and to swim in the nearby pool. The park is also the site of community fairs, horseshoe contests, and road races. *600 East 900 South; 801-972-7800.*

In the southwest corner of the park are the shaded grounds of the **Tracy Aviary,** where you can watch golden and bald eagles, flamingos, peacocks, and hundreds of other unusual birds. Special exhibits educate the public about native Utah ecosystems and their diverse bird life. In the summer, the aviary hosts a bird show and a lory walk (visitors enter an enclosure to feed and observe Australian parakeets). *589 East 1300 South; 801-322-2473.*

Inside Salt Lake City's new Main Library, with the "walkable" wall to the left.

Sugarhouse Park

Sugarhouse Park, now a quiet expanse of grass and hills, reveals a colorful chapter of Salt Lake City history. It was formerly the site of the old Utah State Prison, a facility surrounded by 18-foot-high red sandstone walls that was finally closed down in the 1940s. Labor activist Joe Hill, made famous in a folksong sung by Joan Baez, was executed here. So was a convicted murderer named John Deering, who allowed himself to be wired with an electro-cardiograph as a firing squad prepared to execute him. Though he acted unconcerned, his heart rate jumped to 180 beats per minute shortly before he was shot. The prison physician said Deering would have died even if no bullet had been fired. A monument at Sugarhouse Park reminds visitors of its grim past. *1300 East 2100 South; 801-972-7800.*

Natural Areas

A movement is afoot in Salt Lake Valley to preserve natural areas; converted parklands include the **Parleys Historic Nature Park,** at the mouth of Parleys Canyon, and the **Dimple Dell Regional Park,** near Sandy in the southeast corner of the Salt Lake Valley. Planners hope someday to have a trail system in place along the entire 45-mile stretch of the Jordan River, which cuts the Salt Lake Valley almost in half as it flows from Utah Lake into the Great Salt Lake. Portions of that **Jordan River Parkway** system are in place, with paved paths for pedestrians and bicycles, some equestrian trails, places to put in and take out canoes, park benches, and picnic facilities. A canoe trip from the Raging Waters waterslide complex at 1700 South, past Jordan Park and the International Peace Gardens, through the Utah State Fair Park to the Northwest Community Center is, despite the location in the midst of a bustling city, a surprisingly scenic and quiet float trip. The best part of the Jordan River Parkway system is farther south, however, from 4800 South in Murray to 7800 North in Midvale. Portions of the **Bonneville Shoreline Trail**—which follows, roughly, the shoreline of that ancient lake—allow hikers a view of the city and the feeling of a walk in the mountains. Joggers and bicyclists also enjoy **Memory Grove** and **City Creek Canyon,** located directly behind the State Capitol. The road up the canyon is often closed to automobile traffic, making it an excellent place to walk, run, or ride.

■ ALONG THE EASTERN BENCH

Some of the Salt Lake City's most interesting attractions are located on the eastern bench, a rise between the urbanized valley and the higher Wasatch Mountains left by the ancient Lake Bonneville as its shoreline receded.

■ **UNIVERSITY OF UTAH** *map page 97, D-3/4*

The University of Utah, one of the oldest universities west of the Missouri River, dates back to 1850, when the territorial legislature established the University of Deseret. The home of the first "university" was the parlor of an adobe cabin. Unfortunately, the $5,000 grant appropriated for the school came from an empty treasury, and the venture into higher education—at a time when what was really needed were elementary schools—lapsed into almost non-existence until the late 1860s. The university's revival came in 1869, when Dr. John R. Park took over. Although most of the students had only high school–level skills, Park and his colleagues quickly established schools of law, medicine, education, and mining. The University of Deseret became the University of Utah in 1892 and moved to its present site in 1900. The university headquarters, the John R. Park Building, located on a U-shaped road students call "The Circle," is named in honor of the man who helped revive the institution.

Today the University of Utah—the U—is a visually appealing architectural mix of traditional and contemporary buildings set on a lush, park-like campus of 1,500 acres, with beautiful mountain views. It has a faculty of 2,750 and a student body of more than 28,000. With a reputation as one of the finest state-run institutions of higher learning in the country, it is a leader in technology, computer science, biomedical engineering, genetics, Middle Eastern culture, modern dance, and mining studies.

The affiliated University of Utah Research Park, on 320 acres adjacent to the campus, merges private and public resources by matching 44 companies with 37 university departments; it is a national leader in the number of inventions per research dollar spent. The Huntsman Cancer Institute treats cancer patients and conducts research on curing the disease. And the University of Utah Hospital was the site, in 1982, of the transplant of the first permanent artificial heart into retired Seattle dentist Barney Clark. The transplant, the culmination of 15 years of research, was performed by a team headed by Dr. William De Vries. The heart, the Jarvik 7, was developed by Dr. Robert K. Jarvik, a design engineer who completed medical school at the university in 1976. Clark survived for 112 days.

The University of Utah also provides an educational gathering place for the community. The Utah Museum of Natural History and the Utah Museum of Fine Arts are located on campus. The 15,000-seat Jon M. Huntsman Center and the 45,000-seat Rice-Eccles Stadium, where the opening and closing ceremonies of the

2002 Winter Olympics Games were held, host cultural, artistic, and athletic events throughout the year. Kingsbury Hall and the Simmons Pioneer Memorial Theatre are two of the city's main venues for music, theater, and dance events.

■ THE CAMPUS AND OTHER EASTERN BENCH ATTRACTIONS

Utah Museum of Natural History

In the old university library building, the museum houses exhibits on the ancient Indians indigenous to Utah, the geologic forces that shaped the area, and Utah wildlife, rocks, minerals, and fossils. Mounted skeletons of Jurassic-period dinosaurs in combat—many from the Cleveland-Lloyd Dinosaur Quarry in central Utah—and lifelike dioramas of animals in natural settings delight the youngsters who venture into the museum. Special events and exhibitions are held throughout the year. *1390 East President's Circle; 801-581-4303.*

Utah Museum of Fine Arts

The comprehensive holdings of this museum embrace ancient Egyptian objects, Italian Renaissance paintings, European and American art from the 17th century to the present, sculptures from Southeast Asia, screens and prints from Japan, ceramics from China, Navajo textiles, and objects from African, Oceanic, and Pre-Columbian cultures. Occupying a modern building opened in 2001, only about 10 percent of the permanent collection is on display at any one time. *410 Campus Center Drive; 801-581-7332.*

Red Butte Garden

Just east and south of the university, near the mouth of a canyon by the same name, Red Butte Garden has a huge visitors center filled with interpretive exhibits. Its conservatory houses plants from tropical rain forests and deserts of the world, common plants as well as rare and endangered species. Enjoy a quiet stroll through the adjacent 150 acres of flowers and trees, which hold a meandering stream and waterfalls, quiet ponds, plant collections with explanatory signs, and rolling lawns. In the summer, there is a popular concert series. *300 Walkara Way; 801-585-0556.*

Fort Douglas

The fort, built in 1862 as Camp Douglas, dominates a site just east of the university, a position chosen by Col. Patrick Edward Connor because it gave him and his California and Nevada volunteers a commanding view over the defiant Mormon

A 1930 landscape by Maynard Dixon in the collection of the Utah Museum of Fine Arts.

capital. A variety of examples of military architecture can be seen spread over the grounds of this onetime military post, which has been largely annexed by the University of Utah since its deactivation. A plan to house university students on the grounds neatly meshed with plans to hold the 2002 Winter Olympics in Salt Lake City, and for the duration of the games, the new housing served as the Olympic athletes' village. Two barracks buildings from 1875 hold the **Fort Douglas Military Museum,** tracing military activities from the Dominguez-Escalante Expedition in 1776 to the present. Colonel Connor, who went on to become the "father of Utah mining," is buried in the original fort cemetery. *East side of Wasatch Drive, at 300 South Street; 801-581-1710.*

Utah's Hogle Zoo
The largest and best animal park of its type in the state, Hogle Zoo contains more than 1,100 animals representing more than 250 species. Tropical birds fly freely around a solarium filled with exotic plants. Most children eventually con their parents into taking them for a ride on a replica of an 1869 steam train. As with many Utah institutions, Hogle Zoo has an aggressive outreach program that extends to more than 20,000 students and adults annually throughout the state. There are few school children in the Salt Lake Valley who haven't enjoyed a lecture by a zoo docent. *2600 East Sunnyside Avenue, at the mouth of Emigration Canyon; 801-582-1631.*

This Is The Place Heritage Park
Spend a few hours here for a look back at pioneer times in the Salt Lake Valley, from its 1847 settlement to the coming of the railroad in 1869. A town called **Old Deseret Village** has been established here, made up of original buildings moved from all over the state or newly created replicas. A living-history community, managed by a private nonprofit foundation, the village is peopled during the summer months by tour guides in pioneer garb; visitors can tour Brigham Young's Forest Farmhouse, hear the story of how the Mormon leader's wives and children raised silk worms to produce silk cloth, or watch demonstrations of blacksmithing, adobe brickmaking, and various other crafts. The staff encourage visitors to ask questions and even to join in the work. Special events are held during holidays.

At the entrance to the village, in a replica of an old sugar factory of 1853, is a visitors center relating the story of the Mormons' trek and arrival in the Salt Lake Valley. In front of the visitors center is the This Is The Place Monument, placed there in 1947 to commemorate the 100th anniversary of the Mormons' arrival. You can view the tail end of the route they took—now called the **Mormon Pioneer National Historic Trail**—by driving up Emigration Canyon from the park. The heritage park, visitors center, and monument are open year round. Old Deseret Village is in action as a living-history museum from Memorial Day through Labor Day; during the off-season, the buildings are closed, but a map and booklet for a self-guided tour can be purchased at the visitors center. *2601 East Sunnyside Avenue; 801-582-1847.*

Wheeler Historic Farm
This onetime dairy farm has become a county park and demonstration farm to educate the public on rural life between the 1890s and 1920s. Kids especially enjoy

Pioneer wagons at This Is The Place Heritage Park, which sits near the entrance of Emigration Canyon on the city's east side.

joining the farmer on his rounds of chores, one at 11 A.M. and one at 5 P.M., when they can help gather eggs and milk cows—though old-timers may chuckle at the fact that children actually pay (a small fee) to do these chores. The farm hosts special, old-fashioned celebrations for the holidays; at Halloween, for instance, the woods surrounding the old house become "haunted" as creatures suddenly appear on the trail. Entrance fees include a tour of the farmhouse and a wagon ride. Visitors during the Christmas season see the grounds lit up with twinkling lights and holiday displays. *6351 South 900 East; 801-264-2241.*

■ THE SALT LAKE STAGE

From the very beginning of the pioneer era in Salt Lake City, cultural events played a major role in the life of the community. The first cultural organization in Utah was the Deseret Musical and Dramatic Society, organized at the request of Brigham Young. The group, which presented musicals, concerts, and pageants in the old open-air Bowery structure on Temple Square, made its dramatic debut in 1851 with a melodramatic comedy, *Robert McCaire*, and a farce, *Dead Shot*. In 1853, performances moved to the Social Hall, Utah's first theater, also built at Brigham Young's behest. It has since been demolished, but you can see its foundation at the east end of the ZCMI Center. The Social Hall opened on New Year's Day in 1853 with a prayer dedication and social dancing, followed on January 17 with a double bill of *Don Caesar de Bazan* and *The Irish Lion*.

Theater flourished, and in the late 1850s the aptly named Mechanics Dramatic Association was formed; its members were amateurs who spent their days as laborers and their evenings as performers. Not surprisingly, in those days, a ticket to a show could be bartered for produce—corn, potatoes, ham, and the like. Shortly thereafter, Brigham Young decided to build a real theater, the only one between the Comstock and the Mississippi at the time. Named the Salt Lake Theatre, it opened in 1862, at the corner of 100 South and State streets; again it opened with a double bill, a drama and a farce—you could not expect people to travel vast distances in those times to see only one play. A resident stock company began presenting productions and was so successful that it soon jumped from two performances a week to playing almost every weeknight. Its attractions were heightened by the traveling stars who stopped between Chicago and San Francisco to reprise their famous roles with the support of the local company.

Utah's theatrical ambitions were nourished when Maud May Babcock, the University of Utah's first female faculty member, arrived in 1892 as a part-time elocution and physical culture teacher. When she retired 44 years later, she had founded university departments of speech and physical education; had formed the University Dramatic Club and the Varsity Players, the first American professional theater company sponsored by a university; and had produced more than 300 plays throughout the state.

The Salt Lake Theatre went out of business in 1928, but Kingsbury Hall, a large performing hall on the University of Utah campus still used today, opened in 1930. When Dr. C. Lowell Lees came to the university's theater department in 1943, he brought with him two dreams: to build a replica of the Salt Lake Theatre and to form a theater company with a nucleus of professional actors. Although he quickly managed to bring professional actors to Utah (in one year, 1947, Judith Evans, Orson Welles, and Roddy McDowell all performed at Kingsbury Hall), the theater he envisioned, the Ron W. and Elizabeth E. Simmons Pioneer Memorial Theatre, was not dedicated on campus until 1962, a full century after the dedication of its progenitor.

Pioneer Theatre Company

The company in residence at the Simmons Pioneer Memorial Theatre is the only fully professional resident theater company in Utah, and those familiar with the national "regional theater" scene compare its work favorably with the best being produced today. The company stages seven productions a year, from September through May, including the classics, contemporary dramas and comedies, and Broadway-quality musicals. **Lees Main Stage,** named after C. Lowell Lees, has 932 seats and a proscenium stage equipped with state-of-the-art computerized lighting and sound systems. The downstairs **Babcock Theatre,** a 120-seat facility, is the home of the University of Utah's nationally recognized Department of Theatre. *300 South 1400 East, University of Utah; 801-581-6961.*

Salt Lake Acting Company

This smaller company presents lesser known, more contemporary plays of a sort that many might not expect to see in a town the size of Salt Lake City. Performing in a 200-seat theater, the company supports and develops new works by Utah playwrights and other regional writers, particularly those of national caliber; it also presents the works of such major writers as David Mamet, Emily Mann, Sam Shepard, John Patrick Shanley, Christopher Durang, and Tony Kushner. The theater doesn't shy away from plays with controversial themes and hard language, sometimes challenging conservative Utah values. *Reserve seats well in advance. Marmalade Hill Center, 168 West 500 North. 801-363-7522.*

Other Theater Companies

There are several smaller groups in the Salt Lake area. The **Desert Star Theater** (4861 South State Street, Murray; 801-266-2600), and the **Hale Centre Theatre** (3333 South Decker Lake Drive, West Valley; 801-984-9000) produce plays on a regular basis. Community theater fare, especially musicals, is popular at the Salt Lake Community College's **Grand Theatre** (1545 South State Street; 801-957-3322). **City Rep,** also known as **Salt Lake Repertory Theatre** (638 South State Street; 801-532-6000), puts on five or more productions a year for children.

Capitol Theatre *map page 97, B-3*

Once known as the Orpheum, this building with the colorful tapestry brick and polychrome terra cotta facade was completed in 1913 to host touring vaudeville shows. It fell into disrepair in the early 1970s, when it was used as a movie house. When Salt Lake County voters approved the construction of the Symphony Hall in the 1970s, they also elected to restore the Capitol Theatre (as it's been known since 1927) to its former elegance for use as a performing arts center. Touring national theater companies regularly perform here. In addition, the 1,875-seat theater now serves as the home of the Utah Opera Company and Ballet West. *50 West 200 South; 801-355-2787 or 888-451-2787.*

Rose Wagner Performing Arts Center

Built in 1996 to add performance space for the Children's Dance Theatre, Repertory Dance Theatre, Dance Theatre Coalition, Ririe-Woodbury Dance Company, the Gina Bachauer International Piano Competition, and smaller theatrical productions, the Rose Wagner Performing Arts Center has three theaters— Black Box Theatre, Studio Theatre, and Jeanne Wagner Theatre—of varying sizes. *138 West 300 South; 801-355-2787 or 888-451-2787.*

■ SALT LAKE MUSIC

Music was important to the Mormons from the very beginning. The Mormon hymn "Come, Come Ye Saints" encouraged them during their progress westward, and the Mormon Tabernacle Choir was established only a few weeks after their arrival in the Salt Lake Valley. Besides church music, there was secular music for singing and dancing: simple ballads sung to piano accompaniment, reels picked out on a fiddle. Musical instruments were prized possessions, the last thing a Mormon family would have dreamed of leaving behind. More complex music came later.

■ UTAH SYMPHONY AND OPERA

Although a predecessor, the Salt Lake Symphony Orchestra, was formed in 1892 and put on its first symphony concert that year, Utah did not have a viable symphony orchestra until the **Utah Symphony** was founded in 1940. Initially the group, which now performs throughout the country and internationally and records to great acclaim, struggled artistically and financially. The most important event in its rise to prominence was the hiring of Maurice Abravanel as music director in 1947. As the story goes, the 44-year-old Abravanel, a Greek-born conductor (of Spanish and Portuguese parentage) who was well known in Europe and New York, won the job over a 28-year-old conductor who was also making a name for himself. Symphony board members had interviewed the younger musician in New York City, but found him "too young and inexperienced." That prospect's name was Leonard Bernstein.

Utah was not short-changed, however. Abravanel was offered a one-year contract. But he had come west to build an orchestra of his own and he remained as music director for 32 years, cultivating the public's attendance with popular concerts and outreach programs, traditions that subsequent directors have maintained. In addition to its concerts in Salt Lake City, the orchestra travels to school districts throughout the state and performs for more than 70,000 students per year. It also provides music for Ballet West and for the Utah Opera Company, with which it recently merged, and regularly performs throughout the Intermountain West.

The orchestra played in the Salt Lake Mormon Tabernacle until 1979, when it moved into its stunning new home. Though Abravanel retired for health reasons that year and thus never conducted in it, he was the inspiration for what *Time* magazine called "the most impressive" of all concert halls in the country, and when he died in 1993, it was renamed **Abravanel Hall** in his honor. Six chandeliers with 18,000 beads of hand-cut Austrian and Czechoslovakian crystal grace the 2,811-seat interior, whose decorative accents combine brass, gold leaf, natural oak, and forest-green carpet. In the lobby is an impressive 27-foot-tall red glass sculpture, "Olympic Tower," by Dale Chihuly. The orchestra plays approximately 70 concerts during its September-to-May subscription series in Abravanel Hall. *123 West South Temple; 801-355-2787 or 888-451-2787.*

Opera had its start in Utah in 1918, when two of Brigham Young's grandchildren established the Lucy Gates Grand Opera Company, which lasted until 1923. The current company, **Utah Opera,** was founded in 1978 by Glade Peterson, a Utah native who had a career as a leading tenor in Europe and also sang with the Metropolitan Opera in New York City. In 1985, Utah Opera became one of the first companies of its size to use English super-titles to allow newcomers to understand the words of foreign operas. One of the most popular features of the local arts scene, the company stages four operas a year, often enlisting some of the great American voices for its performances. Like the Utah Symphony, with which it merged in 2002, the company has an active outreach program, through which some 80,000 Utah school children a year are introduced to opera. Most are bused to morning or afternoon performances at the Capitol Theatre, the company's home. Get your tickets well in advance, since many operas in Salt Lake City sell out. *50 West 200 South; 801-355-2787 or 888-451-2787.*

Wearing "something old," a wedding party makes its way across the wintry landscape at This Is The Place Heritage Park.

■ SALT LAKE DANCE

■ BALLET WEST

If Abravanel was the guiding force behind classical music in Salt Lake City, then Willam Christensen—who, with his brothers, had founded the San Francisco Ballet in 1937 and was recognized as one of the pioneers of American dance—was instrumental in making Salt Lake City a center of classical ballet. A Brigham City native, Christensen returned to Utah in 1949 and established the first ballet department at an American university, the University of Utah, in 1951. In 1963 he joined with Salt Lake City arts benefactor Glenn Walker Wallace to establish the Utah Civic Ballet, the first professional ballet company in the Intermountain West. This was renamed Ballet West in 1968, when the Federation of Rocky Mountain States designated it to represent the western United States as the region's official ballet company.

After Christensen's retirement, his successor as artistic director, Bruce Marks, broadened the company's repertoire to include more innovative works, including August Bournonville's classic *Abdallah,* which had not been seen for more than 100 years when Marks's re-creation of it premiered at Ballet West in 1985. "Only a truly classical company, which is what Ballet West has become, could carry this feat off," wrote *New York Times* critic Anna Kisselgoff after watching *Abdallah.* "Ballet West's young dancers bring the ballet back to life on new and valid terms." Today, with 45 members and with Swedish dancer Jonas Kage as artistic director, Ballet West has transcended its regional status to become one of America's leading companies. The company is in residence at the Capitol Theatre. *50 West 200 South; for information: 801-323-6900; for tickets: 801-355-2787 or 888-451-2787.*

■ MODERN DANCE

Classical ballet isn't the only form of dance Utah audiences enjoy. Salt Lake City is also a center for modern dance and boasts of two professional companies—Ririe-Woodbury Dance Company and the Repertory Dance Theatre—in addition to the Children's Dance Workshop.

Repertory Dance Theatre

Known locally as RDT, this 10-member professional modern dance company was founded in 1966 with a grant from the Rockefeller Foundation, which was seeking a modern dance company to preserve the work of the nation's top choreographers.

Salt Lake City was selected because of the prominence of the University of Utah's modern dance instructor, Virginia Tanner; in its early years, RDT was affiliated with the university. Considered a living museum of dance, because the pieces in its repertory span the history of modern dance, the company performs a regular season of three or four programs between October and April. RDT also tours extensively in the United States and abroad, and, like most of Utah's major art groups, is active in outreach, performing for school children throughout the state. The company is in residence at the Rose Wagner Performing Arts Center. *138 West 300 South; for information: 801-534-1000; for tickets: 801-355-2787 or 888-451-2787.*

Ririe-Woodbury Dance Company

Established in 1964 by University of Utah dance professors Shirley Ririe and Joan Woodbury, the Ririe-Woodbury Dance Company each year combines spring, fall, and winter dance performances in Salt Lake City (usually in April, September, and January) with national educational and performing tours. The two founding dancers take particular pride in the pioneering activities that have helped integrate dance into children's curricula throughout the United States.

The company, which employs six full-time professional dancers, is noted for its emphasis on humor, theatricality, and inventive use of media. In addition to performing the works of its co-founders, Ririe-Woodbury has performed works choreographed by dance innovators as diverse as Tandy Beal, Doug Varone, David Rousseve, Murray Louis, and Alwin Nikolais. New additions to their repertory include pieces by Creach/Koester, Laura Dean, Douglas Nielson, and Graham Lustig. The company has performed throughout the world and in all 50 states, including seasons in New York City and at the Kennedy Center in Washington, D.C. The company is in residence at the Rose Wagner Performing Arts Center (138 West 300 South), but also performs at the Capitol Theatre (50 West 200 South). *For information, 801-297-4241; for tickets; 801-355-2787 or 888-451-2787.*

THE WASATCH FRONT

Utah is largely rural, filled with wide open spaces, ranches, and splendid mountain scenery. The Wasatch Front, a roughly 175-mile stretch of land that lies along the western base of the Wasatch Mountains in the north-central portion of the state, contains 80 percent of Utah's residents and stretches loosely from Brigham City in the north to Nephi in the south. The cultural amenities of the Wasatch Front cities satisfy the demands of an increasingly sophisticated population, but Utahns and visitors still feel an occasional urge to escape into the nearby mountains to ski, hike, picnic, fish, or hunt.

■ THE MOUNTAINS

Stretching from the Idaho border in the north to the southern summit of Mount Nebo—its highest point, at 11,877 feet—the Wasatch Range endows one of the most spectacular urban settings on earth. A first-time visitor to the Salt Lake International Airport marvels at the peaks that seem to dwarf the city's modern skyline. Photographers use the reflection of the mountains in the windows of modern skyscrapers to illustrate the beautiful contrast between urban and natural worlds. The mountains are dear to Wasatch Front residents because they provide water for the body and peace for the soul.

The Wasatch Mountains have always been a source of life to the Salt Lake Valley, providing the game that drew both Indians and early trappers into the area. Mormon pioneers drank the water flowing from these snowcapped peaks, and used it to irrigate their crops. Early settlers quarried granite from the mountains to build their temple and cut wood from the forests to construct their homes. Members of Johnston's Army camped at their base and prospected for precious metals in the Wasatch canyons.

Today, the mountains bring skiers from all over the world to experience the thrill of skiing on what Utah's car license plates proclaim to be "The Greatest Snow on Earth." Campgrounds, picnic areas, hiking trails, babbling brooks, small lakes, large manmade reservoirs, and seven congressionally designated wilderness areas provide places to escape urban life and renew one's spirit.

Waterfalls and maples trees in the Mt. Timpanogos Wilderness Area near Provo.

UNWRITTEN RULES

The greatest influence on childhood of the vanished frontier was the freedom we enjoyed. It was an all-inclusive freedom that touched every aspect of our lives. Perhaps I can best suggest it by the relations of the sexes in adolescence, and of this the most vivid symbol I have is a memory from my last year at high school. At noon one day a girl and I were coming back toward Ogden over the foothills when we reached a barbed-wire fence. Helen stopped and modestly bade me look the other way lest I glimpse her calf when she climbed the fence. It was a request absolutely in accord with the Ogden folkways—yet she and I had been alone in the mountains since one o'clock that morning, had climbed a peak and cooked our breakfast on the top. This, in 1914. It was the privilege of young people . . . to wander in the mountains unchaperoned and unsuspected of misbehavior—and, let me say, rightly unsuspected. At a time when elsewhere in America stringent restrictions were put on all such intercourse outside the home, we were quite free to go where we liked at any hours that pleased us. The form which the convention took is amusing: if we went into the mountains to cook supper we must be back before dawn, and if we wanted to cook breakfast we must be careful not to start till after midnight—otherwise we should spend the night together, which was unthinkable.

—Bernard DeVoto, *Forays and Rebuttals,* 1936

On a typical Utah weekend, more cars, campers, and trucks pour out of Salt Lake City and into the mountains than drive into the city. Salt Lake City is one of the few urban regions in the United States where residents can reach the trailhead of a 16,000-acre designated wilderness by driving only 10 minutes from home, or leave work at noon and be skiing at a world-class resort by 1 P.M. The numerous hiking trails, picnic areas, trout-filled streams and lakes, and cozy little restaurants and country inns provide an easy escape from the hurry of urban life.

The seven wilderness areas along the Front are the 30,088-acre Lone Peak, 44,350-acre Mt. Naomi, 28,000-acre Mt. Nebo, 16,000-acre Mt. Olympus, 10,750-acre Mt. Timpanogos, 13,100-acre Twin Peaks, and 23,850-acre Wellsville Mountains. These wild places draw an amazing mixture of people—don't be surprised to see grandmothers at the tops of mountains and babies riding up the trails on their fathers' backs.

Each canyon of the Wasatch, and there are many, holds its own secret. Hiking and fishing are the major summer activities in the canyons east of Salt Lake City. The Snowbird Tram in Little Cottonwood Canyon whisks visitors to the top of 11,000-foot Hidden Peak. Some ride it back down, while others choose to walk. When the snow finally leaves the area around mid-July, the high alpine meadows are covered with wildflowers. After a tram ride to the top, you can hike over to nearby Mt. Baldy, enjoying the clear mountain air and spectacular views. Meanwhile, the hike to the top of 9,026-foot Mt. Olympus, much of which lies in wilderness, is both difficult and rewarding—as are dozens of other hikes along the Wasatch Front.

The drive from Salt Lake City to the hamlet of Henefer—which passes through Emigration Canyon on UT 65, Pioneer Memorial Highway—basically follows the route that the Mormons took into the Salt Lake Valley. Markers along the way depict the progress the pioneers made as they completed their 1,500-mile journey overland from the Missouri River. Later, the Pony Express trail traversed this canyon.

Heading north from Salt Lake City a scenic loop drive connects the towns of Farmington and Bountiful. Forest campgrounds and picnic areas are available along the steep, winding road.

■ PROVO AND UTAH COUNTY *map page 136, D-5/6*

In many ways, Utah County and its county seat, Provo, serve as models for a modern Mormon community. Unlike Salt Lake City and Ogden, which are subject to a considerable spectrum of influences, the population of Utah County is primarily white, middle class, politically conservative, and of the Mormon faith. The influence and culture of the modern Mormon religion is more keenly felt here than in any other urban area of the world.

Ironically, it was two Catholic priests—Francisco Silvestre Velez de Escalante and Francisco Atanasio Dominguez, arriving in September of 1776—who are believed to have been the first white men to visit Utah Valley. In his journal, Father Escalante noted that the group "ascended a low hill and beheld the lake and extended valley of Nuestra Senora de la Merced de los Timpanogotzis (as they called it) . . . surrounded by the peaks of the Sierra." Escalante noted that the river (later named the Provo) running through the valley watered plains sufficient to support, if irrigated, "two and even three large villages."

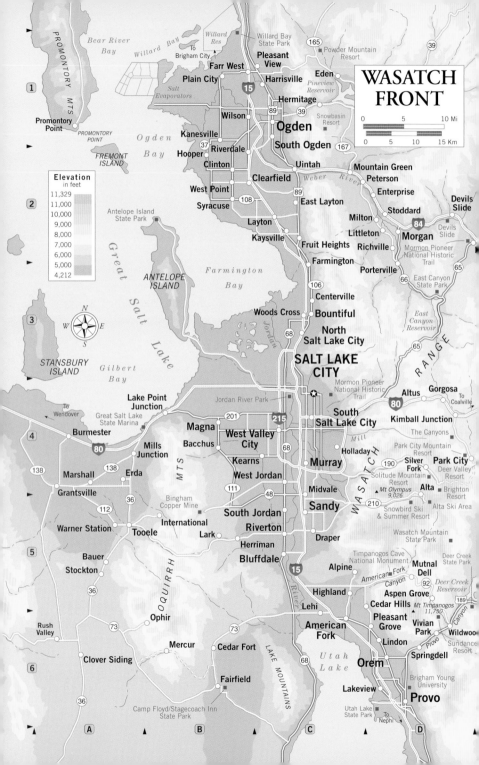

Provo is named after Etienne Provot, a young French-Canadian who explored the valley with a group of trappers in 1825. Though the Mormon pioneers explored Utah Valley three days after reaching the Salt Lake Valley, the first settlers didn't arrive until March of 1849, when John S. Higbee brought 30 families to establish a Mormon colony. As the story is told, the white men were greeted by members of the Ute Indian tribe. After promising not to drive the native Americans from their land, the Mormons constructed a fort, plowed 225 acres of land, and planted rye, wheat, and corn.

■ **BRIGHAM YOUNG UNIVERSITY** *map page 136, D-6*
When Brigham Young University was founded (as Brigham Young Academy) in 1875, with the goal of turning its first 29 students into teachers, few could have imagined its modern scope of influence. Yet today, the Provo-based institution and its 29,900 students play a dominant role not only in Utah County, but around the country. It is no accident that the bumper stickers on the cars of a few BYU sports fans declare the school to be "The University of Utah," a dig at the Provo school's arch rival to the north.

Brigham Young set the tone for the university he founded when, in 1876, he declared to students: "I want you to remember that you ought not to teach even the alphabet or the multiplication tables without the spirit of God." Dr. Jeffrey R. Holland, a modern BYU president, put things another way. "We want our students value-laden and moral," he said. "We want them to be a veritable rod of iron in what is too often a dark and misty ethical void. . . . There's a spiritual power here that goes out into the world. It is a result of our determination to place academic excellence in the context of committed religious faith and wholesome, broad development of the total person. It comes from our insistence on linking Virtue with Truth."

There are few gray areas in BYU's honor code, which students entering the university agree to obey. This includes following Mormon Church rules by maintaining a clean, strong, healthy body as a temple for the intellect and the spirit. The school's code of honor includes such commitments as being honest, observing university regulations, following the dress and grooming standards, refraining from sexual relations outside of marriage, avoiding drug abuse, and abstaining from alcohol, tobacco, tea, and coffee. Dress codes require students to be "modest, neat and clean in their grooming. Shorts, swimming suits, gym clothes and other extremely casual or grubby attire are not considered acceptable wear on campus. Beards are not permitted." By all indicators, BYU students appear to honor the code; *The Princeton Review* rates it the most "Stone-Cold Sober" school in the United States.

The beauty of the BYU campus setting is in keeping with the neatness of the students. The campus is cradled between the lofty peaks of the Wasatch Range and the placid waters of Utah Lake. Because Mormon leaders feel healthy bodies lead to healthy minds, some of the finest physical education and athletic facilities found on any campus in the world can be seen scattered through a campus dominated by grass and wide walkways.

Game day—be the sport basketball, football, track and field, or baseball—is a major event at BYU. The university's 65,000-seat football stadium fills for many community and university events, including the fantastic July 4th Freedom Festival. The school used its pass-oriented offense to win the national football championship in 1984 and is regularly ranked among the top 20 college teams in the United States. The 23,000-seat Marriott Center serves as the home of the BYU basketball team, a place for cultural events, and a setting for the regular Sunday meetings of students with Mormon spiritual leaders. The modern track, one of the finest in the United States, is host to many major track and field events, including the spring BYU Invitational, which dates back to 1915 and brings high school athletes from all over the Intermountain West to compete.

Academically, BYU offers bachelor degrees in approximately 250 academic programs and master's degrees in hundreds more. Researchers at the university tackle such challenges as alleviating the world's food shortage through more efficient agriculture, developing synthetic anti-tumor agents in the fight against cancer, finding low-pollutant energy alternatives, and breaking language barriers with computer-assisted translation. BYU's language program, which helps train the thousands of young Mormon men and women who volunteer for two-year missions all over the world, includes course work in more than 20 languages; the school also offers nearly 20 live-in language houses and daily television broadcasts in many languages.

BYU also serves as a cultural center for much of the Wasatch Front. Many of its performing groups, which include international and American folk dance ensembles, perform throughout the world. Theater-goers enjoy seeing live plays and musicals on campus.

Visitors to BYU can browse through four museums. The **Monte L. Bean Life Science Museum** (1430 North Street; 801-378-5051) exhibits a wide array of natural history scenes, mounted animals, insects, and plants, and also stores scientific collections. Artifacts of ancient Indian cultures from the United States, Central America, and South America can be seen at the **Museum of Peoples and Cultures** (700 North 100 East; 801-422-0020) in Allen Hall. The **Museum of Art** (North Campus Drive; 801-422-8387) houses some of the world's great traveling exhibits as well as a permanent collection of fine art. And the **Earth Science Museum** (1683 North Canyon Road; 801-378-3680) displays several full and partial dinosaur skeletons. Visitors can watch as paleontologists work on BYU's nearly 100 tons of fossils.

Though BYU dominates the list of places to see in the urbanized part of Utah County, there are other cultural and recreational attractions to enjoy.

■ PROVO AREA ATTRACTIONS

Springville Museum of Art

Utah's oldest museum was founded in 1903, when John Hafen, an impressionist landscape painter, donated a painting to Springville High School, hoping to launch a great art collection. By 1935 there were so many paintings in the school that a separate building was required, and the town raised $100,000 to have a museum built by the Work Progress Administration. The Spanish Colonial structure continues to house an impressive collection of works of 20th century American Realism and Soviet Socialist Realism from 1930 to the 1970s. The museum's National Spring Salon, patterned after the great Paris Salons, dates back to 1922 and has brought it to nationwide attention. *126 East 400 South in Springville, 7 miles south of Provo on US 89; 801-489-9434.*

Utah Lake State Park   *map page 136, D-6*

The state's largest natural freshwater lake dominates the western portion of Utah County. Due to the murkiness of the water, though, the lake gets mixed reviews from boaters and anglers. There are three marinas on the lake: one west of Lindon, another south of American Fork, and a third at the state park. The state park marina offers camping and fishing facilities. *4400 West Center; for camping reservations: 801-375-0733 or 800-322-3770.*

■ **ALPINE LOOP** *map page 136, D-5/6*
North of Provo, the American Fork Canyon and Provo Canyon in the Uinta
National Forest provide many recreational possibilities, with most of the sights
connected by a narrow, winding road called the **Alpine Loop**. Take time to hike
one of the trails found along the way, or stop at a turnout and enjoy the view.
Skiing, camping, and fishing are available at Tibble Fork Reservoir, in the North
Fork of American Fork Canyon. The U.S. Forest Service operates a number of picnic areas and campgrounds in the area. Another nice side trip off the Alpine Loop
will take you to **Cascade Springs**, a natural area where flowing water appears out
of the side of a mountain and then disappears again. Interpretive signs along a
boardwalk trail explain the flora and fauna. Kids like to look at the brown trout
swimming in the clear water. The Provo River, flowing through Provo Canyon, is
one of the top wild brown trout fisheries in the state. Since much of the stretch is
governed by special fishing regulations, knowledge of the rules is a must. Another
interesting attraction in Provo Canyon is **Bridal Veil Falls,** which drop 607 feet in
two cascades. *Information and maps are available at the Uinta National Forest
Headquarters in Provo or the Ranger District office in Pleasant Grove. For addresses
and phone numbers, see page 323.*

■ **TIMPANOGOS CAVE NATIONAL MONUMENT** *map page 136, D-5*
This monument is the most famous attraction of American Fork Canyon. The
steep, 1.5-mile hike from the visitors center at the bottom of the canyon to the
entrance of the cave system entails an elevation gain of 1,065 feet and is a summer
tradition for many Utah families. A tour of the three separate caves rewards those
who make the hike on a summer day, offering 43-degree temperatures and many
limestone features—including flowstone formations in subtle shades of green, yellow, red, and white. Martin Hansen discovered the first of the caves in 1887 while
tracking a mountain lion. The other two weren't discovered until 1921 and 1922.
The site received both its lighting and national monument status shortly thereafter.
Tunnels connect all three caverns on the tour. Though a typical cave tour takes
between 45 and 60 minutes to complete, leave three to four hours for both the
hike and the tour. On busy weekends, it's an excellent idea to arrive at the visitors
center early to purchase your tickets, as tours can sell out. Reservations are

Mt. Timpanogos rises from one of Utah's most popular wilderness areas, just north of Provo.

suggested for cave tours and can be purchased from one to 30 days in advance. *Timpanogos Cave Visitor Center is 2 miles into American Fork Canyon on UT 92; 801-756-5238.*

■ SOUTH OF PROVO

■ PAYSON CANYON *map page 184, D-3*

The mountains behind Provo are particularly beautiful. At the top of Payson Canyon, to the south of the city, is a series of little lakes stocked with trout, and some of the fine Uinta National Forest campgrounds provide facilities for horses. There are also two small beaches, a paved nature trail, and some grassy day-use areas at the edge of Payson Lake. *Information and maps are available at the Uinta National Forest Headquarters in Provo or the Ranger District office in Spanish Fork. See page 323.*

If you have time, drive the entire length of the **Nebo Loop,** which rambles from Payson around the east side of magnificent Mt. Nebo, passing what looks like a miniature Bryce Canyon along the way, and ends near the town of Nephi, on the southern boundary of the Wasatch Front.

■ U.S. 89 *map page 184, C/D-3 to 6*

With the exception of the comparatively modern Snow Junior College in Ephraim and a few new subdivisions, the towns along the northern portion of U.S. 89 seem barely changed from pioneer times. These quiet farming communities are perhaps best described as the Utah equivalent of Garrison Keillor's Lake Wobegon. Old historic towns, such as Mt. Pleasant, Spring City, Ephraim, and Marysvale, are being discovered by artists seeking a quiet place to live and work; and there are only a few franchises among the Main Street shops. Western aficionados will be interested in **Burns Saddlery** in Salina (79 West Main Street; 800-453-1281), where a leather craftsman has been on the premises since 1898. Marysvale is home to Utah's oldest historic hotel, **Moore's Old Pine Inn** (60 South State Street; 435-326-4565). Ask for the rooms where Butch Cassidy or Zane Grey slept. Between Fairview, Utah, and Page, Arizona, U.S. 89 has been designated as Utah's Heritage Highway and is being promoted as a place to buy crafts made in Utah.

Robert Redford's Sundance

"To us Sundance is and always will be a dream. What you see, smell, taste and feel here is a dream being carefully nurtured. It is an area whose pledge is to people. What we offer in the form of art and culture, spirit and service, is homegrown and available to all."

—Robert Redford

Robert Redford was not the first person to feel the lure of Sundance. In the 19th century, the Ute Indians found the mountain canyon to be a sanctuary from the summer heat. Then, in the early 20th century, the Stewart family, a group of Scottish immigrants, also discovered the canyon at the foot of Mt. Timpanogos. The family homesteaded the land, raised sheep, and did surveying work. The second generation of the Stewart family saw something altogether different in the snow-covered peaks: the opportunity for recreation in the stunning canyon. In the 1950s they opened Timphaven Ski Resort, with a chair lift, a tow rope, and a burger joint built under and around an ancient tree.

In 1969 Robert Redford purchased the land with a view to creating an arts and recreation community for people who appreciated the beauty of nature and felt responsible for conserving it. During its early years, the "resort" was nothing more

Main Street in Park City during the Sundance Film Festival.

The Egyptian Theatre in Park City is among the Sundance venues.

than a collection of rustic buildings and a restaurant, with such offerings as a dinner-and-movie night and a mountain man rendezvous. But these proved antithetical to Redford's mission to maintain a peaceful environment and respect nature—the deafening roar of muskets and cannons in particular sent wildlife in search of a new home in neighboring states.

Redford studied each of his experiments, while remaining tenacious in his dream of an artistic community. Believing that the Sundance experience was unsatisfactory without overnight accommodations, he gently added cottages to the landscape in the mid-1990s. His success is apparent in the resort's unique character: visitors can choose to ski, hike, or mountain bike, or to spend the day in the Artisan Center, fondly known as the "art shack." Here visitors of all ages can take classes in painting, pottery, drawing, jewelry-making, and a myriad of other arts and crafts.

While there are now two full-service restaurants (one built around the old tree), a deli, grocery store, bar, and a spa at Sundance, all development has been executed with minimum impact to the bucolic mountain surroundings. When guests retreat to their cabins, they are in a setting similar to that of the Stewarts, tucked away in private cabins nestled deep in pine forest.

The Sundance Institute was founded in 1981 with a goal of enhancing the artistic vitality of American film. Each summer the institute hosts film and theater "labs," where emerging filmmakers can hone their art while working with experienced writers, actors, directors, cinematographers, and editors.

The Sundance Film Festival was launched in 1985 and has grown to be the nation's premier showcase for independent filmmakers, not to mention one of filmdom's most talked about social events outside Hollywood. Each winter, film industry movers and shakers descend upon the Wasatch Front, especially Park City, to watch not only each other, but the best of new independent films. Awards are given in categories including cinematography, directing, screenwriting, and acting.

Many films that have become audience favorites and Hollywood award winners were first seen at Sundance—among them *Hannah and Her Sisters; The Big Easy; sex, lies and videotape;* and *Reservoir Dogs.* More recently, *Like Water for Chocolate, Four Weddings and a Funeral,* and *You Can Count on Me* found success at the Sundance Film Festival before ultimately becoming box-office hits.

For more information about the Sundance Institute, call 801-328-3456 or visit http://institute.sundance.org. For more information about Sundance Resort, call 801-225-4107 or visit www.sundanceresort.com. The resort is located on Scenic Route 92, off U.S. 189, in Provo Canyon.

—Janet Lowe

■ MANTI *map page 184, D-4*

The center of Manti—and, in fact, of Sanpete County—is the stately **Mormon Temple,** which sits on the top of a hill at the north end of town. Brigham Young dedicated the site just three months before his death in 1877, but it took workers 11 years to complete the magnificent structure. The highlight of the Sanpete County tourist season comes in June, when church leaders host the Mormon Miracle Pageant, a dramatization of intertwined stories about the founding of the Mormon Church, the *Book of Mormon,* and the journey of the faithful pioneers to Sanpete Valley. The play, a tradition for thousands of faithful Mormons, has been presented here for more than 25 years. As attendance has grown, the production has become more sophisticated, integrating lighting and sound effects. There is seating for 10,000 people at the outdoor pageant, which uses the temple as a backdrop.

For year-round recreation, locals and a few savvy out-of-state visitors venture east into the **Manti-La Sal National Forest.** Small canyons east of Ephraim, Manti, Fairview, and Mayfield lead to tiny fishing lakes, U.S. Forest Service campgrounds, and some fine Nordic skiing and snowmobiling. *For information and maps, visit the Sanpete Ranger District Office in Ephraim. See page 323.*

Palisade State Park, located in the lower part of Six-Mile Canyon on the edge of the forest, provides perhaps the nicest public camping, with fishing, swimming on a pretty beach, and golf on the adjacent eighteen-hole golf course. *Information: 435-835-7275; camping reservations: 800-322-3770.*

Owners of four-wheel-drive vehicles—and the brave drivers of two-wheel-drive cars with high clearance—enjoy negotiating the 150-mile **Skyline Drive,** on the top of the Manti Range, in summer and fall. The autumn leaf displays make this drive particularly appealing. *For information and road conditions call the Ferron Ranger District Office. See page 323.*

■ OGDEN *map page 136, C-1*

Thirty-five miles north of Salt Lake City is Ogden, Utah's third largest metropolitan area. Though Mormon pioneers settled this city, too, Ogden is named after a trapper. Its exciting history was shaped by the 1869 coming of the transcontinental railroad and some awfully colorful characters.

It seems appropriate that Ogden honors the memory of trapper Peter Skene Ogden, because the mountain men were the first non-Indian residents in the area. The current site of the city, built on the deltas of the Ogden and Weber rivers, served as a winter rendezvous site for six or seven years in the 1820s. A particularly memorable gathering took place in 1826, when General William H. Ashley arrived from St. Louis with a hundred well-laden pack animals. "It may well be supposed that the arrival of such a vast amount of luxuries from the East did not pass off without a general celebration," noted Jim Beckwourth, one of the mountain men, in his autobiography. "Mirth, songs, dancing, shouting, trading, running, jumping, singing, racing, target shooting, yarns, frolic, with all sorts of extravagances that white men or Indians could invent, were freely indulged in. The unpacking of the medicine water contributed not a little to the heightening of our festivities."

In 1841, Miles Goodyear became the first pioneer to settle in the Ogden Valley. The Goodyear cabin, the oldest known dwelling constructed by a non-Indian in Utah, still stands on the outskirts of Ogden, where it is now open from mid-May through mid-September as the **Weber County Daughters of Utah Pioneers Museum** (2148 Grant Avenue; 801-621-4891). Goodyear moved out when the Mormons bought his property in 1847. Brigham Young sent a group of 100 families to settle the area in 1849. The community suffered floods, drought, early frosts, insects, cholera, and Indian attacks, supplementing their harvests with thistles and other wild plants. The sego lily, Utah's state flower, helped to save many pioneers from starvation.

The arrival of the transcontinental railroad in 1869 changed the character of the town and also created friction with the Mormons, who disapproved of the saloons and gambling halls that began to spring up. But those animosities slowly dwindled as Ogden became an important railroad, manufacturing, milling, canning, livestock, and agricultural center. The increasing importance of nearby Hill Air Force Base as an employer helped the city continue to grow well into the 1980s. Established in 1939, the base occupies 6,600 acres just south of Ogden and employs more than 8,700 people. Airplane buffs might want to stop at the **Hill Aerospace Museum** and examine the thousands of aviation artifacts and numerous old airplanes. *Five miles south of Ogden, east of I-15; 801-777-6818.*

■ WEBER STATE UNIVERSITY

Another important event in the development of modern Ogden came on January 7, 1889, when 98 students gathered at the old Second LDS Ward meeting house on the corner of Grant and 26th streets for the first day of class at the Weber State Academy. In those lean times, school founders mortgaged their own homes to ensure that classes could be held. The school became Weber Academy in 1908 and broke into the college ranks in 1916 when two years of college work were added to the regular four-year high school curriculum. The name was changed again in 1918 to Weber Normal College and again in 1923 to Weber College, when the high school department was discontinued. The LDS Church transferred title of the college to Utah in 1933. Shortly after the college was moved from downtown to its present site in 1954, Weber State College became a four-year institution. Now, more than 18,000 students attend Weber State University, a modern institution offering undergraduate degrees in a hundred fields of study. With its spacious Dee Events Center, Museum of Natural Science, Collett Art Gallery, Val A. Browning Center for the Performing Arts, and the Layton P. Ott Planetarium, all found on campus, Weber State serves as a center for culture in Ogden. *801-626-6975.*

■ OGDEN MUSEUMS

John Browning, the foremost American inventor of firearms (he made his first gun at the age of 13), helped shape the character of Ogden. Visitors to the city can see his collection of guns and learn about his life by visiting the **Browning Firearms Museum** at **Ogden Union Station,** the old railroad depot. The station also houses an antique auto collection in the **Browning Kimball Car Museum,** geology exhibits in the **Natural History Museum,** and exhibits tracing the history of the railroad in the **Utah State Railroad Museum.** The **Wattis-Dumke Model Railroad** shows, in miniature, tracks, trestles, and other features of the local railroad system, including Ogden Union Station as it was in the 1940s and 1950s (a wooden station from 1869 was replaced by a brick one in 1889, then by another in 1923). There are also two art galleries, one displaying a permanent collection and one for changing monthly shows. *2501 Wall Avenue; 801-629-8446.*

At the **Treehouse Children's Museum,** children can discover the wonders of literature, or attend a children's theater performance. 455 23rd Street; 801-394-9663.

■ OGDEN PARKS AND NATURAL AREAS

The Ogden River winds its way through the middle of town, lined for 3 miles by the Ogden River Parkway, which includes a dinosaur park, a botanical garden, an outdoor convention center, a playground, and sports and picnic facilities. Bicyclists, hikers, and joggers enjoy a paved trail system along the river, while anglers catch wild brown and stocked rainbow trout.

The **Eccles Dinosaur Park** is the habitat of more than 100 life-size reproductions of prehistoric creatures from the Cretaceous, Jurassic, and Triassic periods. They are placed in native Utah foothill vegetation and accompanied by audio effects of dinosaur "roars." A playground with climbable dinosaurs is also a hit. *1544 East Park Boulevard; 801-393-3466.*

The **Ogden Nature Center** offers a wildlife sanctuary with nature trails, tours, and many special events year round. *966 West 12th Street; 801-621-7595.*

A view of the Wellsville Mountains from Cache Valley may be tonic enough for the city-weary traveler.

LAGOON: A PIONEERING AMUSEMENT PARK

Lagoon is one of the nation's oldest amusement parks. It was founded in 1886 by railroad magnate Simon Bamberger, who would later serve as Utah's fourth governor; Bamberger owned the railroad line connecting Salt Lake City and Ogden and built the park to encourage people to ride his train. "Lakeside," as the park was originally called, was originally constructed 4 miles west of present-day Lagoon, on the shores of the Great Salt Lake, but fell out of favor when the lake receded. Eventually, the park was moved to a spot near a pair of ponds and some artesian wells and was renamed "Lagoon."

For many years the park was a tremendous success, but it was closed during World War II and by 1945 was derelict. "There were waist-high weeds all over the place," recalls Peter Freed, who with his brothers Robert and Dave took over the amusement park from the Bambergers in 1945. "It looked like a ghost town. You had to use a lot of imagination to envision it as an amusement park again."

A few remnants of the original Lagoon facilities survive. The oldest building, the Lake Park picnic terrace, dates back to the "Lakeside" days, and a turn-of-the-century carousel—one of fewer than 200 of its kind in the United States—is still in operation. The park's first roller coaster, built in 1921, has retained its original design, although it has been rebuilt many times; it is one of the oldest operating wooden coasters in the country.

When Lagoon was first conceived, it was, like most amusement parks of its time, relatively simple. "The big things in those days," recalls Freed, "were dancing and bathing. We put in the swimming pool, and it was the first one in the area. When we started buying rides, we started out slowly because we didn't have any money. There was nothing like we have now."

In 1953, a fire started near the roller coaster and destroyed most of the west midway. The Freeds rebuilt with a vengeance, and soon Lagoon was one of the largest amusement parks between the Mississippi River and the West Coast.

In the 1950s and 1960s, legendary performers such as Ella Fitzgerald, Louis Armstrong, Johnny Mathis, the Doors, the Beach Boys, the Rolling Stones, and Janis Joplin performed at Lagoon's Patio Gardens. The Beach Boys even composed a song—"Salt Lake City"—which mentioned the park. But, with the advent of the drug culture, the Freeds began to fear that rock-concert patrons wouldn't mix well with wholesome families enjoying the rides, so they turned Patio Gardens into a roller rink, then a game arcade, and built the Lagoon Opera House, where they staged summer theater and musicals.

In 1974, the Freeds purchased the "Pioneer Village" collection of buildings and Utah artifacts, then located near the east bench of Salt Lake City, and brought it all to Lagoon. Their interest in preserving and presenting Utah's pioneer history to the public is understandable, as their maternal grandfather was Brigham Young's older brother. Visitors to Pioneer Village get a sense of what it was like to be an early Utah settler. On view, in one of the best gun museums in the United States, are several of gun inventor John Browning's early prototypes, as well as his tools and workbench. Rare Civil War and Mormon Battalion flags hang near the safe of Mormon leader Porter Rockwell. Kids can be "locked" into an old rock jailhouse, ride a horse-drawn carriage through the streets of the little village, and imagine what school was like inside the old Wanship schoolhouse. Other artifacts on display include Brigham Young's china, a tiny organ that survived the Mormon trek across the plains to Utah, the state's first soda fountain, a drug store, and a rock chapel moved piece by piece from Coalville. There's also the old Charleston post office, a train station moved from Kaysville, and the carriages of some of Utah's most prominent early citizens. Adding to the attraction are the more modern thrills of a log flume ride—a modern-day equivalent of the water chute built at Lagoon at the turn of the century—and Old West shootouts on Main Street.

Lagoon is open from April through October, and considerably more than one million visitors annually come to enjoy the rides and the water park, play games, listen to live music, and view the gardens, exhibits, and fountains. *On I-15, 17 miles north of Salt Lake City (Exit 325) and 17 miles south of Ogden (Exit 327); 801-451-8000 or 800-748-5246.*

Fishing in the Weber and Ogden rivers can be excellent, and Pine View Reservoir in **Ogden Canyon** is extremely popular with local boaters. The beaches are an ideal place to cool off when the temperature climbs in the valley.

One final note about Ogden: don't be surprised if **Ben Lomond Peak,** which dominates the view to the east of the city, looks familiar. It served as the inspiration for the Paramount Pictures logo.

■ **NORTH OF OGDEN** *map pages 202–203, E-2*

The venerable town of **Brigham City** was settled in 1851 as Box Elder Creek, but today this town of 20,000 people honors Mormon leader Brigham Young. Historic displays at the **Brigham City Museum and Gallery** show how residents lived in the 19th century. *24 North 300 West; 435-723-6769.*

Crystal Hot Springs resort in neighboring Honeyville is a wonderful place to soak in naturally heated outdoor pools after a day of downhill or cross-country skiing in the nearby mountains. *8215 North Highway 38; 435-279-8104.*

At harvest time, Wasatch Front residents visit the fruit and vegetable stands located along old U.S. 89 between Ogden and Brigham City, near the town of Willard. Along Fruit Way, as the stretch is called, local farmers sell apples, apricots, peaches, pears, squash, corn, and pumpkins as they come into season.

■ **CACHE COUNTY** *map pages 202–203, E-1/2*

The Wellsville Mountains separate Cache Valley from Brigham City to the west. Cache Valley takes its name from the beaver trappers, who liked to cache their pelts here in the early 1820s.

■ **CHEESE**

Some visitors travel to Logan, in the heart of Cache Valley, to attend summertime professional theater performances at the old Lyric Theater. Others come to marvel at the beauty of Logan Peak, the 9,713-foot summit rising above the picturesque Mormon Temple. Still others, however, make the journey to Logan and Cache Valley because of the cheese.

The dairy industry is one of the major employers in this part of Utah, and some of the best cheese to be found in the state is produced here. Although you can't tour the factories, you can take stock up on cheeses by visiting the factory stores of two producers, the **Cache Valley Cheese Farm Store** (6295 North 2150 West;

435-563-4744) in Amalga or the **Gossner Foods** store (1051 North 1000 West; 435-752-9365) in Logan.

■ **LOGAN** *map pages 202–203, E-1*
The agricultural industry still plays a key role in Logan's economy—and **Utah State University**, established in 1888, is one of the leading agricultural research institutions in the United States. As a land grant school with an enrollment of around 16,500, Utah State supports basic and applied research. The university also has 7,000 acres dedicated to agricultural research; its colleges also teach agriculture, business, education, engineering, family life, natural resources, humanities, social sciences, arts, and science. Off campus, the university's Extension Service offers classes and gives advice to farmers and homemakers at locations throughout Utah. Old Main Hill, where construction started on Utah State's historic administration building in 1889, was planned by the same landscape architects who laid out New York's Central Park.

More important to visitors, Utah State University contributes to the culture of the Beehive State with a variety of museums and performing arts centers. The **Daryl Chase Fine Arts Center** houses a theater and concert hall. The **Nora Eccles Harrison Museum of Art** (650 North 1100 East; 435-797-1414), in a building designed by the internationally acclaimed architect Edward Larabee Barnes, has a collection of more than 4,000 works of art; the museum specializes in American art from west of the Mississippi, from the 1920s to the present.

Be sure to take time to taste the school's famous Aggie Ice Cream while you're on campus. "Lacto ice cream" was first developed at the university in 1922 under the direction of Professor Gustav Wilster. Today, USU employs more than 25 full and part-time students, mostly food science majors, to make the ice cream, which is sold only here and in a few other places in Utah. You can enjoy one of the 33 flavors at the small shop (435-797-2109) in the Nutrition and Food Sciences Building, at 750 North 1200 East.

Designed by Truman O. Angell, the **Logan Mormon Temple** dominates the downtown skyline. Completed in 1885 after Brigham Young selected the site in 1877, the limestone temple with its beautifully manicured grounds ranks with the Salt Lake, Manti, and St. George temples for its striking appearance.

(following pages) Timpanogos Range, a subrange of the Wasatch Mountains, and Utah Lake. The highest peak of the Timpanogos Range is Mt. Timpanogos.

■ **AMERICAN WEST HERITAGE CENTER** *map pages 202–203, E-2*
In the town of Wellsville, 6 miles southwest of Logan on U.S. 91, is the **American West Heritage Center,** an outdoor living-history complex where visitors can glimpse Utah as it was from 1820 to 1920. Exhibits include a Native American village, a pioneer settlement, and a historic farm where demonstrations of plowing, sheep-shearing, fruit and vegetable canning, and cider pressing take place—you may even see a traditional wedding. Numerous events occur throughout the year, including the Fall Harvest Festival, Pumpkin Day, and the always popular Corn Maze—when, for six weeks in September and October, visitors can test their sense of direction in a dizzying corn maze that sprawls across 8 acres.

No Utah event celebrates the heritage of the American West and the trappers better than the eight-day **Festival of the American West,** held here annually from the last Friday of July through the first week of August. The festival gives visitors a chance to pan for gold, visit a military camp, see a Wild West show in a saloon, purchase Indian crafts, and get a feeling for what it was like to live in a mountain man's camp. A pageant combining dramatic action with music and dance helps bring to life the settling of the American West. *4025 South Highway 89/91; 435-245-6050 or 800-225-3378.*

■ **BLACKSMITH FORK CANYON** *map pages 202–203, E-2*
South of Logan, **Blacksmith Fork Canyon** strikes due east of Hyrum. Ducks and geese can be seen in the river and big game is common throughout the canyon. A winter drive might reward you with the appearance of a white weasel scampering across the road.

At the end of UT 101 east of Hyrum sprawls the **Hardware Ranch Wildlife Management Area,** an elk preserve owned and operated by the Utah Division of Wildlife Resources. Workers at the site feed up to 700 elk every winter to prevent the animals from either starving or doing damage to farmers' lands in the valley below. Many families drive up to see the elk in winter, boarding sleighs pulled by Clydesdale horses to get right up beside the hulking beasts. A few elk remain in the meadow the rest of the year, posing for pictures. The canyon also offers camping and fishing in the summer. *Information: 435-753-6206.*

■ **BEAR LAKE** *map pages 202–203, F-1*
From Logan, you can also drive up **Logan Canyon** to marvel at the view of Bear
Lake from the summit. Straddling the Utah-Idaho line at the extreme north end of
the state, Bear Lake supports a state park and several private campgrounds and
recreation areas. The lake contains four distinct kinds of fish thought to be
descended from species found in ancient Lake Bonneville: the Bonneville cisco,
Bear Lake whitefish, Bonneville whitefish, and Bear Lake sculpin. Most fishermen,
however, would rather catch the larger lake trout and Bear Lake cutthroat. In the
summer, power boaters and sailboaters take over the lake. *Bear Lake State Park
information: 435-946-3343; campground reservations: 800-322-3770.*

The Bear Lake area is famous for its jumbo raspberries, so if you're in the Bear
Lake area in July or August, stop at one of the little drive-in restaurants in Garden
City to enjoy a fresh berry malt or sundae. Many Salt Lakers make a special trip up
to Bear Lake to pick or purchase raspberries for jams, jellies, and just munching.

NORTHEASTERN UTAH
MOUNTAINS & DINOSAURS

Northeastern Utah is a place to find adventure. You can paddle canoes down the remote White River in the springtime and watch geese and goslings scramble for cover. You can get drenched by white-water rapids when rafting down the Green River through Dinosaur National Monument's Split Mountain. You can spend a quiet day bird-watching at the Ouray National Wildlife Refuge, and bask in the sun at remote Antelope Flat beach in the Flaming Gorge National Recreation Area.

The Uinta Mountains, the only major range in the lower 48 states that runs east-west rather than north-south, dominate northeastern Utah. Visitors can escape to rocky peaks, grassy alpine meadows, and thick lodgepole forests in the 460,000-acre High Uintas Wilderness Area; it's Utah's largest designated wilderness, and the 17th biggest in the United States. Four of Utah's larger rivers—the Bear, Weber, Provo, and Duchesne—spring from 20 drainages and a thousand-odd lakes in the range. In the small towns and remote highways surrounding the Uintas can be found inns and cafés offering the comfortable charm of the rural West.

■ THE HIGH UINTAS *map page 161, A/C-1/2*

The Uintas look much the same today as they did in the days of the early pioneers. A passage from *Utah: A Guide to the State*, compiled by the Utah Writers' Project under the federal Work Projects Administration and published in 1941, tells some of their story:

> Wandering prospectors, cowboys and sheepherders penetrated the forests and climbed the peaks, leaving only burnt sticks and tin cans to mark their passing. A Swedish prospector was working with his partner in the Rock Creek country. The Swede felt that he had found what he always wanted—gold near running water, lakes, trees, flowers, and a fishing stream right in camp, but his partner yearned for the fleshpots of the mining camps. After many heated quarrels, the partnership was broken up in a fierce fight. The winner—the peace-

Northern Utah's mountains are among the most rugged and wild in the West.

loving Swede—sucked his bruised knuckles and yelled after his ex-partner: 'Yah, now run qvick to Park City vit its hussies and saloons. Anyhow! You are yust a snoose-chewing, coffee-grinding, visky-drinking, ski-yumping, fisk-eating yackass, anyhow!' Homesteading pioneers preferred better land in lower valleys, irrigable with water from these mountains. Some logging was done, but the roads were too rough and the distance to the large centers too far to make it profitable. All factors seemed to conspire to leave the High Uintas a primitive area.

The Uintas remain wild and undeveloped. Visitors searching for nightlife, ski lifts, and fine hotels can find them to the west of the Uinta Basin in Park City. Though a few rustic alpine lodges on the edge of the wilderness area supply bedding and shelter—try Moon Lake, Defas Dude Ranch, or Spirit Lake—the Uintas are really for hikers, anglers, campers, and hunters. One doesn't need to backpack to enjoy the Uintas, however. The wilderness is surrounded by developed U.S. Forest Service campgrounds, which are easily accessible by car. A small fee is charged for use of the facilities.

■ UINTA RECREATION

Mirror Lake Highway *map page 161, A/B-1/2*

The best known and most popular of roads to the Uintas is UT 150, known to locals as the Mirror Lake Highway. The road connects the town of Kamas, Utah, with Evanston, Wyoming. Closed by snow from late October until mid-June in most years, the highway climbs from 6,500 feet at Kamas to the 10,678-foot Bald Mountain Pass, and leads to dozens of developed campsites. Some of the campgrounds are located near lakes regularly stocked with rainbow trout. Trails off Mirror Lake Highway lead to popular backpacking areas. Most hikers are drawn by the wilderness designation on the east side of the road, but the west side (though not a congressionally designated wilderness) possesses many of the same qualities without the crowds. Wise backpackers check with rangers at the Kamas Ranger Station (see page 323) or the Mirror Lake Guard Station to find the least visited lakes and routes.

Most Wasatch Front families seem to have a favorite lake or campground situated along the Mirror Lake Highway, and many make it a tradition to camp there at least once a summer. One of the largest campgrounds surrounds **Mirror Lake**. The lodge on the lake burned down a few years ago, but the site remains popular.

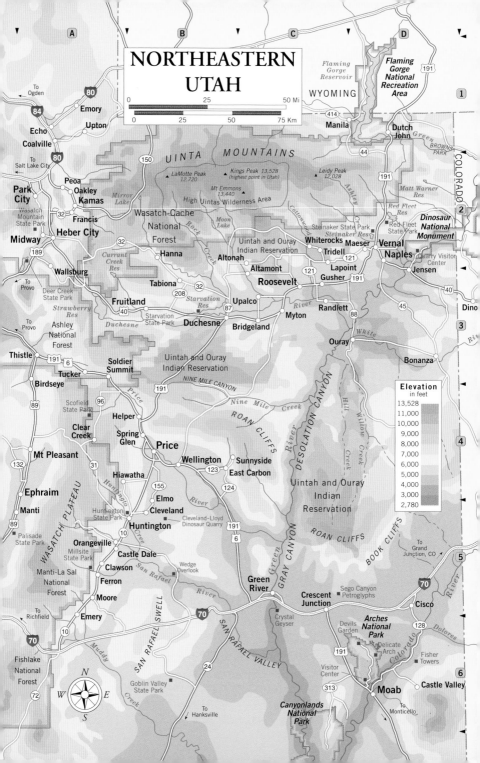

NORTHEASTERN UTAH

A   B   C   D

1
2
3
4
5
6

0   25   50 Mi
0   25   50   75 Km

Flaming Gorge Reservoir

Flaming Gorge National Recreation Area

WYOMING

To Ogden

Emory
Upton

Echo
Coalville

To Salt Lake City

Manila

Dutch John

COLORADO

BROWNS PARK

Green

U I N T A   M O U N T A I N S

LaMotte Peak 12,720
Kings Peak 13,528 (highest point in Utah)
Leidy Peak 12,028
Mt Emmons 13,440

Park City
Peoa
Oakley
Kamas

Francis

Midway
Heber City

Wasatch Mountain State Park

Wasatch-Cache National Forest

High Uintas Wilderness Area

Mirror Lake
Moon Lake

Rock Creek

Ashley Creek

Whiterocks
Maeser
Tridell
Vernal
Naples
Jensen

Steinaker State Park
Steinaker Res
Red Fleet Res
Red Fleet State Park

Matt Warner Res

Dinosaur National Monument

Quarry Visitor Center

Hanna
Altonah
Altamont
Roosevelt

Uintah and Ouray Indian Reservation

Lapoint
Gusher

Wallsburg

Deer Creek State Park

Currant Creek Res

Tabiona

Strawberry Res

To Provo

Fruitland

Starvation Res
Starvation State Park

Upalco
Duchesne
Bridgeland
Myton

Randlett

Ouray

Dino

To Provo

Ashley National Forest

Duchesne

White River

Bonanza

Thistle
Tucker
Birdseye

Soldier Summit

Uintah and Ouray Indian Reservation

NINE MILE CANYON

Nine Mile Creek

Elevation in feet

13,528
11,000
10,000
9,000
8,000
7,000
6,000
5,000
4,000
3,000
2,780

Scofield State Park

Helper
Spring Glen
Price

ROAN CLIFFS

DESOLATION CANYON

Green River

Willow Creek

Hill Creek

Clear Creek

Mt Pleasant

Wellington
Sunnyside
East Carbon

Uintah and Ouray Indian Reservation

Ephraim
Manti

Hiawatha
Elmo
Cleveland
Huntington

Cleveland-Lloyd Dinosaur Quarry

ROAN CLIFFS

BOOK CLIFFS

To Grand Junction, CO

Palisade State Park

Orangeville

Millsite State Park

Castle Dale
Clawson
Ferron
Moore

Huntington State Park

Wedge Overlook

Green River

GRAY CANYON

Crescent Junction

Sego Canyon Petroglyphs

Cisco

Colorado River

Dolores River

To Richfield

Manti-La Sal National Forest

Emery

SAN RAFAEL SWELL

SAN RAFAEL VALLEY

Crystal Geyser

Devils Garden

Arches National Park

Fisher Towers

Castle Valley

Fishlake National Forest

Muddy Creek

Goblin Valley State Park

To Hanksville

Delicate Arch

Visitor Center

Moab

To Monticello

Canyonlands National Park

N
W   E
S

Dawn at Mirror Lake, in the High Uintas Wilderness Area.

Campers willing to drive slightly farther can discover less crowded conditions at North Slope sites like Bridger Lake, China Meadows, and Hoop Lake. Located just south of Mountain View, Wyoming, these quiet places are tucked under some of the highest peaks in the range. Fishing for trout along the creek that flows through China Meadows, or just lying in the tall grass, can be a fine alternative to battling the crowds at better-known places. *Wasatch-Cache National Forest. See page 323.*

East Slope *map page 161, C/D-1/2*
Those wanting to go further afield will enjoy the camping areas at **Browne** and **Sheep Creek lakes**, on the eastern edge of the Uintas. You'll need to follow the dirt roads that head west from the Flaming Gorge National Recreation Area. Streams flowing from these small alpine lakes are teeming with cutthroat trout. Willing anglers should also hike from **Spirit Lake** into the nearby wilderness area, where they will likely be rewarded with excellent fishing. *Flaming Gorge Ranger District, Ashley National Forest Headquarters. See page 322.*

South Slope *map page 161, B/C-2*
The developed U.S. Forest Service campground at **Moon Lake,** on the South
Slope of the Uintas, is a good place to create happy memories. You can rise early
and head for the stream flowing into the lake to catch whitefish and trout for
breakfast. Later, you might want to rent horses for an hour or so and ride into the
forest. A paddling expedition along the shoreline is also a good way to spend the
afternoon. *Vernal Ranger District. See page 322.*

Fishing
The Uintas hold one of Utah's premier fishing regions. Anglers tell stories of walking to a nondescript, unnamed alpine lake and catching hungry trout on each cast.
A simple technique—with a traditional spinning rod, a fly that imitates a mos-
quito, and a plastic bubble for weight—works well here. Anglers soon get wise to
the fact there are many lakes in each drainage. If one lake isn't producing, hiking
100 yards to the next can often change a fisherman's luck.

"We always suggest going into an area with more than one lake," says Glenn
Davis, a retired fisheries biologist with the Division of Wildlife Resources. "That
gives you some alternatives. The lakes closest to the highway get fished heavily.
The Provo River drainage gets hit particularly hard. On the North Slope, there is
high use on Henry's Fork (the trailhead to King's Peak) and Red Castle." Davis
generally recommends fishing the east end of the Uintas, which gets fewer visitors.

The Division of Wildlife Resources manages 650 of these lakes, most of which
contain either cutthroat or brook trout stocked by airplane. A series of 10 booklets,
called *Lakes of the High Uintas,* gives detailed descriptions of lakes, types of fish
stocked, trail access, and camping. It is available from the DWR's offices in Salt
Lake City and Vernal, as well as its other regional offices. *See page 326.*

Backpacking
Hikers seeking information on backpacking in the Uintas will find plenty of
resources. Topographical and hiking maps of the areas can be obtained from the
Wasatch National Forest headquarters in Salt Lake City, or the Ashley National
Forest headquarters in Vernal. U.S. Forest Service district offices can be found
along the roads into the mountains near Flaming Gorge, Vernal, Roosevelt,
Duchesne, and Kamas in Utah, as well as Evanston and Mountain View in
Wyoming. Bait shops and fishing guides sell other maps.

Snowmobiling

Poor access, heavy snow, and extreme cold make winter access to the High Uintas Wilderness Area nearly impossible, but the Mirror Lake Highway is cleared to a snowmobile trailhead near Soapstone Basin. The trail is groomed regularly by the Division of Parks and Recreation. *See page 326.*

■ RESERVOIR RECREATION

Since Utah is one of the most arid states in the country, Wasatch Front residents rely on storage reservoirs to supply much of their water needs. One of the most complicated and expensive components of this water supply system is the Central Utah Project, a huge water-capture and delivery project conceived in 1956 to bring water from the eastern part of the Uinta Basin to the Wasatch Front. The large reservoirs of northeastern Utah, which provide drinking and irrigation water, also possess great recreational value for boaters, fishermen, and campers.

Strawberry Reservoir *map page 161, A-3*

One of the premier trout fisheries in the western United States, the huge Strawberry Reservoir, located 23 miles southeast of Heber City near U.S. 40, was built in 1906 as one of the nation's first reclamation reservoirs. It was expanded to 17,000 acres with the completion of the Soldier Creek Dam in 1973 and the joining with Soldier Creek Reservoir a few years later. Three immense U.S. Forest Service campgrounds give the thousands of fishermen who flock to Strawberry a place to spend the night. Generations of Utahns have spent many a summer afternoon fishing for the large cutthroat trout that have made this place a popular angling spot. *Heber Ranger District. See page 323.*

Deer Creek Reservoir *map pages 202–203, E-6*

Just west of Heber City off U.S. 189 is the Deer Creek Reservoir, also popular with anglers, sailboarders, and sailboaters. Its relatively low elevation draws water-skiers and swimmers. Campgrounds, showers, and picnic areas are at the lower end of the lake. *Deer Creek State Park, 435-654-0171 or 800-322-3770 for camping reservations.*

Jordanelle Reservoir *map pages 202–203, F-5/6*

Just up the Provo River north of Heber City is the newest Central Utah Project reservoir. It features fine facilities for campers and boaters, good trout fishing, and an interesting nature center. *Jordanelle State Park, U.S. 40, 10 miles north of Heber City; 435-649-9540 or 800-322-3770 for camping reservations.*

Starvation Reservoir *map page 161, B-3*
Located near the town of Duchesne, Starvation Reservoir is a quiet alternative for Wasatch Front boaters. Although the fishing here is poor, the beautiful state park offers fine boating and camping facilities. *Starvation State Park, off U.S. 40 west of Duchesne; 435-738-2326 or 800-322-3770 for camping reservations.*

Currant Creek Reservoir *map page 161, A-3*
This scenic lake surrounded by pines and aspens is located 19 miles off U.S. 40 on a bumpy dirt road. Fishing can be spotty, but the Forest Service campground, offering a children's playground and some specially designed units for campers with horses, is one of Utah's best. *Heber Ranger District. See page 323.*

Smaller Reservoirs *map page 161, D-2*
On the eastern side of the Uintas, south of Flaming Gorge, a handful of smaller reservoirs provide some interesting side trips from U.S. 191. Bass and trout fishing, camping, and boating facilities can be found at Steinaker and Red Fleet state parks. Calder, Crouse, and Matt Warner reservoirs on Diamond Mountain are also full of trout. The scenic 74-mile Red Cloud Loop leads to several small reservoirs, some beautiful forest, and Indian petroglyphs in Dry Fork Canyon.

■ FLAMING GORGE NATIONAL RECREATION AREA
map page 161, D-1

The problem with visiting the Flaming Gorge National Recreation Area is that there are almost too many interesting outdoor recreational possibilities, only one of which is fishing in **Flaming Gorge Reservoir,** where anglers tell stories about catching and releasing 30-pound lake trout. Below the **Flaming Gorge Dam,** fly fishermen cast nymphs, streamers, and dry flies to catch beautiful trout on the Green River, as rafters float down the gentle rapids on lazy summer afternoons. Boaters travel to remote campgrounds on the reservoir shore for a quiet evening under the stars and away from the sound of automobiles. As water-skiers zig and zag on the reservoir beneath 1,500-foot red-rock cliffs, swimmers bask in the sun on sandy beaches at Antelope Flat and Mustang Ridge.

Away from the water's edge, hikers climb to the top of Bear Top Mountain for views across the canyons and close encounters with bighorn sheep. Children lead

(following pages) Red Canyon in winter, in the Flaming Gorge National Recreation Area.

their parents on self-guided tours of the Flaming Gorge Dam, dropping 502 feet down in an elevator to the interior of the huge concrete structure, where they see the turbines, generators, and transformers that turn flowing water into electric power. In the winter, snowmobiles go where cars can't because of heavy snowfall. Best of all, visitors to Flaming Gorge can simply find a quiet, shaded campground, and spend their vacation relaxing.

■ FLAMING GORGE ATTRACTIONS

Visitors Centers

First-time visitors to this national recreation area would do well to stop at the **Red Canyon Visitor Center**, located west of Dutch John on UT 44. In addition to receiving information on things to do and places to camp, travelers can study the interpretive display for information about local plants, animal life, geology, and cultural history. The view of Flaming Gorge Reservoir, 1,360 feet below the plate glass window, gives a feeling for the massive beauty of the gorge itself. Take some time to walk around the self-guided nature trail, an easy stroll designed to introduce visitors to the ecology of the area.

The **Flaming Gorge Dam Visitor Center** provides yet more local information. Visitors can view the movie *Flaming Gorge: A Story Written in Water*, which explains the natural and human history of Flaming Gorge from ancient times. *Flaming Gorge Ranger District, Ashley National Forest Headquarters at UT 43/44 in Manila; 435-784-3445.*

Campgrounds

Developed campgrounds abound at Flaming Gorge. Some of the best include **Firefighters Memorial, Lucerne Valley, Buckboard Crossing,** and **Firehole.** Most camping sites are nestled in aspen and pine forests, while a few are found in sagebrush flats. Swimmers might consider staying at Mustang Ridge or Antelope Flat, two campgrounds with beaches located nearby. *For camping reservations call the National Recreation Reservation Service; 877-444-6777.*

Fishing

Though the main recreation season at Flaming Gorge runs from Memorial Day to Labor Day, you can fish on both the Green River and the reservoir itself year-round. Flaming Gorge Reservoir is famous for producing large lake and brown trout; anglers occasionally land lake trout of more than 50 pounds. Guide services and boat rentals are available at Cedar Springs Marina, near the dam; Lucerne Valley, near the Utah-Wyoming border; and Buckboard Marina, in Wyoming. A number of Salt Lake City–based guides also take clients down the Green, which is easily Utah's best river fishery and one of the top trout waters of its kind in the United States. Nine ramps service the power boats and fishing crafts that ply the 91-mile-long reservoir. When you visit the **Flaming Gorge Lodge** near Dutch John, you can see the huge fish caught in the reservoir and talk to anglers who have been out trying their luck. (Because of the complicated regulations designed to protect and produce trophy trout, anglers should study Utah fishing rules closely.) *Flaming Gorge Lodge: 155 Greendale U.S. 191, Dutch John; 435-889-3773.*

Rafting the Green River

A favorite summer activity in the Flaming Gorge National Recreation Area is to rent a raft from the Flaming Gorge Lodge and Flaming Gorge Recreation Services, and take it down the Green River. The river's small rapids provide thrills for experienced adventurers willing to guide their own rafts, as well as a good introduction for beginners with guides. Most boaters enter the river at a ramp below the Flaming Gorge Dam and travel to the Little Hole pullout, just more than 7 miles downstream. A few ride the river all the way down to Brown's Park, a trip that takes the better part of a day, especially if you stop to fish. The concessionaires that rent the rafts will also pick up clients. *Flaming Gorge Recreation Services: U.S. 191 at Dutch John Boulevard, Dutch John; 435-885-3191.*

Geology Driving Tours

There is much to learn about geology at Flaming Gorge. The loop road in **Sheep Creek Canyon**, on the west side of the reservoir, gives travelers an opportunity to view tremendous numbers of geological layers and formations exposed by erosion.

Another driving tour, the 30-mile **"Drive Through the Ages"** on U.S. 191 between Flaming Gorge and Vernal, takes you across the edges of exposed layers that range in age from the merely million-year-old Uinta Mountain Group to the 80-million-year-old Mancos Formation. Interpretive signs along the way point out geological features of interest. *For more information, pick up a free booklet from the Utah Field House of Natural History State Park, 496 East Main Street, Vernal; 435-789-3799, or from any Bureau of Land Management or U.S. Forest Service office. See pages 322–325.*

(following pages) Water play on the Green River.

Ute Mountain Lookout Tower

Early foresters used lookout towers like the Ute Mountain Tower to detect forest fires. The only structure of its kind remaining in Utah, the tower has earned a place on the National Register of Historic Places. Visitors who climb the stairs to the top can see clear into Wyoming. Check with the Flaming Gorge Dam Visitor Center or the Red Canyon Visitor Center for hours and directions.

■ BROWN'S PARK *map page 161, D-1*

Brown's Park is a remote valley lying across the Utah-Colorado border, just below the Wyoming boundary. It received its name from Baptiste Brown, an early fur trader; the area was frequently visited by the mountain men in earlier days. Today, the various parts of Brown's Park are managed by the U.S. Fish and Wildlife Service, the Utah Division of Wildlife Resources, the BLM, and the National Park Service (see pages 322–326). Only one paved road leads into this area—from Maybell, Colorado. But there are dirt roads leading from Dutch John to Clay Basin Creek, and from Vernal to the Brown's Park Waterfowl Management Area.

A point of historical interest in Brown's Park is the **John Jarvie Ranch Historic Site,** on BLM property. In the late 1800s, the ranch was a regular stopping place for anyone traveling through this section of Utah, Colorado, and Wyoming. John Jarvie, a well-educated Scotsman, settled in the Brown's Park area in 1880. A colorful character, he ran a ferry across the Green River, operated a general store, prospected in the nearby mountains, and entertained the locals by playing both the organ and the concertina. He knew, and occasionally hosted, outlaws like Butch Cassidy, the Sundance Kid, Matt Warner, Isom Dart, and Ann Bassett, who was known as the Queen of the Rustlers. Jarvie was murdered on July 6, 1909, by a pair of transient workers from Rock Springs, Wyoming, who were never captured. His body was placed in a boat and pushed out into the Green River. It was found a few days later, just above the Gates of Lodore in the eastern end of Brown's Park.

Today the ranch consists of a dugout that was Jarvie's original house on the property and a stone house built for Jarvie in 1888 by John Bennett, a member of the Wild Bunch gang who was later hanged by vigilantes for his part in a local murder. Also original are the blacksmith shop and some corrals, the latter built of hand-hewn railroad ties. The general store is a replica of the original. Guided tours are available from May through October, and visitors can take a self-guided tour year-round. To get to the ranch follow signs from U.S. 191 that send you down bumpy Brown's Park Road. It's a long ride, but well worth the effort. *435-885-3307.*

■ DINOSAUR NATIONAL MONUMENT *map page 161, D-2*

The lush, alpine forests of the Uintas and Flaming Gorge contrast with the stark, barren valleys of the Uinta Basin and Carbon County to the south. Looking over these desolate landscapes of tan, red, and white rock, it's hard to imagine this as a once-verdant land of ferns, cycads, club mosses, and tall conifers, where dinosaurs roamed. Yet fossils remain to attest to that history.

Giant vegetarians, like the Apatosaurus (once better known as Brontosaurus), Stegosaurus, Diplodocus, and Camptosaurus, as well as sharp-toothed and -clawed carnivores like the Allosaurus, roamed this land 145 million years ago. When these dinosaurs died, some were washed by river floodwaters onto sandbars, where their bones mixed with the remains of turtles, crocodiles, clams, and other animals that lived in the river. Thick sediments piled up on top of them during later centuries. As the sea crept in and out, silica dissolved and percolated through the strata, turning the ancient riverbed into hard sandstone and mineralizing the bones buried within it. When the Rocky Mountains began to form to the east, the developing mountains at what is now Dinosaur National Monument did not push the rock layers from below, but squeezed them from the sides. This action warped and tilted the rock. When rain, frost, and wind wore away the layers of sediment, a bit of the long-buried river bed—and its fossil treasure—began to appear at the top of a jagged ridge.

Thousands of tourists flock to Dinosaur National Monument each year to see this fossilized history of a time no man knew. Although visitors to the monument can enjoy hiking trails, river running, and some fine campgrounds, most folks come to see the fossils still in the rock at the dinosaur quarry. Remains of these ancient creatures dominate famous museums in New York, Washington, Chicago, Denver, and other cities throughout the world. Some of the earliest dinosaur skeletons ever assembled were excavated here in 1909 for the Carnegie Museum in Pittsburgh.

Earl Douglass, a Carnegie Museum paleontologist, was one of the first scientists to search for fossilized bones in the area. "I saw eight of the tail bones of a Brontosaurus in exact position," he wrote on August 7, 1909. "It was a beautiful sight."

Woodrow Wilson designated the place as Dinosaur National Monument in 1915—marking the monument, now being considered for national park status, as America's most important natural display of fossilized dinosaur bones. It was increased to about 78 square miles by Franklin Roosevelt in 1938; additional land acquisitions since then have increased its size to about 325 square miles.

Utah's Jurassic Park

Dinosaur National Monument provides us with a grand view of the Jurassic landscape of 145 million years ago, when the earth's continents were joined together in a single land mass now referred to as the supercontinent Pangaea. As you look about you at the subtle grays and browns of the desert, try to imagine the brilliant green ferns, conifers, and mosses that once grew here, and the behemoth dinosaurs that wandered among them. One of these was Apatosaurus (a.k.a. Brontosaurus), a long-necked and long-tailed vegetarian measuring more than 70 feet in length and tipping the scales at 35 tons. Because Apatosaurus's brain was smaller than ours, though given the job of directing a body as big as 18 station wagons, some people assumed it was dull-witted and spent most of its time sloshing around in swamps. Yet, now we know from studying rock strata in such places as Dinosaur National Monument that Apatosaurus galloped around in herds, probably with its young in the middle, kicking up dust and trampling trees. The smell must have been awful, but this dinosaur may have been fairly smart. After all, Apatosaurus belongs to one of the most successful groups of animals ever to live on the earth.

Other smaller dinosaurs shared the terrain with these monsters, among them the comely Stegosaurus ("roofed reptile"), known for the bony knobs and bumps all over its body, the upright plates on its back and its tail spikes. These animals grew to 20 feet in length and weighed about one-and-a-half tons. Early researchers thought that the back plates served as a defensive weapon, but more recently scientists have suggested that they served as solar panels and radiators regulating Stegosaurus's body temperature.

Roaming around with these oversized vegetarians were meat-eating carnosaurs, who packed their weight behind large heads, powerful necks, stout hind limbs, and small forearms. These included Allosaurus ("strange reptile") and Ceratosaurus ("horned reptile"). Adult Allosaurus was close to 40 feet long with a skull that reached nearly three feet in length; it had sharp, recurved daggers for teeth—serrated on both sides—lining its jaws. It may have sped around on its long, powerful hind limbs and grabbed its prey in the claws on its small, muscular forelimbs. Allosaurus probably fed on whip-tailed Apatosaurus.

As you climb into your two-ton station wagon to leave Dinosaur National Monument, you may feel vaguely relieved to return to the 20th century, where the descendants of Allosaurus—birds—prey on insects and worms.

—Mark Goodwin, scientist at the U.C. Berkeley Museum of Paleontology

Douglass dreamed of the day when a museum could be built next to the quarry where he'd dug out so many unique dinosaur specimens. Visitors today enjoy the realization of that vision: 7 miles north of U.S. 40 from Jensen is the **Dinosaur Quarry Visitor Center,** where the old Carnegie dinosaur quarry has been enclosed, since 1958, in an architecturally novel building. While active excavation has ceased here, visitors can still see dinosaur bones encased in the very cliff face where they were discovered and where paleontologists used to use tools ranging in size from dentists' picks to jackhammers to expose them. Park rangers, who are also paleontologists, are more than willing to answer queries. In summer, rangers invite children to become "junior paleontologists" and get a behind-the-scenes look at the quarry. The kids can examine fossilized bones stored at the quarry, use tools to dig them out of a dirt pit, or explore with their parents two paleontology routes in the park: Tour of the Tilted Rocks or Journey Through Time.

Most visitors spend too little time at Dinosaur National Monument. Take the time to contemplate and study the dinosaur bones entombed in the quarry rocks. Walk to the balcony overlooking the quarry and attempt to piece together the potpourri of fossilized bones into a single dinosaur, while imagining the giant creatures wandering through lush vegetation. Then spend an evening camped at Split Mountain watching the Green River roll slowly through the colorful canyon. Take a walk on the short, self-guided nature trail. You might be inspired to recall the words of John Wesley Powell, who stood near here on a bluff above the Green, 12 years after his 1869 expedition: "We are standing three thousand feet above its waters, which are troubled with billows, and white with foam. Its walls are set with crags and peaks, and buttressed towers, and overhanging domes. Turning to the right, the park is below us, with its island groves reflected by the deep, quiet water. Rich meadows stretch out on either hand, to the verge of a sloping plain that comes down from the distant mountains. These plains are almost naked rocks, in strange contrast to the meadows; blue and lilac colored rocks, buff and pink, vermilion and brown, all these colors clear and bright. . . . We are tempted to call this Rainbow Park." *Dinosaur National Monument, Quarry Visitor Center, UT 149, near Vernal; 435-789-2115.*

The **Utah Field House of Natural History State Park** in nearby Vernal is an excellent place to learn more about dinosaurs. The outdoor Dinosaur Garden contains 18 life-size replicas placed in a natural setting, allowing visitors to view the creatures as something more than fossilized bones. In addition, the park holds skeletal reproductions, archaeological and geological exhibits, fluorescent minerals, and displays of other natural history aspects of the Uinta Basin. Pick up a free souvenir dinosaur-hunting license from the information desk. The museum shop is a good place to purchase souvenirs, such as fossils, children's books, or pieces of dinosaur bone. *496 East Main Street; 435-789-3799.*

■ TOWNS AROUND THE UINTAS

The little towns surrounding the High Uintas offer a special taste of Utah life for those willing to look beyond the gas stations and franchises. Stop in at the general store in one of these hamlets to chat with the proprietor about local history. A small drugstore in **Kamas** is a great place to enjoy a freshly made malt with real ice cream, and in **Roosevelt**, you can stop for a round at the public golf course, the back nine designed by local golfers when there was no money for an architect. If you are in the area on the Fourth of July weekend you can experience one of the finest small-town rodeos in Utah, held every year in **Oakley**.

Heber City still has drive-in restaurants that serve great milk shakes and sundaes. It is also the home of the **Heber Valley Historic Railroad,** which takes travelers across the western part of Deer Creek Reservoir and down into Provo Canyon. There are also specialty trains—the Comedy Murder Mystery Train, the Haunted Canyon Train, the Tube 'n Train, and the Barbecue Train—as well as rides for special events. *Call ahead for a schedule. 435-654-5601.*

This is a wild, hard land, away from the culture of the Wasatch Front's big cities and the fame of southern Utah's red-rock national parks. The lure of the Uintas and of Flaming Gorge, Dinosaur National Monument, and the small towns dotting eastern Utah's landscape draws those in search of solitude, wildlife, and a place still waiting to be discovered.

■ UINTA PARKS AND RESORTS *map page 136, D-5; and page 161, A-2*

Homestead Resort

Founded on hot springs in 1895, the Homestead property has the 55-foot-high Homestead Crater, a hollowed-out, beehive-shape limestone rock filled with warm mineral water in which you can take a therapeutic soak, swim, snorkel, or even practice for your scuba certification test. Tour guides can fill you in on the crater's history and geology. The resort also has an 18-hole golf course with views of the

Heber and Snake Creek valleys and surrounding mountains. The Homestead Trail is joined with those at nearby Wasatch Mountain State Park. *700 North Homestead Drive, Midway; 435-888-7220.*

Wasatch Mountain State Park
The park has 90 holes of golf and a fine campground surrounded by scrub oak trees that turn a blazing orange in the fall. The park was the home of the biathlon and cross-country ski events for the 2002 Winter Olympic Games and is the largest Nordic ski area in Utah. *435-654-1791.*

■ PRICE AREA *map page 161, A/B-4*

Moving west of Vernal to the town of Duchesne, and then southwest on U.S. 191 to the settlement of Helper and the city of Price, travelers can discover another active dinosaur quarry and museum, and some colorful mining and railroad towns. Summer festivals, like Price's **Greek Days** during the second weekend in July, and **International Days** during the second week in August (in conjunction with the county fair) celebrate Carbon County's diversity.

■ PRICE *map page 161, B-4*
A city of nearly 10,000 residents, Price was named after Bishop William Price of the Latter-day Saints, who led an exploring party through Spanish Fork Canyon in 1869. The city serves as a gateway to the canyonlands country to the southeast.

The **College of Eastern Utah Prehistoric Museum,** in the rear of the Price City Hall, contains dinosaur footprints collected from nearby coal mines, an Allosaurus skeleton, fossils of several dinosaurs from the Cleveland-Lloyd Dinosaur Quarry, south of Price, and some of the museum's own discoveries, such as the plant-eating *Gastonia burgei* and the Utahraptor—a savage meat-eating dinosaur nicknamed the Utah slasher. A hairy mammoth found at nearby Fairview Canyon and Indian artifacts found in the area are also on view. (See "Stories in Stone" chapter, page 21.) *155 East Main Street; 435-637-5060.*

Price also serves as a gateway to the eastern edge of the Manti Mountains. State parks at Millsite, Huntington, and Scofield offer fine camping facilities, as do U.S. Forest Service sites near the Joe's Valley, Ferron, and Electric Lake reservoirs. Utah's nicest and least-visited alpine scenery is set away from the Wasatch Front population centers.

■ **NINE-MILE CANYON** *map page 161, B/C-3/4*
Northeast of Price, this 50-mile-long canyon contains some of the finest examples of what archaeologists believe to be petroglyphs from the Fremont culture. Why is a 50-mile-long canyon called Nine-Mile Canyon? According to one story, when John Wesley Powell headed a government expedition through this part of the state in 1869, a mapmaker charting the area made a nine-mile triangulation drawing that he named Nine-Mile Creek. The name stuck with the canyon. Another tale states that the canyon got its name when the Miles family settled the area in the 1880s. Seven daughters and two parents added up to nine Miles. Free brochures—available from the Price Chamber of Commerce or the local BLM office (see page 325)—point out the locations of petroglyphs. The Indians who made them may have inhabited Nine-Mile Canyon as much as 1,700 years ago. The rock art itself depicts both humans and animals. No one knows exactly what the Indians were trying to say with their etchings, but part of the fun of visiting such a site is interpreting the writing yourself. Be sure not to touch the rock, though, as oil from your fingers can harm the images.

■ **HELPER** *map page 161, B-4*
Local railroad and mining industries have left Carbon County with a distinctive religious and ethnic flavor that can still be felt in downtown Helper. Though many of the old stores and hotels are boarded up, enough remain to provide glimpses of this coal-mining town's interesting past. With almost 3,000 present-day residents, Helper was named after the locomotives called "helpers," which were stored here in the late 1800s to help pull trains over the steep grade of nearby Soldier Summit and into the Wasatch Front. The **Western Mining and Railroad Museum** uses old photographs and memorabilia to trace Carbon County's roots. People from other parts of the state enjoy searching payroll lists to find old friends and relatives who once worked here. Other visitors may browse through the exhibits to get a feel both for the diversity of the region and for the hardships endured by miners. *296 South Main Street, 435-472-3009.*

Fields of beeplant illuminate the desert floor in the San Rafael Wilderness south of Price.

GREAT BASIN

Utah's Great Basin is a land of islands and illusions. Totally barren or covered with sagebrush and other desert-loving plants, often it is dismissed as wasteland. Yet in many places, water lies just beneath the surface. Alpine forests on the high mountain peaks and marshes around the Great Salt Lake sustain exuberant islands of life amidst the desolate mud and salt flats.

Mirages are among the first illusions encountered in the Great Basin. Motorists crossing the Great Salt Lake Desert see mountain ranges that seem to float on sky-colored water. But upon approach, the water slowly, mysteriously disappears. In other directions, where there are no mountains, the sky is indistinguishable from the horizon. All is bright and shimmering.

Closer to Salt Lake City, a strong ocean smell assails the nostrils. Seagulls fly overhead. Sailboats race across the bright blue water. Sun seekers wander along white sand beaches. It appears as if one has reached the coast, yet Utah's largest city is 750 miles from the Pacific, almost 1,500 from the Gulf of Mexico, and about 2,200 from the Atlantic.

Through the years, this great, nearly deserted wilderness has seduced thousands with the richness of her mineral deposits. Great Basin names like Disappointment Hills, Confusion Mountains, Skull Valley, and Little Sahara sound like the most uninviting spots on earth. Yet this too is illusory. Today Utah's western desert beckons with an extraordinary wealth of beautiful scenery and fascinating history.

While the masses of people living in Wasatch Front communities are inclined to avoid the Great Basin as much as possible, others are drawn to the solitude. The view from the top of 11,031-foot Deseret Peak is breathtaking. To the east rise the peaks of the Wasatch Range, and on most days, a light gray haze veils the buildings of Salt Lake City. The Great Salt Lake stretches to the north. To the west and southwest, countless basins and ranges, mostly uninhabited, drift off toward the horizon.

There are a handful of popular tourist destinations scattered around the Great Salt Lake, but to appreciate the rest of the Basin, it is necessary to explore with an adventurous attitude. Many a pioneer cursed the heat and the barren landscape of the salt flats and refreshed himself in the cool canyons of the mountains—but from air-conditioned cars, modern tourists can appreciate the beauty of the desert in relative comfort.

Antelope Island, the largest in the Great Salt Lake, is protected as a state park.

About 12,000 years ago, humans lived in caves around the edges of Lake Bonneville, precursor to the Great Salt Lake. The lake at that time contained fresh water, but its salinity increased as it diminished in size, reaching its present level about 9,000 years ago. The Shoshones, Utes, and Goshutes may have collected salt on its shores; mountain men explored the lake for a water route to the Pacific, but found none.

Immigrants bypassed the lake and the salt deserts immediately to its west because they lacked water for their livestock. One hapless exception was the Donner-Reed party, which decided to cross the Great Basin after a California politician, Lansford Hastings, assured them (during a meeting on the Great Plains in 1846) that it was a shortcut to the Golden State. Hastings himself had traversed the territory on horseback. What everyone failed to recognize was that the immigrants' heavily laden wagons would sink into the sludge, and that their oxen would need more frequent water and pasture than did Hastings's horse. The 87-member

SHERLOCK HOLMES IN UTAH

In the central portion of the great North American Continent there lies an arid and repulsive desert, which for many a long year served as a barrier against the advance of civilization. From the Sierra Nevada to Nebraska, and from the Yellowstone River in the north to the Colorado upon the south, is a region of desolation and silence. Nor is Nature always in one mood throughout this grim district. It comprises snowcapped and lofty mountains, and dark and gloomy valleys. There are swift-flowing rivers which dash through jagged cañons; and there are enormous plains, which in winter are white with snow, and in summer are gray with the saline alkali dust. They all preserve, however, the common characteristics of barrenness, inhospitality, and misery.

There are no inhabitants of this land of despair. A band of Pawnee or Blackfeet may occasionally traverse it in order to reach other hunting-grounds, but the hardiest of the braves are glad to lose sight of those awesome plains, and to find themselves once more upon their prairies. The coyote skulks among the scrub, the buzzard flaps heavily through the air, and the clumsy grizzly bear lumbers through the dark ravines and picks up such sustenance as it can amongst the rocks. These are the sole dwellers in the wilderness.

In the whole world there can be no more dreary view than that from the northern slope of the Sierra Blanco. As far as the eye can reach stretches the great flat plainland, all dusted over with patches of alkali, and intersected by clumps of the dwarfish chaparral bushes. On the extreme verge of the horizon lie a long chain of mountain peaks, with their rugged summits flecked with snow. In this great stretch of country there is no sign of life, nor of anything appertaining to life. There is no bird in the steel-blue heaven, no movement upon the dull, gray earth—above all, there is absolute silence. Listen as one may, there is no shadow of a sound in all that mighty wilderness, nothing but silence—complete and heart-subduing silence.

It has been said there is nothing appertaining to life upon the broad plain. That is hardly true. Looking down from the Sierra Blanco, one sees a pathway traced out across the desert, which winds away and is lost in the extreme distance. It is rutted with wheels and trodden down by the feet of many adventurers. Here and there are scattered white objects which glisten in the sun, and stand out against the dull deposit of alkali. Approach, then examine them! They are bones: some large and coarse, others smaller and more delicate. The former have belonged to oxen, and the latter to men. For fifteen hundred miles one may trace this ghastly caravan route by these scattered remains of those who had fallen by the wayside.

—Arthur Conan Doyle, *A Study in Scarlet*, 1887

Donner-Reed party lost four wagons and many animals while crossing the Salt Lake Desert. The delays caused them to reach the Sierra Nevadas late in the season, which in turn caused them to be stranded by the winter's first blizzard, bringing horrible suffering, starvation, and cannibalism. While five people had died before reaching the mountains, 35 more died that winter in the mountains, making it the worst disaster of the California Trail. The story of their ordeal is told in the **Donner-Reed Museum** in Grantsville, northwest of Tooele and on the edge of the salt flats. The museum houses guns and relics abandoned by the party as it struggled to lighten its loads.

■ THE PONY EXPRESS

The Pony Express mail service between St. Joseph, Missouri, and Sacramento, California, was a short-lived business venture developed by William H. Russell, who had experience in east-west transportation in the mid-1800s. While the company reported losses of half a million dollars before closing after only 18 months of operation, it remains one of the West's most romantic stories.

Between 1860 and 1861 young men (preferably orphans because of the risks involved) rode from 75 to 125 miles during a day or night run. Way stations, 10 to 15 miles apart, provided fresh horses and attended to the needs of the rider. The cost to send a letter was five dollars per ounce and the goal was to carry the mail across the country in 10 days. At its peak, the Pony Express route incorporated 190 stations, 420 horses, and 80 riders. The fastest crossing—carrying Lincoln's inaugural address from St. Joseph, Missouri, to Sacramento, California—took seven and a half days.

The 1,900-mile trail entered Utah from Wyoming, cutting through what is now the heart of Salt Lake City before dropping south of the Great Salt Lake. The route crossed the Jordan River where the river cuts through the Transverse Mountains at Point of the Mountain. It then headed west, veering south of the Oquirrh Mountains to the town of Faust, then passed north of Vernon and on to Fish Springs before crossing into the Nevada Territory. Twenty of the 190 stations were in Utah. While there were high hopes that the mail system would eventually gain government subsidy, the Pony Express was thrust into sudden obscurity with the completion of the first transcontinental telegraph line in 1861.

Today, the **Pony Express Trail National Back Country Byway** follows an approximately 133-mile stretch of the route that begins near Fairfield, Utah, and

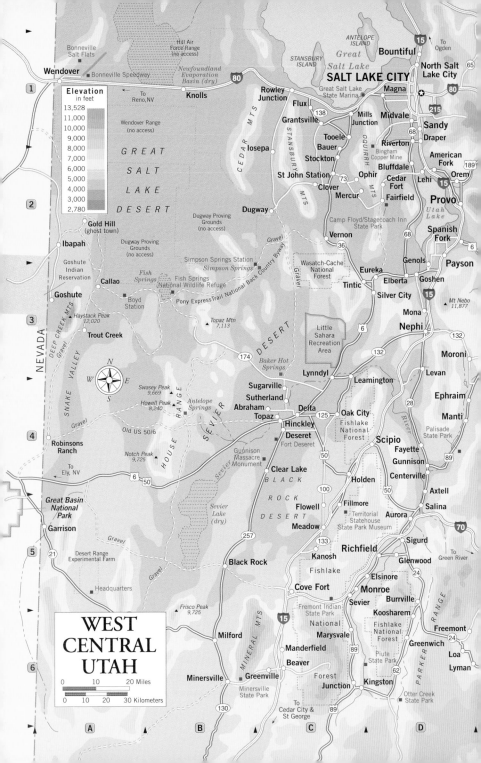

WEST CENTRAL UTAH

Elevation
in feet

13,528	
11,000	
10,000	
9,000	
8,000	
7,000	
6,000	
5,000	
4,000	
3,000	
2,780	

Bonneville
Salt Flats

Hill Air
Force Range
(no access)

Newfoundland
Evaporation
Basin (dry)

ANTELOPE
ISLAND

STANSBURY
ISLAND

Great
Salt Lake

Wendover

Bonneville Speedway

Bountiful

To
Ogden

Knolls

To
Reno, NV

Rowley
Junction

Great Salt Lake
State Marina

SALT LAKE CITY

Magna

North Salt
Lake City

Flux

Flux

Grantsville

Mills
Junction

Tooele

Midvale

Sandy

Iosepa

Bauer

Stockton

Riverton

Draper

WENDOVER RANGE
(no access)

Wendover Range
(no access)

GREAT
SALT
LAKE
DESERT

St John Station

Clover

Ophir

Mercur

Cedar
Fort

Bluffdale

American
Fork

Lehi

Orem

Fairfield

Provo

Utah
Lake

Gold Hill
(ghost town)

Dugway Proving
Grounds
(no access)

Dugway

Camp Floyd/Stagecoach Inn
State Park

Vernon

Spanish
Fork

Ibapah

Dugway Proving
Grounds
(no access)

Simpson Springs Station

Simpson Springs

Eureka

Genols

Payson

Goshute
Indian
Reservation

Callao

Fish
Springs

Fish Springs
National Wildlife Refuge

Wasatch-Cache
National
Forest

Elberta

Goshen

Goshute

Pony Express Trail National Back Country Byway

Tintic

Silver City

Boyd
Station

DEEP CREEK MTS

Haystack Peak
12,020

Mona

Mt Nebo
11,877

Trout Creek

Topaz Mtn
7,113

Little
Sahara
Recreation
Area

Nephi

Baker Hot
Springs

Lynndyl

Leamington

Levan

Swasey Peak
9,669

Sugarville

Moroni

Howell Peak
8,240

Sutherland

Ephraim

Antelope
Springs

Abraham

Delta

Oak City

Manti

Topaz

Hinckley

Scipio

Old US 50/6

Fishlake
National
Forest

Fayette

Palisade
State Park

Robinsons
Ranch

Notch Peak
9,725

Deseret

Fort Deseret

Gunnison

To
Ely, NV

Gunnison
Massacre
Monument

Clear Lake

Holden

Centerville

Great Basin
National
Park

Sevier
Lake
(dry)

BLACK

ROCK

Axtell

Garrison

Flowell

Fillmore

Aurora

Salina

Desert Range
Experimental Farm

DESERT

Meadow

Territorial
Statehouse
State Park Museum

Sigurd

Headquarters

Black Rock

Fishlake

Richfield

Glenwood

Kanosh

Cove Fort

Elsinore

Monroe

Frisco Peak
9,725

Fremont Indian
State Park

Sevier

Burrville

Milford

National

Koosharem

Freemont

Manderfield

Marysvale

Fishlake
National
Forest

Greenwich

Beaver

Loa

Greenville

Piute
State Park

Lyman

Minersville

Forest
Junction

Kingston

Minersville
State Park

To
Cedar City &
St George

Otter Creek
State Park

NEVADA

WEST
CENTRAL
UTAH

0   10   20 Miles

0   10   20   30 Kilometers

The Pony Express.

ends at Ibapah. It is a gravel and sand road that can be unstable when wet. Markers commemorate the trail at other sites throughout the state. Before going, write to the BLM for information, or pick up one of the Utah Travel Council maps that show Pony Express stations. (See page 324 or 327.)

■ CAMP FLOYD/STAGECOACH INN STATE PARK   *map page 184, D-2*
A good place to start off down the Pony Express route is at the **Camp Floyd/ Stagecoach Inn State Park and Museum** in Fairfield, where you can obtain a printed guide describing the route and telling some of the wild tales associated with it. Here you can explore the Pony Express and stagecoach station where Mark Twain and Horace Greeley stopped on their journeys west. Camp Floyd was the site of the army bivouac built in 1858 by Col. Albert Johnston, who was sent to put down a rumored Mormon rebellion that never materialized. *On UT 73, 25 miles west of Lehi; 801-768-8932.*

As you head farther west, you can sometimes see wild mustangs grazing in the valleys along the road. Ancestors of these animals were captured and broken to carry the riders through this unfriendly desert.

■ SIMPSON SPRINGS STATION   *map page 184, B/C-2/3*

While exploring the area in 1859, Capt. James Hervey Simpson described the desert around his namesake outpost as a "somber, dreary wasteland, where neither man nor beast can live for want of the necessary food and over which a bird is scarcely seen to fly." The spring water refreshed Pony Express riders and later, freighters hauling supplies to nearby mining towns such as Gold Hill. Today, there is running water at the BLM campground.

■ THE RAILROAD   *map pages 202–203, D-2*

On May 10, 1869, at Promontory, Utah, the United States was put on its way to becoming a unified world power when the American continent was linked coast to coast by rail. Before the railroad, land routes to the Pacific shore stretched over vast and often hostile terrain, a journey that took wagon trains months to make. The fastest voyage by clipper ship around the tip of South America still required at least a hundred days. With increased migration, Congress began to recognize the pressing need for a rail link between the East and West coasts. Quarrels between the North and the South over which route the railroad should take kept it from being built until the outbreak of the Civil War. President Lincoln and Congress then decided on a northern route in order to keep California with the Republic and to keep the war chest filled with California gold.

To spur interest in the construction project, Congress promised developers free use of building materials from public lands, cash subsidies of $16,000 per mile of track on the plains and from $32,000 to $48,000 per mile through the mountains, and an outright bonus of every alternate, odd-numbered section of public land, which stretched checkerboard-fashion for 20 miles on each side of the tracks.

Employing mostly Irish workers to lay the tracks, the Union Pacific raced westward across the plains from Omaha. The Central Pacific snaked its way eastward from Sacramento through the Sierra Nevada, employing workers mainly from China. Just as many modern contractors seek to bilk the federal government, the railroad companies, too, found ways to get rich. The most blatant example was the laying of 225 miles of parallel track in northern Utah before the government demanded that the two rail lines be brought together at Promontory, joining 690 miles of track from Sacramento with 1,087 from Omaha for a total of 1,777 miles of track. Completed in fewer than four years, the first transcontinental railroad was an engineering feat unequalled in American history.

Visitors to **Golden Spike National Historic Site** can glean the significance of the joining of the rails and the continent through visitors center film shows and displays. The most riveting exhibitions take place outdoors on the anniversary of the event, May 10, and during the Railroaders Festival, usually the second Saturday in August. On those occasions, two full-sized replicas of the engines used in the original ceremony, the *199* and the *Jupiter*, recreate the historical meeting. Shiny and impressive, with thick, black smoke billowing from their stacks, they dwarf onlookers. Puffing and tooting, the engines ease together, head to head, to a squeaking, hissing stop. Engineers dressed in authentic uniforms jump from their cabs and take turns addressing the crowd, telling the tale of the joining of the rails and answering questions. *On UT 83, Promontory; 435-471-2209.*

The original event was not without some humor. "California's Leland Stanford raised his hammer and swung a mighty blow," as the story is told in the WPA's *Utah: A Guide to the State.* "He missed entirely, but the telegraph operator (a line

The railway lines from east and west finally met at Promontory on May 10, 1869.

was connected to the last spike to record the blow), a man of practical foresight, simulated the blow with his key and let tumult loose upon the cities of the country; fire bells, cannon, and factory whistles joined with shouting human voices to signalize the linkage of a continent. At Promontory the two locomotives gingerly nosed their cowcatchers together. To the world the telegrapher tapped out the historic message:

> *The last rail is laid.*
> *The last spike is driven.*
> *The Pacific road is finished.*

Within two weeks of the joining of the rails, more than 300 frame buildings, shanties, and tents were erected at Promontory and nearby Corinne. The rough and lusty population of the latter grew to 7,500, including 5,000 Chinese railroad workers, and a temporary city government was set up to handle them. Col. Patrick Connor, who had set out to weaken the Mormons' stronghold by bringing mining to the Utah Territory, headed the Liberal Political Party, based in Corinne.

Brigham City, 32 miles to the east of Promontory, tried to maintain its status as a quiet religious community by ignoring its unholy neighbors. Mormons took advantage of the railroad, however, to obtain jobs. They were not allowed to work on the trains themselves but kept busy grading the roadbeds.

Present-day Brigham City celebrates the anniversary of the driving of the golden spike with many community activities.

■ Booms and Busts

With the coming of the railroad, mining became a more lucrative business. Brigham Young had discouraged his followers from prospecting, but gold and silver fever spread wherever the precious metals could be found. Boomtowns like Ophir, Mercur, Gold Hill, Eureka, Mammoth, and Frisco sprang up in the Great Basin seemingly overnight. Many still stand in various states of disrepair—fascinating and picturesque, they appeal to historians, antique collectors, photographers, painters, solitude seekers and dreamers. Rockhounds can use guides available in bookstores to locate specimens of fossils and minerals in sites all around the Great Basin.

The adventurous are invited to try their own hand at prospecting. Lucky searchers may find such treasures as ancient gold pans or century-old whiskey bottles. More often, present-day prospectors spend a quiet day contemplating the past preserved in rusting machinery and dilapidated shacks. All visitors should respect property rights and make sure buildings are safe and truly abandoned before entering.

As market conditions and milling methods have changed, Great Basin towns have repeatedly boomed and died. As new methods of extracting metals and minerals from the rocks are developed, some of the towns may be resurrected in the future. Until then, they struggle along and wait for better times, shadows of their thriving former selves.

Train replicas at Golden Spike National Historic Site.

■ **BINGHAM CANYON** *map page 184, D-1*

One of the first discoveries of precious metals was made in 1863 at Bingham Canyon, in the Oquirrh Mountains about 20 miles west of Salt Lake City. Although gold, silver, and lead first drew miners here, the modern quest is for copper, and today, the **Bingham Copper Mine** is the world's largest and most productive. Since 1906, when the open-pit method was first used, several towns have been bulldozed to make way for its ever-enlarging spirals. Visitors on the lip of the mine look out across uncounted spiraling cuts in the rock, which drop dramatically from a few remaining peaks to the rust-red, damp earth at the mine's lowest level. At 2.5 miles wide and a half-mile deep, the pit could easily hold all of downtown Salt Lake City; the tops of the city's tallest buildings would barely reach one-eighth the way up its walls. Astronauts can see the 1,900-acre mine from outer space.

The owner of the mine, Kennecott Utah Copper, was at one time the major employer of Salt Lake City residents. Fluctuations in the copper market and the import of less costly ores from South America resulted in layoffs, however, and Salt Lake City was forced to diversify its employment base. In 2000 mining represented about 1.8 percent of Utah's industrial dollars.

Bingham Canyon and other mining areas throughout the state attracted people from all over the world: Scandinavia, the Balkan States, Western and Central Europe, Asia, and even, during World War II, the Navajo lands to the south. Each nationality settled into its own neighborhood in the narrow canyon.

The immigrants kept a tight hold on their old-world languages and customs. Since mining at Bingham Canyon in those times meant dark tunnels, poor working conditions, and low pay, there were labor disputes and strikes. Old-world dislikes and prejudices crept into the new neighborhoods, often causing fights. But as time passed, fires, floods, and snowslides forced people of different nationalities to help each other. Old lines of division dissolved over time, and the canyon evolved into a cohesive community.

Although this is still a working mine, more widely known as Kennecott Copper Mine, Bingham Canyon Mine has been designated a National Historic Landmark. The Bingham Canyon Mine Visitors Center is open to the public daily from 8 A.M. to 8 P.M., April through October. The visitors center features a video and exhibits explaining mining and copper production; outside is an overlook allowing a view into the mine. *Visitors Center: Off UT 111, 4 miles south of Copperton; 801-252-3234.*

■ BOOMTOWNS AND GHOST TOWNS

Tooele *map page 184, C-1*

West of Bingham Canyon stands the town of Tooele. (One of the tests of native Utahns is whether or not they can pronounce the name of Tooele: TOO-ill-uh.)

The **Tooele Railroad Museum** houses a collection of railroad and mining artifacts, including a scale railway and simulated mine. The museum is open from May through September. *35 North Broadway; 435-882-2836.*

The town also has a **Daughters of Utah Pioneers Museum,** in the old Pioneer City Hall building that served as city hall, courthouse, and jail from 1867 to 1941. The log cabin next door to the museum, built in 1856, was one of the first houses in Tooele. The museum is open on Saturdays from Memorial Day to Labor Day, but guided tours are possible at other times if scheduled in advance. *39 East Vine Street; 435-882-6801.*

Kids of all ages who love fire engines will find plenty of hands-on fun at the **Utah State Fire Museum** on UT 112 between Tooele and Grantsville. The museum houses approximately 60 vintage restored fire engines and related fire-fighting paraphernalia. It is open year-round only on Fridays and Saturdays or by appointment. *Deseret Peak Complex, 2930 UT 112; 435-843-4040.*

Ophir *map page 184, C-2*

South of Tooele is another of Utah's richest mining towns. Ophir was named after King Solomon's fabled mines. By 1900, the town had produced $13 million in ore, including $1 million from the Kearsarge Mine alone. Even as it dimmed, Ophir's fabulous legacy was carried on beyond the boundaries of Utah by Marcus Daly, founder of Anaconda Copper, who earned his grubstake, and much of his know-how, while working at his Zella mine in Ophir. Although a few diehards still inhabit Ophir, it is a favorite of photographers because so much of the old appearance remains. Ophir Canyon is also an excellent place to view bald eagles during the winter months.

Mercur *map page 184, C-2*

The small town that was to become Mercur first came into existence when gold was found there in 1870. Large quantities of the precious mineral never materialized, but gold miners were hard to discourage. As mining of the area continued, the "Mercur lode" was discovered in 1883. Arie Pinedo, a Bavarian miner, thought the vein was cinnabar, and his discovery, along with the town, was named after the by-product of cinnabar: mercury. No significant quantities of mercury were ever extracted, however.

The little boom-and-bust town made news in the late 19th century when the Mercur Gold Mining and Milling Company introduced an Australian process using cyanide to extract gold. Ore from the area was sent to an extraction plant in Denver, where it was determined there was enough gold present in samples to justify building a cyanide plant in Mercur. The subsequent Golden Gate Mill, built in 1898, became the first cyanide extraction plant to be built and operated in the United States. By 1913, however, it was no longer profitable to extract the decreasing amount of gold at the site; four years later the mill was dismantled and closed. One last gasp in 1933 brought another mill to the site, but by World War II, the town had become a ghost town.

Few old buildings survive in Mercur, just south of Ophir. A fire on Statehood Day, January 4, 1876, burned the town completely. Rebuilt, it burned again in 1902 in a fire that began at a Chinese lunch counter. Flash floods rolling down the bare hills finished the city off. The mill itself, however, was always untouched by disaster other than financial.

Eureka *map page 184, D-3*

Farther south, Eureka has been called a living ghost town, not only because many of the buildings and mining paraphernalia have been kept intact for a century, but because a small population of old-timers still call it home. In its heyday, it was the center of the Tintic mining district, one of Utah's biggest and richest. By the end of its first hundred years in 1971, the Tintic's production of silver, gold, and other metals and minerals exceeded $500 million. Eureka's fortunes faded along with those of many other boomtowns, but 700 residents remain.

Gold Hill *map page 184, A-2*

About 100 miles west of Eureka along the old Pony Express route, Gold Hill is one of the most picturesque and complete ghost towns in Utah. Gold Hill started as a gold boomtown in 1892. It died when the gold ran out, but was rebuilt during World War I when tungsten and other minerals were needed for the war effort. One former prospector who didn't strike it rich in Gold Hill but knocked out enough opponents to become the heavyweight champion of the world was Jack Dempsey. The town is 23 miles north of Callao on a dirt road.

Topaz *map page 184, C-4*

Topaz is a ghost town of a different nature. In the wartime hysteria of 1942, about 9,000 Japanese, most of them American citizens, were interned in hastily constructed wood-and-tarpaper barracks here. Although the internment camp closed in 1945, the ghosts of the wrongly imprisoned souls can be felt around remaining streets and foundations. A monument to the injustice has been erected at the northwest corner of the ghost town. To reach Topaz, drive six miles from Delta on U.S. 50/6 to the small town of Hinckley, turn north, and continue 4.5 miles on a partly paved, partly graveled road to its end. Turning left (west), go 2.5 miles on a paved road to its end in Abraham, then turn right (north) and drive 1.5 miles on a gravel road to a stop sign. From there, turn left and drive 3 miles to Topaz on a gravel road.

Near Delta *map page 184, B/C-4*

West of Delta, you can search for souvenirs in the trilobite fossil beds in the House Range.

South of Delta you can find the crumbling remains of **Fort Deseret**, an adobe-walled fort quickly built during the Black Hawk War of 1865.

About six miles southwest of Fort Deseret, is the **Gunnison Massacre Monument.** It marks the spot where Capt. John W. Gunnison and seven of his men were killed by Indians while working on a federal railroad survey during the Walker War in 1853.

■ ISLAND RANGES, INLAND SEA

One of the greatest illusions of the Great Basin is that it is a deserted wasteland that must be crossed in haste as a traveler heads for California. The striking beauty of the mountains of the Great Basin is a well-kept secret. The magnificent desert, marsh, and alpine scenery of this area is showcased in many wilderness areas and wildlife refuges.

The mountain ranges of the Great Basin have been called islands of ecological diversity because slightly different species of plants and animals have developed on each. The intervening mud and salt flats and broad dry valleys kept plant and animal species from migrating and interbreeding.

(following pages) The House Range is typical of Great Basin limestone formations.

The upper reaches of the Stansbury and Deep Creek mountains are untouched wilderness areas. Deseret Peak in the Stansburys, Notch Peak in the House Range, and Haystack Peak in the Deep Creek Range provide fantastic views of the salt and mud flats of the Great Basin. These mountain ranges are home to thousand-year-old bristlecone pines. Miners, pioneers, and outlaws frequented their peaks and canyons. Today hikers in these ranges can sight deer, pronghorn antelope, chukar partridge, bald and golden eagles, and peregrine falcons. Obtain detailed topographical maps from the local U.S. Forest Service offices to help you explore. (See pages 322–324.)

■ **GREAT BASIN NATIONAL PARK** *map page 184, A-4*
U.S. 50/6, which, from Delta, skirts the House Range to Baker, Nevada, has been called the loneliest highway in the United States. Just over the Nevada border, it passes Great Basin National Park, which preserves a spectacular stretch of mountain and high desert, including 13,063-foot Wheeler Peak. Starting in a dry desert valley near Baker, where temperatures often soar over 100 degrees F in the summer, the park road switchbacks up through desert woodlands of mountain mahogany, piñon pine, and juniper to alpine forests of Douglas fir, where it's always cool. *Visitors center on NV 488, 5.5 miles west of Baker; 775-234-7331.*

■ **WILDLIFE AND SAND DUNES**

Fish Springs National Wildlife Refuge *map page 184, B-3*
No streams or rivers leave the Great Basin. The water running off from its mountain ranges ends up mainly in marshes. In the middle of seemingly barren desert, in the midst of such a marshland surrounding freshwater springs, is the Fish Springs National Wildlife Refuge, created in 1959 as a sanctuary for migrating water birds, as well as local wildlife. A self-guiding auto tour makes an 11.5-mile loop for motorists; the route is outlined in a brochure describing various birds that inhabit the refuge seasonally or year-round. Fish Springs was one of the way stations on the old Pony Express and stage route; it's as isolated as ever, reached by a long (about 70 miles) bumpy ride from Sugarville via UT 174. *435-831-5353.*

Waterfowl Management Areas
There are several waterfowl refuges in the Great Basin. Locomotive Springs Waterfowl Management Area is west of Golden Spike National Historic Site. Bear

River Migratory Bird Refuge, Harold S. Crane State Waterfowl Management Area, and Ogden Bay State Waterfowl Management Area border the Great Salt Lake, where the fresh water of the Bear and other rivers enters the salt water. Clear Lake State Waterfowl Management Area is the southernmost of them, more than 20 miles from Delta in the Black Rock Desert. Bird-watching in these areas takes patience but can be rewarding. A variety of birds frequent the refuges. In March, snow geese blanket the Gunnison Bend Reservoir, near Delta, during their northward migration.

Great Salt Lake Islands *map page 184, C-1*
The islands of the Great Salt Lake are actually extensions of the Oquirrh and Stansbury mountains, and are always changing in relation to the lake's water levels: Stansbury Island closely resembles a peninsula now, but may once again be an island should the lake rise. Bison, placed by early pioneers, inhabit Antelope Island. The diverse gene pool of this herd is used to preserve the health of bison herds elsewhere in the country.

Little Sahara Recreation Area *map page 184, C-3*
Remnants of sandbars deposited by Lake Bonneville have accumulated in white dunes in the Little Sahara Recreation Area, managed by the BLM. Off-road vehicles and motorcycles can ply the sands; a separate area is set aside for foot traffic. The three campgrounds in the area have water. *For information or reservations, contact the BLM at 15 East 500 North, Fillmore; 435-743-4116.*

■ LAKESIDE RESORTS *map pages 202–203, D-4/5*

A trip to Utah is not complete without trying out the greatest illusion of them all: walking on water. While no one exactly "walks" on the lake, sitting in water where it is impossible to sink is a fascinating sensation. So is leaving the water and having your skin slowly turn white with salt crystals as you dry. Innocents who try swimming underwater in the Great Salt Lake come up spluttering, with stinging eyes and throats. Look in the water for the tiny orange brine shrimp, the solitary inhabitants of water that is six to eight times as salty as the ocean. Tropical fish food companies harvest these creatures.

The sand on the beaches of the Great Salt Lake is also an illusion. Unlike most sand, it is not made of tiny pieces of rock, but, rather, pellets cast out by the digestive system of the brine shrimp. Small crystals of calcium carbonate, a mineral found in the lake, grow around each pellet to form rounded to elongated gray or yellowish-gray grains of sand. Each grain is called an oolite (fish egg) because of its shiny spherical shape.

Past entrepreneurs have built elaborate bathhouses and pavilions to capitalize on this unusual natural wonder. Unfortunately for them, lake levels have fluctuated too radically to allow any successful permanent structures.

The first attempt to promote tourism on the Great Salt Lake was made by John W. Young, the third of Brigham's 25 sons. Near the railroad stop of Farmington, he built a resort that he named Lake Side. Within the year, Jeter Clinton opened a competing resort on the south shore called Lake Point. Both resorts offered steamboat rides, and a skipper of one of the steamboats soon built another lake resort, Lake Park, to the north. It boasted a large dance pavilion and covered pier, elegant dressing rooms, a restaurant, and a saloon. It also had the best sandy beach. Unfortunately, after 50 years of massaging by thousands of tourist feet, the sand turned to mud, and Lake Park failed.

In 1893, Saltair was born. "Saltair," wrote historian Dale L. Morgan in *The Great Salt Lake*, "caught everybody's imagination." It was connected with Salt Lake City, 16 miles away, by a train that ran on "pile-supported track 4,000 feet out into the lake to reach the pile-driven, crescent-shaped platform. The 2,500 ten-inch pilings were driven into the lake bottom through salt dissolved by steam. Upon this platform was built a large two-story pavilion, with picnic tables and restaurant overlooking the lake on the ground floor, and an immense ballroom, locally thought to be the largest in the world, on the upper floor." Rows of bathrooms served thousands at a time. Because there was no beach, bathers descended directly into the waters of the lake. Amusement park rides assured that everyone had a good time.

The other resorts faded. After Lake Park burned to the ground in 1904, Saltair was the only one remaining until lake levels dropped in the early 1930s and two new resorts were built: J.O. Griffith's Black Rock Beach a few miles south of Saltair, and Ira Dern's Sunset Beach a short distance east of Black Rock.

Despite fluctuations in the lake levels, these three resorts continued to entertain tourists transported to them by railroad and automobile through World War II. In those years, hundreds of people came to the large Moorish-styled Saltair pavilion for ballroom dancing. But ballroom dancing went out of style and the lake level

Saltair was Salt Lake City's answer to Coney Island.

dropped. Saltair burned down in the sixties, and nothing came along to replace it until 1981.

A new incarnation of Saltair, opened in 1993, is located south of the original. While the not the popular swimming destination of the original, the facility houses a souvenir shop and a concert and dance hall. *I-80 west, Exit 104, Magna; 801-250-4400.*

The best place to enjoy Great Salt Lake swimming and vistas is at **Antelope Island State Park.** To reach the island, the largest in the Great Salt Lake, take Exit 335 near Layton off Interstate 15 and drive west on UT 108. A 7-mile paved causeway leads to the island, where visitors can enjoy beaches, hiking and mountain bike trails, horseback-riding concessions, buffalo corrals, a visitors center with interpretive displays, campgrounds, a small marina, and a historic ranch. *801-725-9263 or 800-322-3770 for camping reservations.*

■ THE SPIRAL JETTY *map pages 202–203, D-3*

Visitors to the Great Salt Lake who accidentally encounter Robert Smithson's earthwork *Spiral Jetty* walk away wondering if it was built by visitors from another planet or college students with too much time on their hands.

The fact is, Smithson built the earth sculpture—a 1,500-foot coil of black basalt rocks—in 1970. The artist was one of many who chose to build site-specific art outdoors in the West, away from the commercialism of urban galleries. He built the spiral out of black basalt rocks taken from the shoreline of the Great Salt Lake, arranging them to a height just above the surface of the water so people could walk on the earthwork as if on a pier. At the time the Spiral Jetty was constructed, the lake was unusually shallow because of drought. When the water levels rose, the jetty disappeared under the water and was generally only seen from the air. Toward the end of the 20th century, lake levels again began to drop and the jetty became visible once again.

Spiral Jetty is located at Rozel Point, about 100 miles northwest of Salt Lake City. The art is accessed by driving a 15.5-mile dirt road. Detailed directions are available at the Golden Spike National Historic Site. The jetty is not visible during times of high water.

■ BONNEVILLE SALT FLATS *map pages 202–203, A-5*

Stretching over 30,000 acres, Utah's Bonneville Salt Flats are, like the Great Salt Lake, what remains of the ancient Lake Bonneville. During the Ice Age, the lake covered one-third of present-day Utah as well as part of nearby states. Today the flats are for the most part devoid of life. Only the hardy in search of strange, surrealistic desert experiences venture beyond the interstate and into this land of white salt and mirages.

To most people, the salt flats are a wasteland, a place to spend a few minutes gazing at stark whiteness and sparkling salt crystals from a freeway rest stop before wandering on into the air-conditioned casinos less than 10 miles to the west in Wendover, Nevada. To those who run mineral industries, the salt flats are a gold mine—within the area, 15 different salts, potassium, and manganese are gathered from evaporation ponds. Another group of people look at the Bonneville Salt Flats and in their mind's eye see sleek racing cars, because for them these salt flats are a world-famous racing strip—the **Bonneville Salt Flats International Speedway.**

Travelers along Interstate 80 can stop at the rest area next to the Salt Flats and walk out on the salt. Displays explain the history of the speedway—a straight strip in the desert, 9 miles long and 80 feet wide, where many land speed records have been set. The first trials began in 1896 when W. D. Rishel, a bicycle racer and promoter out of Salt Lake City, rode and carried his bicycle across the flats. But it was Sir Malcolm Campbell, of Great Britain, who first put Bonneville Speedway on the map. The year was 1935, and his speed as he raced across the salt was 301.13 miles per hour. Other racing pioneers soon followed. Craig Breedlove became the first to break the 400 and 500 mile-per-hour speed barriers; then on November 15, 1965, his *Spirit of America* racing machine sped across the salt at a record 600.601 miles per hour. Gary Gabolich's rocket car, *Blue Flame* flew across the raceway at an amazing 622.4 miles per hour in 1970.

Each year between August and October, the Utah Salt Flats Racing Association arranges times trials and races that allow participants to establish land speed records. Spectators are welcome to talk to the race car drivers and watch them as they attempt to set records. There are more than 200 different classes of races, based on body style, engine type, and type of fuel. There is an admission fee for the pit and spectator areas and a registration fee for those wanting to participate in a race. For more information on events contact the USFRA (801-256-1805).

In spring and winter, the salt flats are usually covered with water because surface moisture at this time neither penetrates nor evaporates readily; rather, the water is blown about the surface by the wind until it evaporates. As it moves over the surface, the water smoothes the salt, making it almost perfectly flat—this is said to be one of the only places in the United States where one can see the curvature of the earth over dry land.

Due to its unique geology, history, and scenic beauty, the Bonneville Salt Flats were designated an Area of Critical Environmental Concern in 1985. Freeway building and mining activity have caused deterioration, making land speed record attempts difficult, but the Bureau of Land Management and salt-mining interests are cooperating to correct, or at least to alleviate, the problem.

The salt flats are located north of I-80, just east of Wendover. Signs indicate where vehicles can drive onto the flats, but be careful not to join the ranks of unwary would-be racers who have become mired in the grey-green mud.

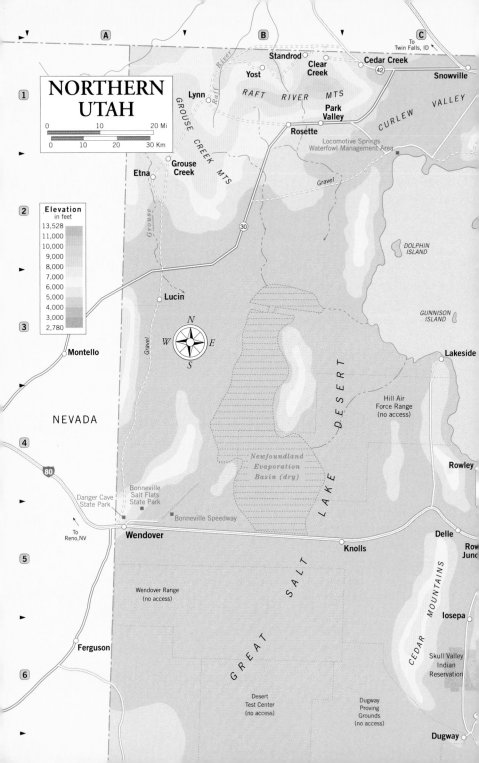

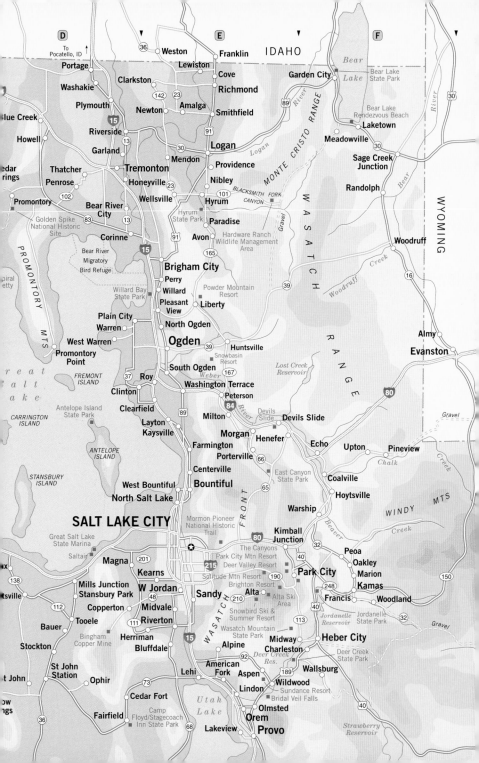

SOUTHERN UTAH

"By whatever name it might be called," once wrote longtime Utah author Ward Roylance, "this great province is as distinctive in its own peculiar personality as, say, the Alps of Europe, the Amazon Basin of South America, the Sahara of Africa, the steppes or Himalayas of Asia."

Indeed, southern Utah is a magical, almost surreal place. Deep canyons, towering red rock walls, spires, pinnacles, and hoodoos stand in an explosion of color. Remote, seldom-visited blue-green mountain ranges offer cool respite from the desert heat, along with excellent camping, fishing, and summer drives. The Colorado, Green, and San Juan rivers are packed with white-water rafting adventure and ancient archaeological sites. Mountain bikers pedal over steep slickrock domes and rock climbers hang like lizards off thousand-foot sandstone walls. But tourists may also watch Shakespeare performed in a replica of the Globe Theater in Cedar City, or listen to world-class chamber music next to the Colorado River in Moab.

Five of America's most dramatic national parks draw visitors from all parts of the world. Southern Utah is also home to four national monuments, 19 state parks, three national forests, and three ski areas. There are millions of acres designated as wilderness, wilderness study areas, or primitive areas, which are managed by the U.S. Forest Service and Bureau of Land Management.

In fact, the issue of wilderness in Utah is complex and volatile, especially in southern Utah. The topic often polarizes residents throughout the region as they, along with the federal government, attempt to strike a balance between preservation and public use. For many people who travel to the region, the lands in southern Utah are as wild and primitive as any they will ever see.

As more tourists discover the national parks—Arches, Canyonlands, Bryce Canyon, Capitol Reef, and Zion—it is becoming increasingly difficult to find the kind of solitude enjoyed by early visitors. It is worth the effort, however, to explore the parks and other public lands in greater depth, to veer off the beaten path or to visit off-season. That's when you will discover the real magic of southern Utah.

An evening in June at Dead Horse Point State Park, looking into Canyonlands National Park. Prince's plume (Stanleya pinnata) *blooms in the foreground.*

WILD PLACES I

It's a tough country to visit. It's an even tougher country to live in. So powerful is the sun in summer, one adopts a perpetual squint. Summer can bring biblical periods of forty days of heat well over one hundred degrees, reducing you to a lizard state of mind, no thought and very little action. You sleep more and you dream. It is a landscape of extremes. You learn sooner or later to find equilibrium within yourself; otherwise you move.

Desert as teacher.
Desert as mirage.
Desert as illusion, largely our own.

What you come to see on the surface is not what you come to know. Emptiness in the desert is the fullness of space, a fullness of space that eliminates time. The desert is time, exposed time, geologic time. One needs time in the desert to see. . . .

For those who have not experienced the sublime nature of Utah's canyon country, I invite you to imagine what it might be like to see and feel the world from the inside out. If you do come visit, prepare to be broken open like a rock fallen from a once-secure place.

—Terry Tempest Williams, *Red: Passion and Patience in the Desert*, 2001

This country awakens all five senses. Smell the sagebrush after a fall rainstorm. Feel the cool waters of the Green River as you enjoy a moonlight swim after a day of canoeing. Listen to the howl of a coyote on a dark night in Horse Pasture Canyon. Taste the dust stirred up after driving a four-wheel-drive vehicle over the challenging bumps of Canyonlands' Elephant Hill. Watch the sun set from the edge of Grandview Point on a late December afternoon, as the shadows spread over three mountain ranges and the canyons of the Colorado River.

While southern Utah is a rugged, daunting landscape, civilization—in the form of towns, gas stations, grocery stores, restaurants, and motels—is seldom far away. With a little common sense, a full tank of gas, and plenty of drinking water, you can safely explore even the most remote corners of this incomparable region.

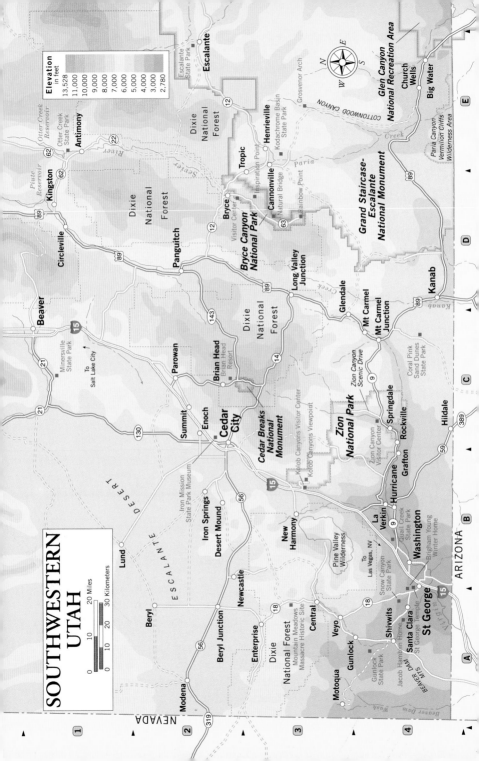

■ SOUTH TOWARD CEDAR CITY

■ FILLMORE *map page 184, C-5*

Interstate 15 leads south 160 miles from Salt Lake City to Fillmore, a town of more than 2,000 residents. Because the site was near the geographical center of the Utah Territory, Brigham Young designated Fillmore as Utah's original territorial capital in 1851, even though no town then existed. Visitors can tour the old Territorial Statehouse, Utah's oldest government building, now the **Territorial Statehouse State Park Museum.** Completed in 1855, it is actually the first of four wings the building was supposed to have. Although several territorial legislatures met here, the lack of facilities and antagonism between the U.S. government and the Mormons eventually caused the legislature to move to Salt Lake City. *50 West Capitol Avenue; 435-743-5316.*

■ UTAH STATE HIGHWAY 133 *map page 184, C-5*

When traveling south along Interstate 15, detour along the old UT 133 and visit towns like Meadow and Kanosh. This is a part of Utah where getting off the beaten track pays dividends. There are few museums or tourist facilities; instead, visitors can stop at old general stores to enjoy a soft drink and some pleasant conversation with local merchants, who often have the time to talk about the history of their towns. Old pioneer homes, many restored to their original condition, dot the four-lane main streets decreed by Brigham Young, and the old pioneer cemeteries reveal interesting bits of history and family names. In the Kanosh cemetery, look for the headstone marking the burial place of old Chief Kanosh, who was the Paiute leader when the pioneers first settled this area.

Corn Creek Canyon leads into the Fishlake National Forest east of Kanosh. A small, developed campground sits next to a clear mountain stream full of wild brown trout. Mule deer roam in the oak brush, and a few pieces of ruddy-colored stone jut out above the canyon, hinting at the red-rock grandeur farther south.

■ BEAVER *map page 184, C-6*

There are more than 200 historic houses of architectural interest scattered around Beaver, which was settled by Mormon farmers who came north from Parowan in search of pasturage for their cattle. When gold and silver were found in the San Francisco Mountains to the west, non-Mormon miners rushed to Beaver. Tensions between the two groups, and threats of Indian attack, prompted the army to build

WILD PLACES II

Something will have gone out of us as a people if we ever let the remaining wilderness be destroyed; if we permit the last virgin forests to be turned into comic books and plastic cigarette cases; if we drive the few remaining members of the wild species into zoos or to extinction; if we pollute the last clear air and dirty the last clean streams and push our paved roads through the last of the silence, so that never again will Americans be free in their own country from the noise, the exhausts, the stinks of human and automotive waste. And so that never again can we have the chance to see ourselves single, separate, vertical and individual in the world, part of the environment of trees and rocks and soil, brother to the other animals, part of the natural world. . . . We need wilderness preserved—as much of it as is still left, and as many kinds—because it was the challenge against which our character as a people was formed. The reminder and the reassurance that it is still there is good for our spiritual health even if we never once in ten years set foot in it. It is good for us when we are young, because of the incomparable sanity it can bring briefly, as vacation and rest, into our insane lives. It is important to us when we are old simply because it is there—important, that is, simply as an idea.

—Wallace Stegner, "Wilderness Letter," 1960

Fort Cameron. One stone building from the fort still stands on the east edge of town, across the highway from the golf course. The ornate **Beaver County Courthouse** now houses a historical museum of pioneer and mining exhibits, as well as a courtroom and a dungeon-like jail in the basement. Open June through the first week in September. *90 East Center Street; 435-438-2922.*

■ **CEDAR CITY** *map page 207, C-2*

After passing through Beaver and Parowan, visitors reach Cedar City. With about 20,000 residents, it's the second-largest settlement in southern Utah. Boosters call it the "Festival City," because of numerous special activities hosted by Southern Utah University. The **Utah Summer Games,** an Olympic-style extravaganza with athletes from around the state competing in more than 40 sports, from archery to wrestling, ushers in the summer festivities, but the main event is the **Utah Shakespearean Festival,** which runs from late June or early July through mid- to late October.

■ UTAH SHAKESPEAREAN FESTIVAL

The **Adams Shakespearean Theatre**, dedicated in 1977, is one of the world's most accurate reproductions of Shakespeare's Globe Theatre. The theater is so authentic, in fact, that the British Broadcasting Corporation filmed part of its own Shakespeare series there. During the festival, theatergoers can choose from three Shakespearean plays in the Adams Shakespearean Theatre, on the Southern Utah University campus, and three or more other classical or contemporary productions in the other festival venue, the Randall L. Jones Theatre, dating from 1989.

Literary and production seminars, special workshops, backstage tours, foyer entertainments, and an orientation to the evening's performance are also presented amid the Elizabethan action. The nightly Greenshow adds to the festivities with jugglers, puppeteers, and vendors dressed in costume. The audience is invited to join skits and impromptu plays.

The Utah Shakespearean Festival in Cedar City attracts more tourists than any other annual event in southern Utah.

Southern Utah's love of Shakespeare actually dates back to pioneer times. According to R. Scott Phillips, managing director of the festival, Mormons who settled nearby Parowan staged a Shakespearean play three weeks after moving in from the north.

The festival was founded by Fred C. Adams, who left New York City to come West in 1959, tried producing a popular Broadway musical for southern Utah residents, and discovered little interest. Challenged, he organized a production of *Romeo and Juliet*. Much to his delight, the play sold out its initial three-night run, and two more nights as well.

When Interstate 15 bypassed Cedar City's Main Street in 1962, city fathers became nervous that the town might die. The local Lions Club put up $1,000 for the first Shakespearean

Festival in 1962. *The Taming of the Shrew, Hamlet,* and *The Merchant of Venice* were performed on an outdoor platform supporting a partial replica of an Elizabethan pavilion. This first festival was put on by an original company of 20 people and drew 3,276 patrons, giving organizers enough of a profit to mount a second season.

Nowadays, some 350 workers and actors—including a couple of dozen full-time employees—labor to produce the festival. More than 150,000 theater patrons enjoy a season lasting from late June through late October and featuring about 150 evening performances. This mammoth undertaking, which produces millions for the local economy, won a Tony award in 2000 for "Outstanding Regional Theatre." *351 West Center Street; information: 435-586-7880; box office: 435-586-7878.*

■ IRON MISSION STATE PARK MUSEUM   *map page 207, C-2*
For a glimpse of Cedar City's pioneer past, spend some time browsing through this state park on Main Street. The town earned its "Iron Mission" nickname because iron was produced here, making the city exceedingly important to Mormon self-sufficiency in the territory's early days. The park illustrates pioneer life with a collection of horse-drawn vehicles, including a Wells Fargo stagecoach, buggies, surreys, mail carts, horse-drawn farm machinery, an old milk wagon, and even a one-horse sleigh. The most popular item is probably the stagecoach that Butch Cassidy reputedly riddled with bullets during his gang's escapades in the Four Corners section of Utah. *635 North Main Street; 435-586-9290.*

The Robert Redford–Paul Newman movie *Butch Cassidy and the Sundance Kid* gave even more notoriety to this already famous Western outlaw. According to folklorist Dave Stanley, who chronicles the history and folklore associated with southern Utah's national parks and monuments, southern Utah abounds with tales and evidence of the outlaw Robert LeRoy Parker, alias Butch Cassidy.

"He and the Sundance Kid and the rest of the Wild Bunch have been tracked through Bryce Canyon, Capitol Reef, and Canyonlands, especially in the Robbers' Roost country between Hanksville and Moab," writes Stanley. "Many of the Butch Cassidy stories treat him as a Robin Hood figure who robbed the rich and helped the poor. One tale concerns a local widow whose ranch was threatened by foreclosure. Butch and the boys robbed the local bank and

(following pages) Sandstone formations in Cedar Breaks National Monument.

delivered the cash to the woman, who paid off a surprised banker when he showed up at the ranch to evict her. On the way back to town, Butch held him up again and made off with the money."

Cedar City's festivals and proximity to major national parks, monuments, and forests have brought many amenities not found in cities of similar size. Restaurants, modern motels, and a community that welcomes out-of-towners make it a comfortable place to visit.

■ CEDAR BREAKS NATIONAL MONUMENT
map page 207, C-2/3

Cedar Breaks was named by Mormon pioneers who settled Cedar City in 1851— named erroneously, however, because the "cedars" growing near the base of the cliffs were actually juniper trees. The pioneers referred to the steep badland topography as "breaks."

With a drop of 2,500 feet and a diameter of more than three miles, Cedar Breaks is shaped like a gigantic amphitheater. Stone spires, columns, arches, and canyons in hues of tan, red, and orange change color and texture as the sun moves across the sky. Particularly enchanting is the short walk along the Alpine Pond Trail in early summer, when high meadows are ablaze with wildflowers.

Visitor facilities and the Cedar Breaks Scenic Drive close each winter, but Highway 143 remains open through the northeast corner of the park, and the North View Overlook is accessible. The rest of the park is accessible on snowshoes or cross-country skis. When sufficient snow falls, snowmobiles are permitted on designated routes; however, snowmobilers need to check with the park's administrative headquarters for current snow conditions. *From Cedar City, take UT 14 south for 18 miles to UT 148, then go north 4 miles; 435-586-9451.*

Visitors fortunate enough to glide quietly on cross-country skis around the rim of the amphitheater will find the view on a clear winter day breathtaking. Ancient bristlecone pines frame vistas of snow-covered red and tan rock below, and the icy silence magnifies the majesty of the entire place. About 30 miles of marked trails and another 185 miles of backcountry routes are available in Cedar Breaks National Monument and in and around the town of Brian Head.

In the summer months, hikers can take a rugged 10-mile trail into Rattlesnake Creek and the nearby U.S. Forest Service Ashdown Gorge Wilderness Area, located on the western boundary of the national monument. The trail descends an incredible 3,400 feet into the gorge. Smart backpackers arrange to be picked up at the bottom of the hike rather than try to climb back out.

Those who don't enjoy camping may wish to rent a condominium or hotel room at Brian Head Resort, a ski resort that offers off-season rates in the summer. Excellent mountain biking opportunities can be enjoyed, as one of the resorts' lifts is available to carry mountain bikers to mountaintop trailheads. Information, trail maps, guide services, and rentals are available at the shop inside the hotel. Brian Head Resort offers a variety of other summer activities, including photography workshops, star-gazing parties, music festivals, and hikes.

Summer visitors to Cedar Breaks often take side trips to **Panguitch** and **Navajo lakes.** Both have rustic lodges and U.S. Forest Service campgrounds. Mountain bikers are discovering the challenging and scenic dirt roads and trails in this area.

■ ZION NATIONAL PARK *map page 207, B/C-3/4*

The Great White Throne, Angels Landing, Temple of Sinawava, the Guardian Angels, the Pulpit, Mount Moroni, the Tabernacle: the names of Zion's canyons, peaks, and rock formations reveal much about the nature of this land and the reverence for it held by the pioneers who settled here. Zion is Utah's oldest national park and one of its most beloved tourist destinations.

Nephi Johnson is believed to have been the first non-Indian to enter Zion Canyon, which he did in 1858. Isaac Behunin built the first cabin near the site of the present-day Zion Lodge in 1863. Zion first came under federal protection in 1909, when it was designated Mukuntuweap National Monument. Ten years later it became a national park.

Zion may be Utah's most accessible national park. Visitors can enjoy a stay in its lovely lodge, or walk along paved hiking trails to the more popular attractions. Large developed campgrounds, a children's nature center, visitor facilities at both Zion Canyon and Kolob Canyon, ranger-guided hikes, naturalist programs, and evening campfire talks provide even more options for visitors. Just outside the park's southern boundary in the tiny town of **Springdale** are restaurants, motels, stores, and the O.C. Tanner Amphitheater, where theater-goers enjoy live performances with Zion Canyon as a wonderful backdrop.

(following pages) Winter adds a touch of white to Zion's familiar reds and greens.

The Great White Throne is a popular emblem of Zion, Utah's oldest national park.

Yet, for all its civilized manner (and, in the summer, its crowds), Zion is essentially a wild place full of unexpected adventures for those willing to escape the confines of their cars and do some exploring. An easy stroll of just over a mile takes you to the popular **Emerald Pools.** Few who grip the chains on the **Angel's Landing Trail** to keep from falling off the lip of a sheer sandstone cliff will forget the thrill. The truly adventurous hiker may choose to get wet in the "Narrows," a popular hike in the waters of the Virgin River. The Riverside Walk is an easy, meandering trail suitable for baby strollers and for wheelchairs with assistance.

Still, even a drive through the park is breathtaking. From April through October, a shuttle bus takes visitors through the canyon, stopping at the lodge, view points, and trailheads. (Although the Zion Canyon Scenic Drive is accessible only by shuttle in summer, UT 9, crossing the park east to west, is open to private cars.) In Zion Canyon, the rock walls tower 2,000 to 3,000 feet above the road. Negotiating the switchbacks up to the **Mount Carmel Tunnel** and motoring past windows cut in the tunnel walls, you hardly dare to glance down at the chasm below. Emerging into daylight again, you find yourself on the edge of a great petrified sand dune carved into a checkerboard pattern, where large trees grow sideways out of bare rock. Appropriately, the feature is known as **Checkerboard Mesa.** Zion is a four-season park. Fall rewards visitors with sights of blazing orange oaks and yellow cottonwoods shimmering at the bottom of gigantic crimson cliffs. Winter brings snowcapped sandstone peaks, ice formations, and cold solitude. Springtime visitors hear the roaring Virgin River, swollen with runoff, and smell plants coming to life after a winter hibernation. Summer brings blazing heat, which sends visitors scrambling to a cooling waterfall or the shade of a narrow canyon.

Parents visiting the park in the summer may want to consider signing their children up for the Junior Ranger Program.

More and more adventurers explore Zion by backpacking into canyons. In the remote Kolob region of the park, some 45 miles east and north by road from Zion Canyon, backpackers can hike to Kolob Arch; with a span of 310 feet, it is the world's longest. Backcountry explorers may not always see wildlife like cougar, ringtail cat, bobcat, coyote, mule deer, and fox, but they can see signs of these critters in the dry sandy washes or on the banks of the tiny creeks that flow through this land of standing rocks.

The main section of Zion National Park has two entrances, both on UT 9; one is 33 miles east of I-15 and the other is 12 miles west of U.S. 89. The Zion Canyon Visitor Center is in this southern section of the park. A second section of the park, the northern Kolob Canyons section, is accessible just off I-15, 18 miles south of Cedar City. The Kolob Canyons Visitor Center is at its northwest border. *435-772-3256.*

■ ST. GEORGE *map page 207, A/B-4*

As one motors south from Cedar City to Zion and then to St. George, it is easy to feel the change in the climate and see the difference in the landscape. The elevation at Cedar City is 5,800 feet. St. George, where locals claim the sun spends the winter, is 2,880 feet. The skyline of this bustling city is still dominated by the brilliant white Mormon Temple, but southern Utah's largest town enjoys newfound prosperity. The weather here is similar to that of Phoenix or Palm Springs, drawing thousands of Utahns south to swim, play golf and tennis, and bask in the winter sunlight. The city accommodates them with fine restaurants, modern hotels, pools and spas, and more than half a dozen golf courses.

In 1861, upon Brigham Young's request, 300 Mormon families from Salt Lake City were led south by George A. Smith. (The town was named in honor of Smith, who was considered, after the Mormon tradition, a latter-day saint.) On orders from Brigham Young, who wanted Mormons to be independent from the outside world for their clothing, the settlers planted cotton—hence the area's nickname, "Utah's Dixie."

Floods, drought, and disease hit the Mormons hard in Utah's Dixie. But the final blow to the cotton mission arrived with the completion of the transcontinental railroad in 1869, when cheaper cotton from the deep South became readily available.

Travelers entering the Virgin River Valley from any direction still thrill to the sight of the spectacular **St. George Temple**, framed by the red sandstone hills and dark green juniper and piñon pine trees. Completed in 1877, it is the oldest temple still in use by the Latter-day Saints. *400 East 200 South; 435-673-5181.*

Take time to explore other local pioneer sites, like the **Mormon Tabernacle**, the **Daughters of Utah Pioneers Museum, the Brigham Young Winter Home**, the **Old Cotton Mill**, and the **Jacob Hamblin Home** in nearby Santa Clara, all of which provide glimpses of what early life was like here. St. George is also an ideal base for exploring Zion National Park, less than 40 miles to the east. Zion, however, is only the most famous of the area's attractions.

■ SIDE TRIPS FROM ST. GEORGE

Recreation Areas
North of St. George, the **Pine Valley Mountains** are a good place to escape the summer heat. **Pine Valley Recreation Area** and **Pine Valley Wilderness** are two promising hiking destinations, while boating, fishing, and other watery activities are available at nearby **Gunlock Reservoir, Baker Dam Recreation Site, Quail Creek Reservoir**, and **Sand Hollow State Park**.

Mountain Meadows Massacre Historic Site *map page 207, A-3*
West of the Pine Valley Mountains, just off UT 18, is the Mountain Meadows Massacre Historic Site. A simple monument marks the place where 120 members of a wagon train bound for California were attacked and executed by an alliance of Mormons and local Indians in 1857. Though the tightly knit

Brigham Young's winter home in St. George.

Mormon community tried to cover up the incident, John D. Lee, who was in charge of Indian affairs in southern Utah at the time and was believed to have been one of the leaders of the massacre, was brought to justice 20 years later, and executed in this same place.

Beaver Dam Wash *map page 207, A-4*

Naturalists and birdwatchers visiting the St. George area should not miss a fascinating oasis called Beaver Dam Wash, located south of the town of Shivwits in the extreme southwestern corner of the state. The southern region of the Great Basin, the western portion of the Colorado Plateau, and the northern part of the Mojave Desert all merge here at Utah's lowest elevation, 2,000 feet above sea level. Brigham Young University, which worked with the Nature Conservancy to purchase the area, manages Beaver Dam Wash (also known as Lytle Ranch) as a natural preserve. It may take some work to find it, but it's worth it. Take Old U.S. 91 northwest through Santa Clara and Shivwits (about 25 miles), then continue for another 20 miles across the summit of the Beaver Dam Mountains southwest to Castle Cliff, a large cliff on your left topped by a wooden flagpole. Immediately beyond the cliff is the only unpaved road to the right. Take this road about 11 miles to the west. Several yellow and black road signs along the way will guide you to the preserve.

Snow Canyon State Park *map page 207, A-4*

If you have time to visit only one park (aside from Zion) in the St. George area, don't miss Snow Canyon, 5 miles north of St. George off UT 18. With hot showers and hookups for trailers, the scenic campground at Snow Canyon is among the best in this part of the state. If you hike to the small arch in the canyon, try to find the Indian pictographs on the canyon walls. Kids like to play in the sand dunes, while more adventurous visitors can take flashlights into the lava tubes. Many a photographer has stood at a Snow Canyon overlook and marveled at the contrasting colors of the red sandstone and black basalt formations of lava. *Snow Canyon State Park; 435-628-2255 or 800-322-3770 for camping reservations.*

Grafton *map page 207, B-4*

Near the town of Rockville, a few miles from the south entrance to Zion National Park, the ghost town of Grafton brings photographers by the dozens to snap pictures. Paul Newman fans will recognize the town's schoolhouse, store, and cabins as the setting of the bicycle scene in *Butch Cassidy and the Sundance Kid*. A nearby graveyard (you may need to ask locals for directions) preserves interesting hand-carved headstones. But visit soon: with the building of housing developments around it, Grafton is becoming less of a ghost town every day.

Kanab *map page 207, D-4*
This pretty town, 41 miles southeast of Zion on the Utah-Arizona border, is close to both Lake Powell and Arizona's Grand Canyon. The town has been a center of the Western movie industry for many years. The **Frontier Movie Town** (297 West Center Street; 800-551-1714), a replica of a frontier town that is something of a museum with a back lot made up of salvaged movie sets, has been built to show tourists a bit of the old West. Admission is free. Also, be sure to visit the **Kanab Heritage House** (100 South Main Street), an 1895 Queen Anne–style Victorian built by one Henry Bowman. A Mormon, he lived in it only two years before being called away on a mission. A photo of the next owner, Thomas Chamberlain, along with his six wives and 55 children, is in the sitting room. The house is open from May through October.

Coral Pink Sand Dunes State Park *map page 207, C-4*
Stark, ruddy-colored hills of sand are the main attraction at this state park west of Kanab. The small campground provides an out-of-the-way experience that differs greatly from the larger, crowded campgrounds at Zion. Visitors to the dunes can enjoy watching ATVs tackle the sand or walk into a small area reserved especially for hikers. *12 miles off U.S. 89; 435-648-2800.*

Pipe Spring National Monument
One of the West's most vivid pictures of pioneer life is re-created in the living history program at Pipe Spring National Monument on Arizona State Highway 389, southwest of Kanab. Stepping through the gates of the visitors center is like being whisked away in a time machine. The place is just as it was in pioneer times. In the summer, docents dressed in period garb act the parts of pioneers and profess to knowing nothing about the 20th century. *Take UT 89 south from Kanab to Fredonia, Arizona, turn west onto AZ 389, and drive 15 miles; 928-643-7105.*

The color of the dunes at Coral Pink Sand Dunes State Park near the Arizona border is enhanced by the setting sun.

■ BRYCE CANYON NATIONAL PARK   *map page 207, D-2/3*

Bryce is not actually a canyon at all, but a series of 14 huge amphitheaters that extend a thousand feet down through the pink and white limestone of the Paunsaugunt Plateau. It has been described as the most colorful national park in the world. Depending on the season, the hour of the day, and the weather, the fantastic rock formations, or "hoodoos," visible from **Inspiration** and **Rainbow points** turn vivid shades of white, orange, yellow, red, and purple. When you first approach Bryce, take time to sit on a bench at the edge of one of the amphitheaters and contemplate the extraordinary scene before you. The rock formations took on their unusual shapes because the top layer of rock is harder than the layers beneath it, causing the layers to erode at differing rates. If erosion cuts away too much of the soft rock beneath the cap, the hoodoo falls.

This astonishing landscape was named for Ebenezer Bryce, pioneer cattleman and the first permanent settler in the area. His description of the landscape, oft repeated today, was quite succinct: "It's a helluva place to lose a cow."

It's hard to resist striking out on the trails for such enchanting destinations as **Queen's Garden, Navajo Loop, Peekaboo Loop, Under-the-Rim,** and **Fairyland.** Unfortunately for hikers who may not be in the best of shape, the walks down into the Bryce amphitheaters are deceptively easy. Climbing back out can be a real chore, especially during the hot summer months; the trails have elevation gains ranging from 300 to more than 800 feet. The easiest hike is the 1.5-mile **Queen's Garden Trail,** which begins at **Sunrise Point** and takes about two hours to complete. The **Rim Trail,** which runs along the lip of the amphitheaters, offers outstanding vistas into the canyon and for 100 miles across the horizon. A small portion of the trail, between Sunrise Point and **Sunset Point,** is paved.

Less crowded trails wander through the meadows of the Paunsaugunt Plateau, on the west side of the park. In the spring, sego lilies, penstemons, asters, clematis, evening primrose, scarlet gilias, Indian paintbrush, and wild iris turn this part of Bryce into a garden full of wonderful color. Ancient bristlecone pines, more than 2,000 years old, still inhabit Bryce Canyon.

Though all of Utah's five national parks experience four distinct seasons, the extremes are greater at Bryce Canyon because of its high elevation (the park reaches 9,105 feet at Rainbow Point). This means temperatures in winter dip well below freezing. Winter can be a great time to see Bryce, however. Few people venture into the park, and the contrast of the red rock hoodoos and white snow adds a dimension to the landscape unavailable in the summer. While the trails are often snow-covered, a good pair of hiking boots and warm clothes will allow you a wonderful experience. No trains of horses, sounds of automobiles, or long strings of other hikers will disrupt your solitude.

The 38-mile (round-trip) scenic drive through the park takes in 13 overlooks and takes about three hours to complete. You can drive into the park year-round, although there is an optional shuttle bus service in operation from mid-May through September.

Bryce Canyon National Park Visitor Center is 1.5 miles south of the park entrance, which is 4.5 miles southeast of the intersection of UT 12 and UT 63 (24 miles southeast of Panguitch); 435-834-5322.

Many who visit Bryce Canyon end their exploration of this part of Utah with the national park instead of continuing east on UT 12, where some of the state's best-kept secrets can be unlocked. This road brings travelers to some of the most remote and isolated towns and backcountry; the stately alpine forests give this part of Utah an entirely different look from that of Zion or Capitol Reef.

■ KODACHROME BASIN STATE PARK

map pages 228–229, A/B-5

Kodachrome Basin is a scenic little valley full of towering monolithic chimneys unlike anything else in the world. Its very name—chosen by the National Geographic Society, with the film company's permission—attests to its picturesque color, yet because Kodachrome Basin is located off the main highway on the northern edge of Grand Staircase–Escalante National Monument, it receives fewer visitors.

Geologists believe Kodachrome Basin State Park was at one time similar to Yellowstone National Park, but that its hot springs and geysers eventually filled up with sediment and solidified. Through time, the sandstone surrounding the solidified geysers eroded, leaving large sand pipes.

Taking a hike to Shakespeare Arch helps introduce visitors to the ecology of the desert. The small rock formation was discovered by the superintendent of Kodachrome Basin one afternoon while he was searching for a coyote den. The trail passes such typical plants as juniper, sagebrush, buffaloberry, Indian rice grass, false buckwheat, saltbush, snakeweed, yucca, Mormon tea, and rabbitbrush.

The 24-unit campground, located in the midst of the rock spires and piñon/juniper forest, ranks among the best of its kind in the state, largely because each site is set so far from its neighbors. A concessionaire provides a small grocery store and guided horseback, wagon, and stagecoach rides, as well as cabins. *Located 9 miles southeast of Cannonville; 435-679-8562 or 800-322-3770 for camping reservations.*

■ HEADING SOUTH

Kodachrome Basin State Park is only a tiny pocket of beauty in a larger area designated as the Grand Staircase–Escalante National Monument. **Cottonwood Road,** which leads south from Cannonville to Kodachrome Basin and on into the monument, is paved, but it becomes a considerably rougher dirt road beyond the park, so check with park rangers before attempting to drive it, and don't go when the road is wet. **Grosvenor Arch**, an unusual, yellowish-tan span, is named in honor of the founder of the National Geographic Society. Continuing south, you will reach the unusual rock formations of **Cottonwood Canyon,** called the **Cockscomb** because they resemble the top of a rooster's head.

Fresh snow on Queen's Garden Trail in Bryce Canyon National Park.

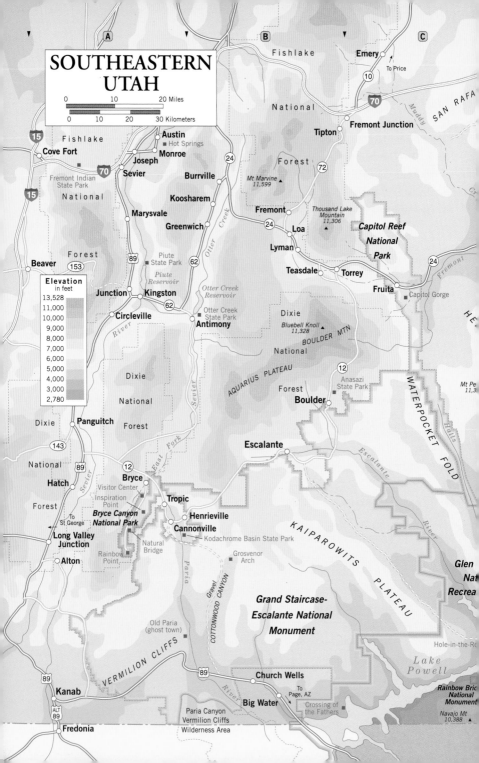

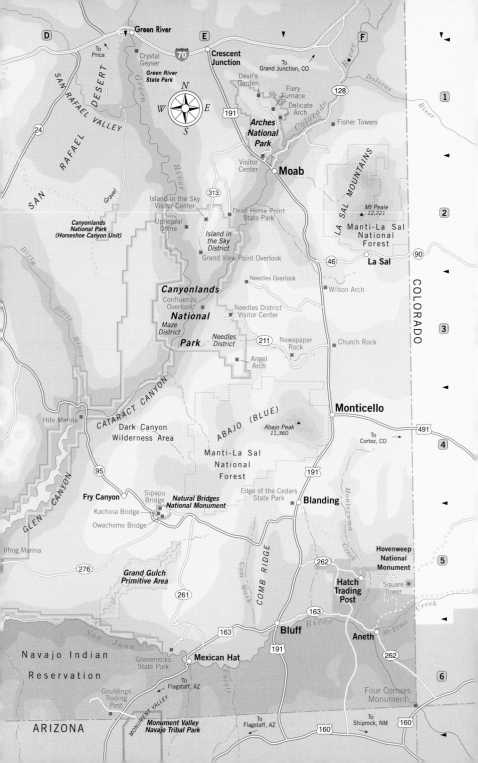

The Paria River runs through the Kodachrome Basin, eventually leading into the **Paria Canyon–Vermilion Cliffs Wilderness Area** on the Utah–Arizona border. Backpackers, who sometimes must wade through waist-deep water, tell many stories of the narrow, twisting canyons of the Paria River.

■ GRAND STAIRCASE–ESCALANTE NATIONAL MONUMENT   *map pages 228–229, A to C-3 to 6*

When President Bill Clinton designated the new Grand Staircase–Escalante National Monument in September 1996, he told millions what a few southern Utah red rock fanatics knew all along: that the new 1.7-million acre monument contains some of the world's wildest and most intriguing desert country.

"On this remarkable site, God's handiwork is everywhere," said Clinton. "In the natural beauty of the Escalante Canyons and in the Kaiparowits Plateau. In the rock formations that show layer upon layer millions of years of geology. In the fossil record of dinosaurs and other prehistoric life. In the remains of ancient American civilizations like the Anasazi Indians."

Unfortunately, the president never actually set foot on the monument he created with his signature. He made the announcement on the edge of Arizona's Grand Canyon—to the irritation of many of Utah's already disgruntled elected officials, who had boycotted the ceremony. They had instead wanted a long-proposed coal mine on the Kaiparowits Plateau, to provide jobs for rural Utahns and income for the state.

The new national monument may have detractors in Utah, but it does protect and highlight a region with great diversity of scenery: it's a wild land of arches, goblins, hoodoos, and assorted canyons. The Escalante River and its tributaries worked with rain and wind to form most of these natural areas. The river is believed by most historians to be the last major river "discovered" by government surveyors in the continental United States.

The region is still hard to explore today, thanks to its lack of access, difficult terrain, and challenging topography. Both U.S. 89, on the monument's southern border, and UT 12, on the northern edge, are paved, but between them, only a few rugged dirt roads (which will give visitors a brain-jarring ride) offer vehicle access into the rugged terrain. For hikers, too, there are few truly developed or marked

Lower Calf Creek Falls near the Escalante River.

Rough Going

We crossed the river on the 1st of Feb. all safe; was not half as scared as we thought we'd be, it was the easiest part of our journey. Coming down the hole in the rock to get to the river was ten times as bad. If you ever come this way it will scare you to death to look down it. It is about a mile from the top down to the river and it is almost strait down, the cliffs on each side are five hundred feet high and there is just room enough for a wagon to go down. It nearly scared me to death. The first wagon I saw go down they put the brake on and rough locked the hind wheels and had a big rope fastened to the wagon and about ten men holding back on it and then they went down like they would smash everything. I'll never forget that day.

—Elizabeth Morris Decker as quoted in *Hole-In-The-Rock,* David E. Miller, 1959

---

trails into the interior. Some of the more popular hiking routes, such as those through **Coyote Gulch** and **Harris Wash,** lure hikers with the promise of lush gardens in the midst of desert terrain, narrow slot canyons, waterfalls, and towering arches. Many other special places remain rather difficult to reach, largely untouched and explored only by those willing to take long day hikes or several-day treks— but they're well worth the effort. There are multi-colored slot canyons so narrow in places that it is impossible to see the sky. The **Kaiparowits Plateau** offers unmatched vistas of wide open country in a seldom-visited desert that may be the loneliest wilderness this side of Alaska. Destinations with such foreboding names as **Spooky Gulch, Devils Garden, Peekaboo Canyon,** and **Death Hollow** are inviting only to those willing to spend the physical effort to see the country on its terms.

Before doing much exploring in this area, it's a good idea to stop at one of the visitors centers to pick up literature, safety information, maps, and historical background. *Kanab Visitor Center: 745 East Highway 89, Kanab; 435-644-4680. Cannonville Visitor Center: 10 Center Street, Cannonville; 435-679-8981. Escalante Interagency Visitor Center: 755 West Main, Escalante; 435-826-5499.*

There are only two developed campgrounds within the national monument: the 13-unit Calf Creek campground and the five-unit Deer Creek camping facility at the northern end of the monument. Nearby Escalante Petrified Forest State Park, Kodachrome Basin State Park, and Bryce Canyon National Park offer the best alternative camping facilities. Motels, restaurants, and gas stations can be found in towns such as Kanab, Tropic, Escalante, and Boulder.

Perhaps the best-known destination in the Escalante area is **Calf Creek Falls,** 15 miles east of the town of Escalante. Small natural arches, thousand-year-old Indian rock art, an Ancestral Puebloan dwelling, and a moderate hike to a refreshing waterfall make this a special destination. Summer visitors can fish in the pools along Calf Creek for brown trout.

■ HOLE-IN-THE ROCK   *map pages 228–229, C-6*
The Hole-in-the-Rock expedition, which took place in 1879–80, is a telling story of the faith of the early Mormon pioneers. Directed by their Mormon leaders, who were seeking to open new lands for cultivation, a colonizing mission of more than 200 people from various towns of southwestern Utah set out for a shortcut into the San Juan area of southeastern Utah. With them on what turned out to be a 290-mile journey were 82 wagons with teams of two or more horses, about 200 additional horses, and more than 1,000 head of cattle.

The Colorado River formed a major obstacle along the route, but when the pioneers discovered the Hole-in-the-Rock, a narrow slit in a 2,000-foot cliff overlooking the river, they believed a road could be blasted through the crack that would allow them to drop down the cliff and cross the river. Their success is testament to their tenacity—even after blasting, their "road" was nothing more than a wagon-wide slot that dropped 1,800 feet in less than three-quarters of a mile. It was too steep to walk down, so the women and children sat down and slid to the bottom. Wagons were lowered at near perpendicular angles, with as many men as possible hanging onto the attached ropes to slow the descent.

Today, some of the **Hole-in-the-Rock Road** has been drowned by Lake Powell. Enough signs of the original trek remain, however, that boaters on Lake Powell or drivers willing to brave the rugged 61-mile county-maintained gravel road can still view the places where pioneers struggled. The road passes **Dance Hall Rock,** a huge sandstone amphitheater where dances kept pioneer morale high, then leads to the crevice above the Colorado, where the party used blasting powder and picks to open a passage to the river.

■ ANASAZI STATE PARK   *map pages 228–229, B/C-4*
The park conserves the remains of an ancient village constructed on top of a mesa and inhabited from approximately A.D. 1050 to 1200. With a year-round water supply, fertile fields, a broad view of the surrounding countryside, and abundant wild game, wood, and stone, the village was able to support about 200 people.

(The park retains the name formerly used for this culture—Anasazi—although the preferred term today is "Ancestral Puebloan," a name more acceptable to their descendants.) The park museum explains how the villagers lived, while a reconstructed pueblo allows visitors to see for themselves. You can try your hand at grinding corn the Indian way with a mano and metate. *460 North Highway 12, in Boulder; 435-335-7308.*

■ **BOULDER MOUNTAIN** *map pages 228–229, B-3/4*
UT 12, one of America's most beautiful drives, passes through the town of **Boulder** and climbs north to Boulder Mountain, in Dixie National Forest. It's a good place to go to escape the heat and to enjoy glimpses of Capitol Reef and the Waterpocket Fold to the east, the Aquarius Plateau to the west, and the Escalante canyons, Straight Cliffs, and Kaiparowits Plateau to the south. From any of the three developed Dixie National Forest campgrounds along the road, visitors can hike into one of the many lakes that are teeming with brook trout.

■ **CAPITOL REEF NATIONAL PARK** *map pages 228–229, C-2 to 4, and page 235*

Capitol Reef gets its name from two geological curiosities of the **Waterpocket Fold,** a 100-mile bulge in the earth's crust containing eroded pockets that catch water after each rainfall. Early settlers thought that the mountains, which dominate the landscape of the national park, resembled a coral reef. One of the white sandstone outcroppings, meanwhile, **Capitol Dome,** resembles that monument in our nation's capital.

Inside the park, influences of Mormon pioneer settlers remain in and around the little town of **Fruita:** a barn, a farmhouse, rock fences, an 1896 one-room schoolhouse, and acres of fruit orchards. These groves provide beautiful displays of blossoms in the spring, shade during the hot summer months, and fruit—apples, cherries, peaches, apricots, pears—in the late summer and fall. The public is invited to pick them and pay a small per-pound or -bushel price. The campground is located in the midst of one of these orchards. Deer and skunks—which often get too friendly with campers—frequent the area. The old weathered barn, situated against the red-rock cliffs guarding the campground, is one of the most frequently photographed structures in southern Utah.

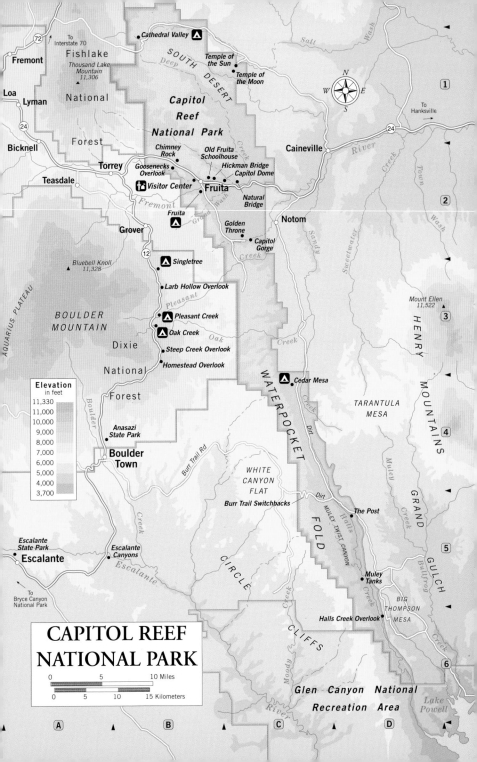

CAPITOL REEF
NATIONAL PARK

To Interstate 70
72
Fremont
Fishlake
Thousand Lake
Mountain
11,306
National
Loa
Lyman
24
Forest
Bicknell
Torrey
Teasdale

Cathedral Valley

SOUTH DESERT

Deep

Temple of
the Sun

Temple of
the Moon

Capitol
Reef
National Park

Salt

Wash

To Hanksville
24

Caineville

1

N
W   E
S

Chimney
Rock

Old Fruita
Schoolhouse
Hickman Bridge
Capitol Dome

Goosenecks
Overlook

Visitor Center   Fruita

Fruita

Natural
Bridge

Golden
Throne

Capitol
Gorge

Notom

2

Grover
12

Bluebell Knoll
11,328

Singletree

Larb Hollow Overlook

AQUARIUS PLATEAU

BOULDER
MOUNTAIN

Dixie

National

Forest

Pleasant

Pleasant Creek

Oak Creek

Steep Creek Overlook

Homestead Overlook

Oak

Creek

Mount Ellen
11,522

3

HENRY

Cedar Mesa

WATERPOCKET

TARANTULA
MESA

MOUNTAINS

4

Elevation
in feet

| 11,330 |
| 11,000 |
| 10,000 |
| 9,000 |
| 8,000 |
| 7,000 |
| 6,000 |
| 5,000 |
| 4,000 |
| 3,700 |

Boulder

Anasazi
State Park

Boulder
Town

Burr Trail Rd

WHITE
CANYON
FLAT

Burr Trail Switchbacks

Dirt

Dirt

Muley

Creek

The Post

FOLD

MULEY TWIST CANYON

Halls

GRAND

5

GULCH

Creek

Bullfrog

Escalante
State Park
Escalante

Escalante
Canyons

Creek

Escalante

CIRCLE

CLIFFS

Moody

River

Muley
Tanks

Halls Creek Overlook

BIG
THOMPSON
MESA

Creek

6

To
Bryce Canyon
National Park

Glen Canyon National
Recreation Area

Lake
Powell

0   5   10 Miles

0   5   10   15 Kilometers

A   B   C   D

The **Fremont River,** a lifeline for the fruit orchards and cottonwoods, runs through the middle of the park along UT 24. It takes its name from the Fremont Indians, whom archaeologists believe inhabited this area as long ago as A.D. 800. They left petroglyphs and storage bins, called moki huts, along the walls of the canyons.

Capitol Reef has a fine paved road, but no trip can be complete without at least one hike. Walking to **Hickman Bridge** or through **Capitol Gorge** and **Grand Wash** helps visitors appreciate the fascinating geology of the park's water pockets, or "tanks." Kids can scramble up the easy-to-climb sandstone and through the little stone alcoves, playing hide-and-seek for hours. Longer, more difficult treks take walkers to **Cassidy Arch, Frying Pan Canyon** (where a shout turns into an echo heard several times over), **Spring Canyon,** and the **Golden Throne.** An excellent hiking guide detailing the most popular trails is available at the visitors center.

Only a few of the roads in Capitol Reef are unpaved, but it is good to check on conditions before setting out, as wet weather can make roads impassable. Solitude seekers can take longer hikes from the **Burr Trail**, a partially paved road cutting down the eastern boundary of the park, with one spur south to Lake Powell and another west to Boulder. The **Upper** and **Lower Muley Twist canyons** are among the most popular backpacking destinations. At the north end of the park, four-wheelers can explore the rugged dirt road leading to **Cathedral Valley,** where huge monolithic sandstone buttes resemble cathedrals in the desert. To the south, the Burr Trail leads past farms and cattle ranches where lush green alfalfa and deep red soil color the landscape. After a harrowing drive up narrow switchbacks, the trail enters a sandstone canyon not unlike Zion's. Mountain bikers especially like traversing the Burr Trail in fall, spring, and even winter. This is dry country most of the year, so carry in your own water.

As is the case in all of Utah's national parks, backpackers need a permit, which is free. No other accommodations or restaurants are found inside Capitol Reef National Park, although tiny Wayne County hamlets like Torrey, Teasdale, Bicknell, and Loa furnish some unexpected treats. There has been a recent building boom of franchise hotels, and several B&Bs have opened, especially in Teasdale. *Capitol Reef National Park Visitor Center is 11 miles east of Torrey on UT 24; 435-425-3791.*

■ SAN RAFAEL SWELL *map pages 228–229, C/D-1*

The stretch of Interstate 70 between Salina and Green River cuts through Fishlake National Forest, the heart of the red-rock San Rafael Swell and Sinbad Valley, without passing through a town for more than 100 miles. Some devotees argue that this is one of the most scenic portions of interstate highway in the entire national system. The Swell itself has been described as the jagged remains of a dinosaur backbone, an exposed sandstone coral reef, a saw blade, and a scene from the Arabian Nights. It's desolate but interesting country with a colorful history. Many believe it is worthy of national park status.

Early Mormon settlers built the Fruita schoolhouse circa 1896. It closed in 1941 due to lack of students.

The San Rafael Swell arches up from the landscape like a dinosaur's backbone.

North of Interstate 70 at **Buckhorn Draw,** travelers can view the pictographs and petroglyphs left by ancient Indians who roamed this area thousands of years ago. Backpackers, horseback riders, and off-road-vehicle enthusiasts can discover places like the Little Grand Canyon, Wedge Overlook, Temple Mountain, the Muddy River, Crack Canyon, Iron Wash, and Little Wildhorse Canyon. Outlaws and cattle rustlers once hid in the narrow, winding canyons of the San Rafael Swell.

Maps and information for exploring the San Rafael Swell are available from the Price Chamber of Commerce and BLM offices in Price, Hanksville, and Salt Lake City (see pages 324–325). There are also several good hiking guidebooks.

■ GREEN RIVER   *map pages 228–229, D/E-1*

The 57-mile drive on U.S. 6/191 between Price and Green River gives glimpses of some of Utah's wildest, most desolate country. **Desolation Canyon,** a stretch of the Green River that's popular with rafters, is hidden from the road by the

Tavaputs Plateau, Roan Cliffs, and Beckwith Plateau to the east. To the west, the northern portion of the San Rafael Swell looms on the horizon. On some stormy evenings, the sun plays tricks with the clouds, and thunderbolts slash across one part of the sky while a rainbow graces another. Save for the tiny coal-mining communities of East Carbon and Sunnyside to the east, there are no towns on this stretch of highway, leaving drivers free to relax while enjoying the grand vistas.

At first sight, the town of Green River may seem desolate and bleak, but closer inspection reveals that this farm and tourist town has some interesting prospects. Built at an easy ford of the Green River, it's famous for its fine-tasting watermelons. Folks from all over Utah flock here in September to celebrate Melon Days, enjoy the early fall weather, and buy melons from roadside stands.

Giving a taste of the rapids, canyons, and lore of the Colorado and Green rivers, the **John Wesley Powell River History Museum** offers telling glimpses of the famous explorer's journeys, as well as interpretive hands-on exhibits, art displays, a river runners' hall of fame, a fine art gallery, and a multimedia presentation. *885 East Main Street; 435-564-3427.*

The **Green River State Park** south of town hosts campers in a lovely, shaded, grassy campground. It does fill at times during the summer, but nearby private campgrounds almost always have space available. A nine-hole golf course winds its way along the river near the campground. The park serves as a launching point for some rafting trips (on both the Green and Colorado rivers) and offers a fine stretch of flat water for canoes. *150 South Green River Boulevard; 435-564-3633 or 800-322-3770 for camping reservations.*

■ **GOBLIN VALLEY STATE PARK** *map pages 228–229, D-2*

Southwest of the town of Green River, UT 24 heads back toward Capitol Reef along the edge of the San Rafael Swell. A favorite destination here is Goblin Valley State Park, roughly midway between Interstate 70 and Hanksville, 17 miles beyond a clearly marked turnoff.

Goblin Valley is filled with stone goblins, ghosts, and toadstools that range in height from 10 to 200 feet. They stand like families of red goblins poured out, one by one, by a giant wizard and left frozen in time. These natural formations were made by uneven weathering of the sandstone; the softer material was removed by wind and water, leaving thousands of harder sections in unusual shapes.

There is something wonderful about wandering through the maze of goblins, toadstools, and other hoodoos at night under a full moon. Children love to play hide-and-seek and turn this valley into a giant playground. It is easy to see the role rain plays in shaping Goblin Valley. Thunderstorms turn the hollows between the goblins into shallow streams resembling the chocolate river in *Willie Wonka and the Chocolate Factory*. Because there are few plants here, the mud flows rapidly off the formations. Minutes after the storm ends, the streams disappears into the sand, and the goblins take on new shapes.

Arthur Chaffin, who once owned and operated the Hite Ferry on the Colorado River, stumbled upon Goblin Valley in the late 1920s while searching for an alternate route between Green River and Caineville. He called it Mushroom Valley. The area received protection as a scenic area in 1954, when it was under the control of the Bureau of Land Management, and officially became a state park on August 24, 1964.

Plan on spending at least several hours there, or better yet, stay a night at the state park campground. Showers, drinking water, and a trailer dump station are all available. *435-564-3633 or 800-322-3770 for camping reservations.*

At nearby Hanksville, travelers can either head west to Capitol Reef National Park, or south to Bullfrog and Hite marinas on Lake Powell in the Glen Canyon National Recreation Area.

■ **LAKE POWELL** *map pages 228–229, B to D-4 to 6*

The 186-mile-long reservoir known as Lake Powell came about as a result of the creation of the Glen Canyon Dam, between 1956 and 1966, to impound the water of the Colorado River. Although the dam is in Arizona, near Page, most of Lake Powell, and its meandering, 1,960-mile shoreline, is in Utah. The surrounding Glen Canyon National Recreation Area itself consists of more than 1.25 million acres, or 1,963 square miles. Most of that is accessible only by boat, some of it can be reached by automobile, and other parts can be explored by hikers or rafters.

If you're not into water sports but still want to see some of the lake, take UT 276 to **Bullfrog Marina** and ride the small John Atlantic Burr Ferry to Halls Crossing. Inaugurated in 1985, the ferry provides an alternative route to southeastern Utah for vehicles and trailers of all sizes. **Bullfrog** and **Halls Crossing** are the preeminent marinas at the upper end of the reservoir, offering powerboat and houseboat rentals, beaches, and campgrounds; Bullfrog is also the location of the

National Park Service visitors center. Tourists who don't want to steer their own boat can stay in modern lodges overlooking the lake at either Bullfrog or Wahweap Marina, near Page, and take a guided tour boat ride. *Bullfrog Visitor Center; 435-684-2243.*

Houseboating is an especially popular way to see Lake Powell. Some of the larger boats sleep up to 12 people. With gas available at the Dangling Rope Marina near Rainbow Bridge, boaters don't have to return to the main docking areas for days at a time. There are arches to discover, Indian ruins to find, and narrow canyons that lead into fine hiking areas. Take a moonlight summer swim in the warm waters, or rent a water-ski boat.

Avid fishermen will want to avoid the crowds of summer by renting a powerboat in either April or May or from mid-September to late October. Fishing for large- and smallmouth bass, striped bass, crappie, northern pike, walleye, and channel catfish is best during those times of year.

Many years of drought in Western states have brought water levels at Lake Powell to unprecedented lows. In 2003, the water was 89 feet below normal, causing the closing of some facilities previously accessible by boat. Boat ramps that have traditionally been underwater are now dirt. Before embarking on boating trips, be sure to check with lake officials regarding closures.

The Glen Canyon Dam and the Glen Canyon National Recreation Area were born in controversy, and they continue to polarize people in the West. In 1996 the Glen Canyon Institute and Sierra Club proposed that Lake Powell be drained and Glen Canyon restored to its former beauty. Just as construction of the dam affected local economies, water supplies, energy sources, and ecology, so does the proposal to drain the dam.

■ **RAINBOW BRIDGE NATIONAL MONUMENT** *map pages 228–229, C-6* Probably the most famous sight along Lake Powell is Rainbow Bridge. With a height of 290 feet and a span of 270 feet, it is the world's largest natural bridge. This spot, sacred to the Navajo Indians, was made famous in Zane Grey's *Riders of the Purple Sage.* A national monument since 1910, it is accessible only by boat or by a 13-mile hike across Navajo Nation land, for which a permit is required. In Grey's day, only a few hearty souls made the long and difficult hike. Now thousands of boaters visit the monument annually. Rainbow Bridge is adjacent to and administered by the Glen Canyon National Recreation Area. *For information: 928-608-6404; or the Navajo Nation Parks and Recreation Department: 928-871-6647.*

WATER IN AN ARID LAND

One who understood the limits of the West . . . was John Wesley Powell, the one-armed Civil War major who . . . headed . . . the forerunner of what was to become the Bureau of Reclamation. Much has been written of Powell's prescience, which was formidable, but in the end he was a failure. Although a powerful and shrewd bureaucrat, he was unable to get his most important program through Congress, because it alienated too many interests. . . .

Most of what Powell proposed was the result of his travels through Utah, which contained a unique communal society dependent on the diversion of water and readily able, through its religious institutions, to accomplish this purpose. . . .

Powell preached the uniqueness of arid lands and their need for special institutions. He . . . proposed that instead of the rectangular grid survey useful to the east on flat, equally watered lands, the arid West should be divided into watersheds, such as the Colorado River basin. . . . Powell knew that the West did not have an unlimited amount of land that could be irrigated or an inexhaustible supply of water, two false impressions spread widely by various boosters. He was read out of the Reclamation movement for declaring at the National Irrigation Congress in Los Angeles in 1893, "Gentlemen, it may be unpleasant for me to give you these facts. I hesitated a good deal but finally concluded to do so. I tell you, gentlemen, you are piling up a heritage of conflict and litigation of water rights, for there is not sufficient water to supply the land."

—Philip L. Fradkin, *A River No More*, 1981

■ **HENRY MOUNTAINS** *map pages pages 228–229, C/D-3/4*
The Henry Mountains dominate the horizon to the northwest of the upper end of Lake Powell and furnish their own special kind of recreation. The dry, rugged character of the Henrys have kept them in a wild, natural state. Thousands of acres around the two highest peaks in the range, Mount Ellen and Mount Pennell, have been proposed for wilderness designation. John Wesley Powell named the range after Professor Joseph Henry of the Smithsonian Institution, one of his supporters. Prospectors have searched the Henrys for gold and other minerals since the turn of the last century. Robbers' Roost, an important stopping point on the famed **Outlaw**

Lake Powell's 1,960 miles of shoreline provide Utahns with a host of recreational opportunities.

Trail that stretched from Canada to Mexico, is found here. The remote canyons also made fine places for cattle rustlers to hide their bounty. The nearby **Dirty Devil River,** which now pours into Lake Powell, received its moniker because Powell and his men claimed "it stinks like a dirty devil." *Maps and hiking information are available at the BLM's Henry Mountain Field Station in Hanksville; 435-542-3461.*

The Utah Division of Wildlife Resources introduced 18 buffalo into the western foothills of the Henrys in 1941. Now hunters harvest surplus animals of what is one of the few wild, free-roaming buffalo herds in the country. In addition, the area is home to mountain lions, mule deer, snipe, chukar, blue grouse, and jackrabbits. Backpackers and four-wheel-drive enthusiasts seeking solitude enjoy dispersed recreation opportunities in this part of the state.

■ MOAB *map pages 228–229, E/F-2*

The town of Moab, with a population of just over 5,000, serves as the tourist hub of southeastern Utah. Though Monticello, Blanding, Bluff, and Mexican Hat to the south all have a few tourist amenities, Moab offers much more than motels, concessionaires, restaurants, and shops. It is, first and foremost, an incomparable base of operations for exploring the extraordinary canyonlands area of southeastern Utah—in particular, Arches and Canyonlands national parks and the La Sal Mountains. It is also the preeminent base of operations for river trips, bicycle excursions, hikes, and four-wheel-drive expeditions through the red-rock country. On top of that, thousands of visitors from all over the United States come for the special yearly events, like the Moab Half-Marathon in March, the Easter Jeep Safari, the Labor Day Jeep Jamboree, 24 Hours of Moab, and the October Fat Tire Festival for mountain bikers.

One word of advice to spring, summer, and fall travelers: arrive early in the day to get lodging or, better yet, make reservations. Though it occasionally snows in the winter and temperatures can dip down below freezing, off-season travelers to this part of Utah generally enjoy relatively mild weather and have trails and canyons to themselves. April and October are ideal months to visit, but they can be crowded, and those who truly don't like to share their outdoor experiences with 4x4s or mountain bikes should skip Easter week, when the Jeep Safari is on, and October during the Fat Tire Festival.

Founded in the 1870s by Mormon farmers and ranchers, after a colonizing mission attempt in 1855 failed, Moab was named for the biblical kingdom at the edge

The Colorado River town of Moab is the gateway to Arches National Park.

of Zion, the promised land. The town itself is located in a green valley on the edge of the Colorado River and is surrounded by high sandstone cliffs. Moab remained a quiet ranching community until the early 1950s, when a uranium boom tripled the town's population in three years and turned old prospectors like the near-legendary Charlie Steen into millionaires overnight. Steen earned and lost a fortune in just a few years. His home, named Mi Vida after the mine that made him rich, sits high above town and now houses a restaurant with a scenic view, the **Sunset Grill** (see page 306). The town also became a center of potash mining, but as is the case in many mining ventures, the boom went bust and Moab turned to tourism for its survival.

Scenic country with a Western flavor helped turn Moab into a movie center. John Wayne films like *Rio Grande* and *The Comancheros,* the biblical movie *The Greatest Story Ever Told* with Max von Sydow, and, more recently, *Indiana Jones and The Last Crusade, Thelma and Louise, City Slickers II,* and *Geronimo* were filmed in the area.

While Moab is most known for its recreational opportunities, it is also home to the **Moab Music Festival,** which has been held every year since 1992. Performers come from all over the world to perform in a variety of Moab area venues, including a pavilion on the banks of the Colorado River and a concert tent tucked into the red rocks of canyon country. A special fund-raising performance occurs 33 miles downriver on the Colorado. Performers and attendees float downstream on a jet-boat and enjoy classical music in a natural amphitheater with stunning acoustics, while red-tailed hawks soar above. The main festival is held in September, but a June river concert is a special treat too. *435-259-7003.*

The **Moab Arts Festival** fills the Swanney City Park each year on Memorial Day weekend with artists and artisans from across the West. The springtime weather often affords opportunities for recreation as well as art. *435-259-2742.*

First-time visitors to Moab should stop first at the **Moab Information Center** for free brochures on Moab-area movie locations, walking tours of the city, car tours, restaurants, mountain bike trails, jeep trails, rental equipment, winter activities, hiking trails, and other kinds of recreation. *Main and Center Streets; 435-259-8825 or 800-635-6622.*

■ Moab Recreation

Mountain Biking

Moab's reputation as the mountain-bike capital of the world is well-established. Some feel this town is to mountain biking what Aspen, Colorado, is to skiing. The first thing one will likely notice when driving toward this town is the number of mountain bikes being hauled on the top of automobiles and trucks. Though **Rim Cyclery** (94 West First North; 435-259-5333) was among the first to recognize Moab's mountain biking potential, many other shops in town rent bikes and offer information. The **Slickrock Bicycle Trail,** originally designated for use by trail machines and motorcycles, has been taken over by mountain bikers who enjoy the challenges of riding their all-terrain bicycles over the pale orange Navajo sandstone petrified dunes. The area is almost entirely devoid of vegetation and provides excellent traction for trail bikes. A 2.3-mile practice loop will give you a good idea of whether your skills will stand up to the challenge of the full route, which is 10.3 miles long and most suitable for advanced riders. Overlooks at Updraft Arch, Negro Bill Canyon, Shrimp Rock, Abyss Viewpoint, and the aptly named Echo Point provide glimpses of the Colorado River, the La Sal Mountains, and Arches National Park.

The four-wheel-drive roads and trails enjoyed by off-roaders for years also provide excellent overnight or all-day mountain-biking potential. The White Rim Trail in Canyonlands National Park, Monitor and Merrimac, Kane Creek Canyon Rim, Pritchett Canyon, Hurrah Pass, and the Gemini Bridges all provide challenging adventures.

River Rafting

Moab has long served as a base for river-running adventure. Day and night jet-boat trips and one-day rafting trips make seeing the canyons relatively easy, but to really get to know the country, a longer expedition is in order. Most Colorado River trips into Cataract and Westwater canyons begin in Moab. A three-day Cataract Canyon trip will give you the thrill of shooting some of North America's most difficult rapids; you can also swim in the river, camp under the stars, explore side canyons on foot, and enjoy the hospitality and knowledge of a seasoned guide. Some trips include a scenic flight back to Moab from Lake Powell.

4x4 Adventures

Thousands of miles of old cattle and mining roads, many unmaintained relics from the past, offer some excellent, rugged, four-wheel-drive experiences. If you like a challenge for your machine, this is the place. The old jeeper's creed of "never move a rock if you can drive around it—or over it" certainly applies on dozens of routes. Rental vehicles and guided trips are available in Moab. Also keep an eye out in town for Fran Barnes's books and maps, which are among the best for the backcountry driver.

Hiking

The scenic route between Moab and Cisco, UT 128, crosses the Colorado River north of **Fisher Towers**. The towers, isolated remnants of a 225-million-year-old floodplain, gained some fame in 1964 and 1974 when helicopters placed cars atop the pinnacles to make some automobile commercials. A 2.2-mile hiking trail around the base of the towers takes about three hours to complete.

Hikers should also investigate the uncrowded trails that cross the country around Moab outside the boundaries of Arches and Canyonlands national parks. **Portal Overlook, Corona** and **Bowtie arches, Mill Creek Canyon, Negro Bill Canyon, Hidden Valley,** and **Hunters Canyon** often reward explorers with contemplative solitude. Listen to the wind as it whistles through Corona Arch at sunset; it's an almost unearthly experience.

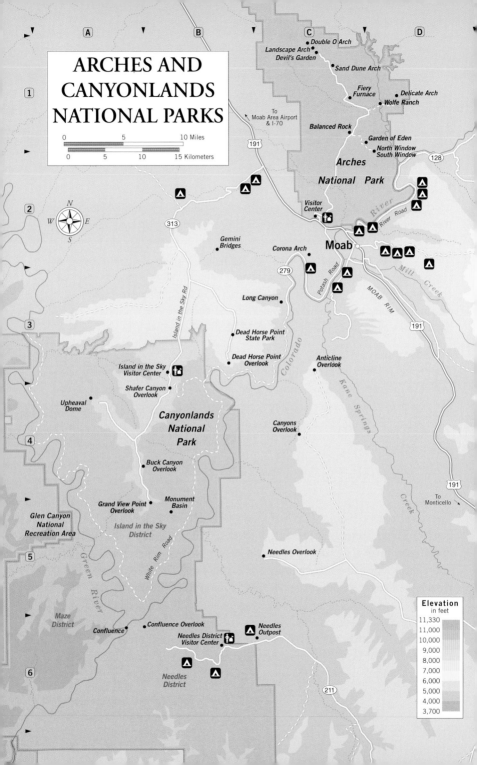

ARCHES AND CANYONLANDS NATIONAL PARKS

0   5   10 Miles

0   5   10   15 Kilometers

A   B   C   D

Double O Arch

Landscape Arch
Devil's Garden

Sand Dune Arch

Fiery
Furnace

Delicate Arch

Wolfe Ranch

To
Moab Area Airport
& I-70

Balanced Rock

191

Garden of Eden

North Window
South Window

128

Arches

National   Park

313

Visitor
Center

River

River Road

Moab

Gemini
Bridges

Corona Arch

279

Potash Road

Long Canyon

Island in the Sky Rd

Dead Horse Point
State Park

Dead Horse Point
Overlook

Colorado

Anticline
Overlook

Kane Springs

MOAB RIM

Mill Creek

191

Island in the Sky
Visitor Center

Shafer Canyon
Overlook

Upheaval
Dome

Canyonlands
National
Park

Buck Canyon
Overlook

Canyons
Overlook

Glen Canyon
National
Recreation Area

Grand View Point
Overlook

Monument
Basin

Island in the Sky
District

White Rim Road

Green River

191
To
Monticello

Creek

Needles Overlook

Maze
District

Confluence

Confluence Overlook

Needles District
Visitor Center

Needles
Outpost

Needles
District

211

Elevation
in feet

11,330
11,000
10,000
9,000
8,000
7,000
6,000
5,000
4,000
3,700

N
W   E
S

1

2

3

4

5

6

■ ARCHES NATIONAL PARK   *map pages 228–229, E-1; and page 248*

The late Edward Abbey—legendary iconoclast, cynic, and author of some of the best essays and fiction written about the deserts of southern Utah—wrote his most famous book, *Desert Solitaire*, while working as a seasonal park ranger at Arches National Park. He awoke the first day of his job and wrote: "This is the most beautiful place on earth."

Just driving into the entrance of the park, four miles north of Moab, is a thrilling introduction to what lies ahead. The park contains more than 2,000 natural arches, more than any other area in the world. The arches were created by the effect of wind and rain on Entrada sandstone, which was laid down as coastal sand dunes some 150 million years ago. Every year, more than half a million people come here for the spectacular scenery and the simple joys of hiking through soft sand and over slickrock.

Arches National Park is divided into six sections: Courthouse Towers, The Windows, Delicate Arch, Fiery Furnace, Klondike Bluffs, and Devil's Garden. Even lazy walkers can enjoy some of the park's trails, which for the most part are short, easy, and interesting. One of the best introductions to the park is the 2.5-hour, 2-mile ranger-led walk through the **Fiery Furnace**. Winding their way through a maze of narrow canyons, many hikers lose all sense of direction within moments and express relief that the ranger knows where he is going. Or does he? In places, visitors must squeeze through narrow spots on the trail, their bodies touching the walls on both sides.

Even toddlers enjoy short walks through **The Windows.** A quarter-mile hike in this section leads to **Double Arch,** which appeared in *Indiana Jones and the Last Crusade.* Another favorite kids' hike is **Sand Dune Arch,** a 4-mile trek through a narrow canyon. Beneath the arch is a large sand dune. Children have been known to spend an enchanted day playing in the trail's fine, pink sand.

The longest series of maintained trails in Arches can be enjoyed in the **Devil's Garden** area at the end of the paved road, just north of the campground. The 5-mile loop trail, with only a gentle 200-foot gain in elevation, leads through narrow fins to **Double O Arch** and **Landscape Arch.** At 291 feet long and 188 feet high, Landscape is the longest span in the park and the second longest in the world. No fewer than 60 arches, in fact, are found in this area. Take time to enjoy views of the fins, Salt Wash, and the La Sal Mountains along the way.

WOLFE RANCH

When John Wesley Wolfe left Ohio to move to what is now Arches National Park in 1889, he left behind his wife, his daughter, and grandchildren. Wolfe hoped his family might want to join him as soon as he built a house and got settled on the ranch, but his letters home did little more than discourage them.

"We have started a cattle spread in the Utah desert," Grandpa wrote. "We call it the $\overline{DX}$ (pronounced Bar DX). Fred and I live in a little log house on the bank of a wash that is sometimes dry, sometimes flooded from bank to bank with roaring muddy water.

We are surrounded with rocks—gigantic red-rock formations, massive arches and weird figures, the like of which you've never seen. . . .

The desert is hot in summer, cold in winter. The air is so dry, your lips parch. Sometimes a sudden sand storm threatens to blow our cabin down. But you should see it when it does rain! Waterfalls pour off every cliff. It is a sight to behold!

It is quiet and peaceful here," Grandpa Wolfe's letter continued. "The DX Ranch is a day's ride from the nearest store. . . . "

That was enough for Grandma Wolfe. Never, she vowed, never would she move her children to that isolated, primitive land!

—Maxine Newell, *A Story of Life at Wolfe Ranch,* no date

While Mrs. Wolfe never made the trip west to live, Wolfe's daughter, Flora, his son-in-law, Ed Stanley, and his two grandchildren, Esther and Ferol, did join him and his son Fred. For three years the family lived on the isolated ranch, but by 1908 Esther was 10 and a formal education was long overdue. The young family moved to Moab before finally returning to Ohio in 1910. John Wesley Wolfe sold his ranch and returned with them.

There is probably no other hike in the world as spectacular as the trek to **Delicate Arch.** The arch, once dubbed "The Schoolmarm's Bloomers" by local cowboys, graces the covers of many Utah books and is the star attraction of Arches National Park. The improbable natural wonder is a freestanding arch of salmon-colored sandstone, about 65 feet high, and with an opening nearly 35 feet wide. The rigorous, shadeless 1.5-mile trail that leads to it begins at the historic **Wolfe Ranch,** built by Civil War veteran John Wesley Wolfe, who tried to make a living out of this desolate country in the late 1800s. The beauty of the hike is that the arch itself isn't visible until the last possible second. Viewing it for the first time can be compared to seeing the Statue of Liberty for the first time—a stunning sight that almost takes your breath away. Visitors tend to sit for hours contemplating the view in wonder and awe, especially at sunset, when the light and shadows play tricks with the arch and the natural amphitheater around it. *Arches National Park Visitor Center is 5 miles north of Moab on U.S. 191; 435-719-2299.*

■ CANYONLANDS NATIONAL PARK *map pages 228–229, E-3; and page 248*

Edward Abbey described the Canyonlands country of southeastern Utah best when he called the place "the least inhabited, least developed, least improved, least civilized, most arid, most hostile, most lonesome, most grim bleak barren desolate and savage quarter of the state of Utah—the best part by far."

In terms of sheer acreage, Canyonlands is the largest of Utah's five national parks. First designated as a park in 1964, it was expanded to its present size in 1971. It is the least developed and most difficult to tour.

The park is divided into three principal districts. Island in the Sky is a broad, level mesa wedged between the Green and Colorado rivers. It serves as a kind of observation platform for the other two wards of this rugged park: the Needles District and the Maze District. A separate chunk of parkland, the Horseshoe Canyon Unit, lies northwest of the main body of the park.

Check with the visitors centers for information on overnight backpacking, mountain biking, and four-wheel trip permits. Park headquarters is in Moab, 2282 SW Resource Boulevard; 435-719-2313. There are visitors centers in the Needles and Island in the Sky districts, and at Hans Flat Ranger Station in the Maze District.

■ ISLAND IN THE SKY *map page 248, A/B–3 to 5*

The park's **Island in the Sky District** is reached by UT 313, which runs west from its junction with U.S. 191, 6 miles north of the turnoff to Arches National Park. One spur of UT 313 leads to Dead Horse Point State Park; the other leads into Canyonlands to the Island in the Sky Visitor Center and beyond.

You can survey much of the park from the **Grand View Point Overlook**. On a quiet, cold winter morning, the distant peaks of the La Sal, Henry, and Abajo mountains stand like snow-covered sentinels in the midst of twisting, convoluted

A view toward the Maze from the Green River Overlook in Island in the Sky.

canyons. To the south, the Needles jut like monoliths erected by some ancient culture. Rock formations with descriptive names like Lizard Rock, the Doll House, Chocolate Drops, the Maze, and the Golden Stairs rise up in the southern background near the canyon of the Colorado River. Take some time to be alone in this outpost, to contemplate the vast tract of wilderness below you.

Long hiking trails and rugged dirt roads lead down to the **White Rim Trail**, remote arches, and interesting side canyons. Only the hardiest backpackers and experienced four-wheel-drive enthusiasts should attempt these routes. Everyone else can enjoy shorter hikes into places like Mesa Arch, Whale Rock, and Upheaval Dome.

Do you enjoy a mystery? Then come up with your own theory of how **Upheaval Dome** was formed. The latest thinking is that this 3-mile-long, 1,200-foot-deep crater in the Island in the Sky District may have been caused by a meteorite, but other scientists theorize that it is a collapsed salt dome. Before coming up with your own theory, you may want to hike the 8-mile trail that completely surrounds the crater.

The eastern spur of UT 313 leads to **Dead Horse Point State Park,** stopping short of Canyonlands National Park. Dead Horse Point is a promontory standing 2,000 feet above the Colorado River and offering a magnificent view. Standing on the edge of this cliff gives a perspective on the depth, size, and majesty of the canyon country. Cowboys used to trap wild mustangs on the promontory by closing off the narrow neck of the formation. According to one legend, the gate was once left open so a band of corralled mustangs could return to the range. Instead, they remained on the point, dying of thirst within sight of the river below; hence the name of Dead Horse Point. The state park has a visitors center and a campground. *On UT 313, 35 miles southwest of Moab; 435-259-2614 or 800-322-3770 for camping reservations.*

Traveling south from Moab toward the **Needles District,** you'll come to the turnoff (32 miles south of Moab) to **Needles Overlook Road,** which takes you to **Needles Overlook.** The view of the district from here is simply staggering, well worth the detour.

Seven miles farther along on U.S. 191, UT 211 heads west toward the **Needles District Visitor Center.** Along the way it passes **Newspaper Rock,** managed by the Bureau of Land Management. This wall of sandstone is covered with Indian petroglyphs that date as far back as 1,500 years ago. Several theories have been proposed to explain the meaning of the rock graphics. Contemporary Indians recognize some symbols; the Hopi, for instance, still use some in their religious ceremonies. Some graphics have been found to have direct connections to astrological occurrences; archaeologists have used others as maps to find water. The strange anthropomorphic figures have also been interpreted as records of extraterrestrial visits. Or was all this writing simply the doodling of passers-by, like the graffiti of our time? Form your own conclusions. *On UT 211, 12 miles west of U.S. 191; 435-587-2141.*

■ NEEDLES DISTRICT *map page 248, A/B-6*
The Needles District is an amazing landscape of wind-carved sandstone fins and spires. Plan on spending a day or two here camping in their midst and hiking to **Roadside Ruin, Cave Spring,** or **Pothole Point.** Lovers of cowboy lore should visit the reconstructed line camp next to Cave Spring.

Few 4x4 drivers will ever forget an expedition over **Elephant Hill,** one of the wildest, roughest, most challenging stretches of "road" in the entire West. Narrow

EDWARD ABBEY'S CANYON COUNTRY

The canyon country of southern Utah and northern Arizona—the Colorado Plateau—is something special. Something strange, marvelous, full of wonders. As far as I know there is no other region on earth much like it, or even remotely like it. . . . Nowhere else have we had this lucky combination of vast sedimentary rock formations exposed to a desert climate, a great plateau carved by major rivers—the Green, the San Juan, the Colorado—into such a surreal land of form and color. Add a few volcanoes, the standing necks of which can still be seen, and cinder cones and lava flows, and at least four separate laccolithic mountain ranges nicely distributed about the region and more hills, holes, humps and hollows, reefs, folds, salt domes, swells and grabens, buttes, benches, and mesas, synclines, monoclines, and anticlines than you can ever hope to see and explore in one life-time, and you begin to arrive at an approximate picture of the plateau's surface appearance. . . . The canyon country does not always inspire love. To many it appears barren, hostile, repellent—a fearsome land of rock and heat, sand dunes and quicksand, cactus, thornbush, scorpion, rattlesnake and agoraphobic distances. To those who see our land in that manner, the best reply is, yes, you are right, it is a dangerous and terrible place. Enter at your own risk. Carry water. Avoid the noonday sun. Try to ignore the vultures. Pray frequently.

—Edward Abbey, *The Journey Home*, 1977

slots barely wide enough for a vehicle to get through, silver stairs of sheer rock, and steep inclines force off-roaders to put their machines in the lowest possible gear. At one point in the 10-mile loop, four-wheel-drives are forced to back to the edge of a steep cliff in order to make the turn.

■ **MAZE DISTRICT** *map page 248, A-5/6*
The remote Maze District, located on the west side of the Colorado River, can be reached only by jouncing over some 60 miles of dirt road branching off UT 24 near the Goblin Valley State Park turnoff. Only hikers and four-wheel-drive vehicles should attempt the last few miles.

Few hikes anywhere compare with a turn through the Maze. If you hike into this pristine area, bring a good topographical map and know how to read it. This is difficult, seldom-traveled country.

■ **Horseshoe Canyon Unit** *map pages 228–229, D-2*
The road to the Maze passes through a section of Canyonlands National Park detached from the main body of the park: the Horseshoe Canyon Unit. Some of North America's most outstanding ancient Indian rock art can be found here in the **Great Gallery.** The huge, ghost-like pictographs on the canyon walls are believed to have been made by a culture predating the Ancestral Puebloans.

Many people, upon seeing the Great Gallery for the first time, stop in their tracks and gasp. Life-sized apparitions seem to float out of the wall above your head. The armless, legless figures wear mask-like, ghost-like faces and appear as souls from another world.

Large graceful cottonwoods grow along the trail to the bottom of the canyon. In places the water surfaces to nourish cattails, horsetails, reeds, and willows. Seeping water in occasional alcoves nurses delicate flower gardens and lacy ferns.

■ Mountain Escapes

■ **La Sal Mountains** *map pages 228–229, F-2*
Though desert, vast and dry, seems to dominate the landscape around Moab, just to the east rise the cool, verdant peaks of the La Sal Mountains, proffering summer respite in their forests of aspen and pine. Cleared of snow from May through October, the **La Sal Mountain Loop** transports drivers into the mountains from UT 128 north of Moab and from U.S. 191 to the south. The 60-mile loop takes about four hours to drive. As you gain elevation, the piñon and juniper trees give way first to oak, then to larger pines and aspen, and finally to spruce and fir.

Those planning to explore the La Sal Mountains on foot should stop by the visitor information center in Moab for a copy of the U.S. Forest Service's excellent guide to the range's hiking trails. Many of these were made by miners who explored the country a century ago. *Main and Center Streets; 435-259-8825 or 800-635-6622.*

Increasing numbers of cross-country skiers discover the fine, untracked powder of the La Sals each year. A hut-to-hut system is available for those interested in a multi-day expedition.

(following pages) Hikers at Dead Horse Point State Park.

■ **ABAJO MOUNTAINS** *map pages 228–229, E/F-4*
About 50 miles below Moab, west of Monticello, the **Abajo Mountains** provide another welcome furlough from the desert heat. Also called the Blue Mountains, the Abajos rise to elevations as high as 11,360 feet. The high alpine country here is remote and little visited. The remote **Dark Canyon Wilderness Area** on the western edge of the mountains offers views to the north of the Needles District.

■ **TRAIL OF THE ANCIENTS**

The heart of Ancestral Puebloan country is a vast circle—sometimes referred to as the Grand Circle—embracing the Four Corners area of Utah, Colorado, New Mexico, and Arizona. Within this area thousands of acres of public land have been set aside to preserve Ancestral Puebloans villages and ruins. Visitors can become acquainted with the ancient culture and enjoy some spectacular scenery by following the Trail of the Ancients. The trail has more than one variant, depending on which of numerous Ancestral Puebloan points of interest the visitor wants to see, but it can include UT 95 from Hanksville to Blanding; U.S. 191 between Blanding and Bluff; and U.S. 163 and UT 262 eastward from Bluff to Aneth and on toward Mesa Verde National Park in southwest Colorado. It can also include UT 275 north from UT 95 to Natural Bridges National Monument; UT 261 south from UT 95 towards Mexican Hat and from there U.S. 163 east to Bluff; as well as UT 262 east to Hovenweep National Monument. Brochures can be obtained at any of the sites along the trail.

■ **EDGE OF THE CEDARS** *map pages 228–229, E/F-4/5*
At **Edge of the Cedars State Park** you will find the remains of an immense kiva. Such structures are common around Mesa Verde in Colorado and Chaco Canyon in New Mexico, but the Great Kiva here is the northernmost one of its kind in Utah. It was probably roofed and the roof's flat surface used by many clans for dances and ceremonies. The roof of a smaller kiva nearby has been restored. At Edge of the Cedars you have a chance to actually climb down into the chamber and sit for a moment of contemplation. The park's museum traces the settlement of San Juan County by Ancestral Puebloans, Utes, Navajos, and Euro-American settlers; it also houses one of the largest Ancestral Puebloan pottery collections in the Southwest. You can buy Native American arts and crafts in the museum shop. *660 West 400 North, Blanding; 435-678-2238.*

■ NATURAL BRIDGES NATIONAL MONUMENT

map pages 228–229, E-4

This national monument is famous for three impressive natural bridges spanning White Canyon. A 9-mile loop road connects the three, which have Hopi names: **Kachina,** a representation of Hopi gods; **Owachomo,** a flat-rock mound; and **Sipapu,** the gateway to this world from the other world below. Dwelling sites of Ancestral Puebloans have been found at the monument, and it's easy to see why they wanted to live here. The trail down to White Canyon leads through a desert garden. A stream runs through the bottom of the canyon, and tracks of coyote, ringtail cat, deer, and other small game line its banks. **Horsecollar Ruin,** an Ancestral Puebloan site (so named because the doorways to two of its structures resemble horsecollars), is accessible from the trail between Sipapu and Kachina bridges.

President Theodore Roosevelt established the national monument in 1908 after *National Geographic* magazine publicized the three great bridges. Unfortunately, fame also brought vandalism, as it does all too often today. Consider the story told by Zeke Johnson, who was the custodian of the monument in 1926:

> A group of boys was going out to the bridges from Blanding, and I told them not to scratch their names on rocks inside the monument. One man who went along with the boys (I will just call him John Doe) told his boy that man Zeke Johnson had no police authority over those rocks, and he and his son wrote their names on top of Sipapu Bridge and dug it deep.
>
> Well, of course I explained the law and told him to get back out and rub it off, and he told me to go "places." The invitation to go some place was repeated several times, and I found it necessary to write to the director of national parks in Washington, D.C. The defendant got a letter telling him that unless he immediately complied with Custodian Johnson's instructions he would have a ride at his own expense from Blanding to Washington, D.C., to be arraigned before the U.S. Government. He soon hunted me up and asked what he should do. I said just do as I told you, track back out there and take off those initials. He offered me twenty bucks if I would do it, but I told him nobody could do it but him, and it was a five-day horseback trip in those days. Since then he has been a help

to me. Several initial-cutters have been caught, and when they tried to lobby with me I just told them to step across the street and talk with Mr. John Doe. I can't give you chapter and verse, but the law is very plain, and I am obliged to enforce it.

On UT 95, 40 miles west of Blanding; 435-692-1234.

■ **GRAND GULCH PRIMITIVE AREA** *map pages 228–229, D-5*
The Grand Gulch area, south of the Natural Bridges National Monument, preserves a winding, many-fingered canyon where numerous rock art panels can be found along the walls. Archaeologists have determined that the area was occupied by the Ancestral Puebloans as early as A.D. 200, though it was apparently then abandoned and reoccupied two centuries later.

If you're planning to explore Grand Gulch, it's wise to check in with the Kane Gulch Ranger Station or call the BLM Monticello Field Office (see page 325). *On UT 261, 4 miles south of UT 95.*

■ **BLUFF** *map pages 228–229, E/F-5/6*
Bluff, 27 miles south of Blanding, is a small Utah town on the Trail of the Ancients. Nearly every cliff or canyon slope within a 50-mile radius of town harbors some sign of its ancient inhabitants. Visitors should be aware of hazards when exploring Indian dwellings here. Many archaeological sites are located in inaccessible cliffs, and people have been injured trying to climb into ruins by treacherous routes. Rattlesnakes and scorpions can be found in this part of the country, too, so go slow and be observant. Backcountry trails and roads can become treacherous in a flash flood.

Guided tours of the backcountry by foot or four-wheel-drive are available at Recapture Lodge Tours in Bluff, and to the south at Goulding's Trading Post near Monument Valley Navajo Park.

■ **HOVENWEEP NATIONAL MONUMENT** *map pages 228–229, F-5*
Hovenweep, 42 miles south of Bluff, is a curiosity in the Ancestral Puebloan world because of its distinctive square towers—the Ancestral Puebloans usually built round towers. Six separate ruined settlements are found here.

Deep alcoves such as this one offered natural protection to Ancestral Puebloans seeking shelter.

The Mystery of Everett Ruess

In January of 1931 19-year-old Everett Ruess hitchhiked from his home in Los Angeles to Monument Valley, which straddles the border of Utah and Arizona.

Ruess wandered the deserts and canyons in southern Utah and northern Arizona, painting, writing letters home, and absorbing the landscape, which he found "fiercely, overpoweringly beautiful." He made his way by trading his art or poetry for food, sometimes picking up an odd job here and there.

He interrupted his journey in 1932 to return to Los Angeles, but found himself becoming increasingly disconsolate with city life. In the spring of 1934, he returned to his beloved desert. He wrote to a friend, "Once more I am roaring drunk with the lust of life and adventure and unbearable beauty."

Ruess's fascinating journeys in Navajoland and the canyons of southern Utah are captured in letters he sent home to his family. They are collected in the book *A Vagabond for Beauty*. His last letter home was posted to his brother on November 11, 1934, from Escalante, Utah.

"As to when I when I shall visit civilization, it will not be soon, I think. I have not tired of the wilderness; rather I enjoy its beauty and the vagrant life I lead, more keenly all the time. I prefer the saddle to the streetcar and star-sprinkled sky to a roof, the obscure and difficult trail, leading into the unknown, to any paved highway, and the deep peace of the wild to the discontent bred by cities."

On November 19, 1934, Everett said goodbye to the friends he had met in Escalante and set out with his burros. In Soda Gulch he encountered a couple of sheepherders and spent two nights with them before heading south to paint at Hole-in-the-Rock, on the historic Mormon Trail.

Everett's parents did not expect to hear from him for two months, but when three months had passed, they wrote a letter to the postmaster in Escalante. All of Escalante, especially those residents who had spent time with Everett, were propelled into the search for the friendly, albeit unusual, young man.

In Davis Gulch they quickly found Everett's two burros in a small corral he had constructed. They followed his tracks and found that they led out of the canyon on an old Indian trail before dead-ending at a place only scaleable by an agile human being. Here they found only milk cans, candy wrappers, and impressions in the sand where he had laid his bedroll. His bedroll itself, his cook kit, paintings and supplies, journal, and money were not found.

All newspaper accounts suggest that Everett fell to his death into a deep crevice where he could not be found. Indeed, the tortured landscape and maze of cliffs, canyons, and boulders made this a realistic assumption. Even Everett had written

Everett Ruess and his traveling companions.

earlier of his own "reckless self confidence": "Hundreds of times I have trusted my life to crumbling sandstone and nearly vertical angles in the search for water or cliff dwellings."

The missing camp supplies remain a key ingredient to the mystery. Some speculate that one of the searchers found them and hid the discovery so he could keep the Navajo rug and money; other theories suggest that they were stolen from his camp by wandering cowboys even before the burros were found by searchers.

Most residents of Escalante thought rustlers were probably involved in the young man's disappearance. Cattle rustling was common along the Escalante River, and just prior to Everett's arrival there, rumors began circulating that local cattle owners had hired an undercover agent to obtain evidence. Did Everett innocently wander into the midst of a cattle crime and end up dead at the hands of bad guys? Many locals believed so, but the possibility of foul play was never seriously investigated.

In 1957 archaeologists came across some camp remains in Cottonwood Canyon, 10 miles southwest of Davis Gulch. Among the equipment was a box of razor blades from the Owl Drug Company in Los Angeles. While the scientists thought for sure they had found Everett's gear, his mother could not positively identify any of the items. The lower portion of the canyon and the old campsite are now filled by the waters of Lake Powell.

The mystery of Everett Ruess is still a topic of conversation into the 21st century. What is known about him is that he wanted to wander as long as he lived. He wrote of his own death:

"When the time comes to die, I will find the wildest, loneliest, most desolate spot there is."

Indeed, Everett Ruess had wandered into—and never returned from—a place that remains one of the largest wild areas in the continental United States.

—Janet Lowe

Boulder House in Hovenweep National Monument was occupied by the Ancestral Puebloans around A.D. 900.

Hovenweep, a Ute word meaning "deserted valley," was inhabited by Ancestral Puebloans who migrated from Mesa Verde, nearly 100 miles to the east, around A.D. 900. Perhaps they were migrants, maybe even outcasts. They lived in scattered villages and cultivated corn, beans, squash, and melons. Studies of tree rings have allowed archaeologists to determine that by 1200, annual rainfall had decreased substantially, prompting the Indians to abandon the outlying farm villages and rebuild new ones near canyons with permanent springs. The style of the towers and the location of the dwellings in the cliffs suggest that the inhabitants of

Hovenweep may also have been preparing for attack by other Ancestral Puebloan clans or Shoshone raiders looking for food and water. Each tower contained only one small doorway protected by a parapet. Most towers also have peepholes pointing outward—away from the canyon.

Archaeologists have offered another theory concerning the use of the towers. At least three sites at the monument, including the major ruin, **Square Tower,** may have been used as observatory sites. Certain windows in the towers are situated in such a way that sunlight enters only during the summer and winter solstices and the autumn and vernal equinoxes, striking particular points marked on the interior walls.

When the last springs dried up, Hovenweep's Ancestral Puebloans were forced to leave, archaeologists surmise, and join the Zuni Pueblo in western New Mexico. By 1300, the Hovenweep region was deserted. *20 miles north of Aneth; 970-562-4282.*

■ **MONUMENT VALLEY** *map pages 228–229, D/E-6*
Famous the world over, the majestic buttes of Monument Valley are another wonderful example of Utah's geological patrimony. The valley's unique rock formations have served as the backdrops for many famous Western movies—you fully expect John Wayne to ride by at any moment. Traditional Navajo hogans dot the landscape, because Monument Valley occupies part of the 16-million-acre **Navajo Indian Reservation,** which covers large areas of Arizona and New Mexico and also reaches into Utah's rugged southeastern corner. In addition to visiting **Goulding's Trading Post** (435-727-3231), be sure to drive the 14-mile loop road through the **Monument Valley Navajo Tribal Park,** a 30,000-acre area that has some of the best-known monuments. Or go to the visitors center and join one of the Navajo-guided tours, which will take you to areas not otherwise open to visitors. *Off U.S. 163, 21 miles south of Mexican Hat, at the Utah-Arizona border; 435-727-5870.*

■ **FOUR CORNERS MONUMENT** *map pages 228–229, F-6*
The Navajos also manage the entrance to the small Four Corners Monument, the only place in the United States where a visitor can stand in one spot and be in four states—Utah, New Mexico, Colorado, and Arizona. Besides the marker, there's also a visitors center here, as well as a demonstration center where Navajo artists, potters, rug weavers, silversmiths, and other jewelers sell their crafts. *For information, call the Navajo Nation Parks and Recreation Department: 928-871-6647.*

S K I I N G   U T A H
T H E   G R E A T E S T   S N O W   O N   E A R T H

The snowstorm raged through much of the night, dumping prodigious amounts of fluffy powder on ski slopes throughout Utah. Cars full of skiers anxiously waited for the canyon roads to be cleared and for the avalanche rangers to declare the resorts safe.

As the roads opened, the skies began to clear. A few clouds rolled off to the eastern horizon just as the sun peeked over the mountain, bathing the ski slopes in light. Skiers quickly unloaded their cars, buckled their boots, snapped into their bindings, and hopped aboard the chairlifts. The untouched powder was knee deep. This was the kind of day Utah skiers love.

There is a certain magic surrounding Utah ski resorts that has its source in what many have called the best-quality skiing snow in the world. And there's a reason Utah's snow conditions are often better than those in surrounding states. According to National Weather Service personnel in Salt Lake City, most of the winter storms that affect Utah have their origins in the northern Pacific Ocean. The storms move southeastward across the Sierra Nevada and Cascade mountains, where they lose some of their moisture. When they hit the high Wasatch and Utah's south-central mountains, orographic lifting (induced by the presence of mountains) occurs and squeezes out much of the moisture. This is what produces the colder, drier powder for which Utah is noted.

The secret of Utah's uniquely wonderful powder is the structure of the individual snow crystals. Under cold, relatively dry conditions, light crystal-type snowflakes called dendrites are produced. These snowflakes are thin and symmetrical in shape, and they float down through the cold atmosphere, accumulating like fluffy down or powder on Utah's mountains. Often cold northwest winds will follow a storm and prolong this powdery snowfall over the higher mountains. When deep enough, the powder gives skiers the feeling they are floating on air as they ski down—and that's what makes the Greatest Snow on Earth.

Visitors to the Wasatch Front have a choice of 11 ski resorts, all within an hour's drive of the airport. In addition, hundreds of roads in the national forests are ideal

At Brian Head Resort in southern Utah.

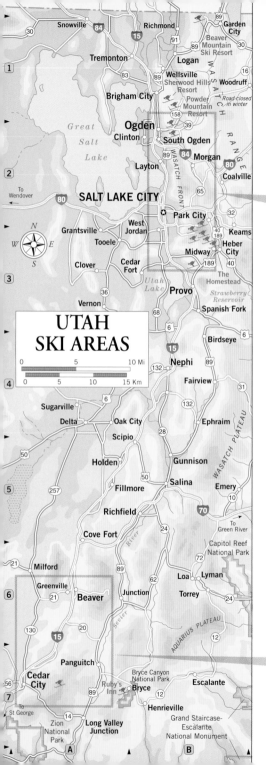

UTAH
SKI AREAS

0   5   10 Mi
0   5   10   15 Km

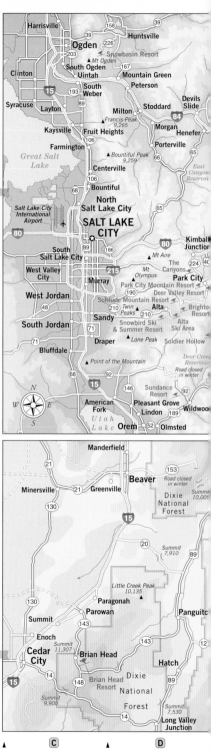

for cross-country skiing. Contact Ski Utah for the *Utah Winter Vacation Planner*. It contains information on specific resorts as well as on lodging, ski pass rates, seasons, hours, and other important details. *150 West 500 South, Salt Lake City, UT, 84101; 801-534-1779; www.skiutah.com.*

■ HISTORY OF SKIING IN UTAH

Skiing began in Utah during the early 1900s, when a few miners and trappers adopted skis to get around the mountains during winter. Robert F. Marvin was one of the few miners to leave a first-hand account of early ski equipment and technique. "Let me tell you about Alta, before it became effete and a play-place for kids, before it was converted from a mining camp to a ski resort," wrote Marvin in an unpublished manuscript. "Let me tell you of the men who lived and labored there, of men who plied their trades as miners, as haulers of ore and freight, as hewers of wood. Let me describe the lives they lived and the works they wrought with strong backs and calloused hands and precious little help from things mechanical."

Alta was not in those days a ski resort. There were no hotels, no accommodations—and almost no skis. In 1916 the onset of winter found exactly two pairs of skis in the camp, not counting the stubby, broad and double-edged skis the Finlander miners brought in from the old country. I had to send far away for my first pair, all the way to St. Paul, where someone had begun to manufacture them. When the skis came, they were hickory, thick and heavy and exactly 11 feet long. The thinking was that the longer the skis were the better they would ride atop the snow and not sink in. I was about the only person in camp long-legged enough to make a kick turn with them, and it was an effort like a high-kickin' chorus girl's. Ski poles we had none; they were to us an unknown. Instead, we had a single long pole, usually cut from creek-side brush, preferably water birch because the bark was so smooth. This pole we used like an oar or gee-pole, always on the uphill side, right or left. Also, there was no ski harness, only a leather toe-strap (sometimes tied to the ankle with a short length of cord to prevent the skis going home by themselves in case of a tumble). With this primitive gear, we "rowed" ourselves uphill and down to all the places your tows and lifts take you now, and beyond; to the top of Baldy on occasion.

A ski jumper at Ecker Hill, near Salt Lake City, in 1933.

The Utah ski industry grew from these humble beginnings. Alta, the second-oldest resort in the United States (behind Sun Valley, Idaho), constructed its first lift in 1938. It was followed by Snowbasin in Ogden Canyon and Brighton in Big Cottonwood Canyon. Construction of the huge Park City complex—one of the few Utah resort areas that can compare in size and scope to Colorado's Aspen and Vail or California's Mammoth Mountain—started in 1963. The Canyons and the exclusive Deer Valley followed, as did other Wasatch Front resorts, like Robert Redford's Sundance, east of Provo; Powder Mountain, in Ogden Valley; Solitude, in Big Cottonwood Canyon; and Beaver Mountain, in Logan Canyon. Snowbird, a huge, modern complex located below Alta in Little Cottonwood Canyon, appeared on the scene in the early 1970s, bringing with it an often acrimonious debate over how much development should take place in the canyons east of Salt Lake City. Organizers of the 2002 Winter Olympics kept the Games out of Salt Lake City's watershed and the resorts in Big and Little Cottonwood canyons, but the debate continues over how much development is a good thing in the Wasatch canyons. Development and ski resort expansion has slowed considerably since the Olympics.

Each Utah resort occupies its own niche. The giant resorts, such as Park City, Deer Valley, and The Canyons, rank with the top ski areas in the world in terms of facilities, number of runs, and nightlife. Smaller resorts, such as Beaver Mountain, Brighton, and Alta, bring to mind simpler times in the ski business when only the quality of the snow and the ski runs seemed important.

Ticket price ranges are listed in this book as:
inexpensive = under $35; **moderate** = $35–50; **expensive** = over $50.

■ LITTLE COTTONWOOD CANYON   *map page 268, D-3*

Little Cottonwood Canyon is just a short drive east of Salt Lake City. Alta and Snowbird, the two resorts located just a few miles from one another at the top of Little Cottonwood Canyon, could not be more different.

■ ALTA   *map page 268, D-3*

With its world-famous powder and comparatively low lift rates, Alta provides a reminder of what skiing in the United States used to be like. Its eight lifts service a mountain that compares favorably with any other ski resort on earth, and its lodges are small, quaint, and few in number.

Even on holiday weekends, when a skier may have to wait in line for 40 minutes before boarding an Alta lift, the wait seems worth the effort. Alta has a well-deserved reputation for having some of the best powder in the world; its moguls, tree skiing, and deep powder challenge even the most expert of skiers. It is also an excellent place for beginners to learn the sport. Its slopes are well-groomed, and the Sunnyside Lift services one of the longest and best beginner slopes in Utah.

Lodging at the resort ranges from elegant to rustic. Alternatively, the Utah Transit Authority bus service, which brings skiers from downtown Salt Lake City to Alta for a small round-trip fare, makes staying in town and then skiing at Alta a relatively easy proposition.

Alta Ski Area

P.O. Box 8007, Alta, UT 84092-8007; 801-742-3333 or 801-359-1078; www.alta.com.

Distance from Salt Lake City airport: 33 miles.

Terrain: 2,200 skiable acres, more than 54 runs: 25 percent rated as beginner, 40 percent intermediate, and 35 percent advanced.

Lifts: One quad, three triples, four doubles, five surface tows.

Snowmaking: 50 acres.

Vertical drop: 2,020 feet.

Top elevation: 10,550 feet.

Ticket prices: Moderate.

Facilities: Child care, ski schools, rental shops.

Dining: Three restaurants on mountain, several base restaurants.

Accommodations: Some small lodges at base. Call 801-359-1078 for information.

Snowboard facilities: None; snowboards are not allowed.

Cross-country skiing: Not groomed, but popular at nearby Albion Basin.

Spring sunrise on Superior Peak as seen from Alta in the Wasatch Mountains.

■ **SNOWBIRD** *map page 268, D-3*

Snowbird is an unabashed giant, working hard to create an image of technological wonder. From the monolithic cement condominiums at the resort base to the gleaming red-and-blue trams that whisk skiers to the top of 11,000-foot Hidden Peak, Snowbird presents itself as a gleaming, well-planned, modern ski area. The shopping centers, restaurants, tennis courts, swimming pools, convention center, spa, and bars reflect the vision of founders Dick Bass and Ted Johnson. Skiers straight off the slopes can head to a spa to enjoy a massage, nail care, herbal wraps, and hair care, or visit the shops, restaurants, bank, post office, laundry, medical clinic, and pharmacy.

Snowbird is a slightly more difficult resort to ski than Alta, although a dual lift ticket allows you access to both resorts. Runs at Snowbird range up to 3.5 miles in length. Only 27 percent of the runs are rated for beginners, with 38 percent for intermediate and 35 percent for experts. Advanced skiers take the tram and the Peruvian and Little Cloud lifts to ski the expert runs. The vertical drop of 3,240 feet is the sharpest at any Utah resort.

Snowbird Ski & Summer Resort
P.O. Box 929000, Snowbird, UT 84092-9000; 800-453-3000 or 800-232-9542; www.snowbird.com.
Distance from Salt Lake City airport: 29 miles.
Terrain: 2,500 skiable acres, more than 89 runs: 27 percent beginner, 38 percent intermediate, 35 percent advanced.
Lifts: One aerial tram, three quads, seven doubles, one rope tow.
Snowmaking: 400 acres.
Vertical drop: 3,240 feet.
Top elevation: 11,000 feet.
Ticket prices: Expensive.
Facilities: Mountain school, ski school, alpine slide (summer), ice skating rink, tubing hill, climbing wall (summer), helicopter skiing.
Dining: 15 eateries on mountain or lodge, from fine dining to burgers and beer.
Accommodations: Four slopeside lodges with 1000 total rooms.
Snowboard facilities: Two terrain parks and one half-pipe.
Cross-country skiing: None.

■ BIG COTTONWOOD CANYON   *map page 268, D-3*

■ BRIGHTON   *map page 268, D-3*

Named after William S. Brighton, who constructed a small hotel in 1874 in Big Cottonwood Canyon, Brighton bills itself as the place where Utah learns to ski. Some have said that people learn to ski at Brighton, enjoy expert powder skiing at other resorts, and then return to Brighton when they get older and their knees start going bad.

Brighton does boast good powder skiing, and about 39 percent of its runs are rated for experts. Powder hounds love blasting through the deep stuff on the Scree run near the Millicent Lift or skiing between the pines under the Snake Creek triple chair after a heavy snowfall. The Crest and Great Western Express quads serve a wide area, all but eliminating lift lines. The resort features the state's best night skiing, good snowboarding, and several trails that connect to its Big Cottonwood neighbor, Solitude.

Brighton Resort
12601 Big Cottonwood Canyon Road, Brighton, UT 84121; 801-532-4731 or 800-873-5512; www.brightonresort.com.
Distance from Salt Lake City airport: 35 miles.
Terrain: 1,050 skiable acres, 66 runs: 21 percent beginner, 40 percent intermediate, 39 percent advanced.
Lifts: Two high-speed quads, two triples, three doubles.
Snowmaking: 200 acres.
Vertical drop: 1,745 feet.
Top elevation: 10,500 feet.
Ticket prices: Moderate.
Facilities: Ski school, rentals, largest night-skiing area in Utah.
Dining: Three small restaurants.
Accommodations: One small lodge.
Snowboard facilities: Three terrain parks, two half-pipes.
Cross-country skiing: Solitude Nordic Center.

Big Cottonwood Canyon in a winter storm.

■ **SOLITUDE** *map page 268, D-3*

Solitude might be described as a poor man's Snowbird. The skiing terrain, like Snowbird's, possesses many mogul-laden hills and places to enjoy great powder after a heavy storm. The resort offers two high-speed quad detachable chairlifts, capable of moving skiers up the mountains twice as fast as a normal chair but slowing to allow them to load and unload. There are also four double chairs and two triple chairs serving 64 different runs.

Solitude was opened in 1957 by a colorful miner named Bob Barrett, an independent sort who believed in doing things his own way. He ran into trouble with Salt Lake City officials trying to protect the Big Cottonwood Canyon watershed, as well as with U.S. Forest Service bureaucrats charged with issuing special-use permits for the part of the resort that rested on federal property. Barrett was a do-it-yourself buff, and his lifts, unique to Solitude, became legendary for both their construction and their numerous breakdowns. Now under new ownership, Solitude's modern base facilities resemble a Swiss village.

Solitude Mountain Resort
12000 Big Cottonwood Canyon, Solitude, UT 84121-0350; 801-534-1400 or 800-748-4754; www.skisolitude.com.
Distance from Salt Lake City airport: 28 miles.
Terrain: 1,200 acres, 64 runs: 20 percent beginner, 50 percent intermediate, 30 percent advanced.
Lifts: Two quads, two triples, four doubles.
Snowmaking: 90 acres.
Vertical drop: 2,047 feet.
Top elevation: 10,035 feet.
Ticket prices: Moderate.
Facilities: Skating rink, mini-movie theater, billiards, kid-friendly gaming room.
Dining: Gourmet eateries on mountain and in Solitude Village, including a ski-in yurt serving five-courses.
Accommodations: The Inn at Solitude Village.
Snowboard facilities: Terrain Park.
Cross-country skiing: Solitude Nordic Center.

■ PARK CITY SKI AREAS *map page 268, D-3*

In the late 1960s, Park City's Main Street was on the verge of turning into a ghost town. Old mining equipment seemed to litter the landscape, the railroad station was abandoned, and wooden shacks clung precariously to the hills. Mining activity in the old community, which had produced some of Utah's richest and most eccentric community leaders, had all but ceased. A few curious tourists made the 32-mile drive from Salt Lake City during the summer to shop for antiques or have a soda at the old fountain and listen to some colorful characters tell stories about the fires, the different cultures, the 30 Main Street saloons, and the wealthy mining magnates that were all part of the history of this place. Fewer than 2,000 residents lived in what had once been a booming town.

What a contrast to the current day's bustling atmosphere. Three of Utah's largest ski areas sit just outside of town: Park City Mountain Resort, The Canyons, and Deer Valley. Though Main Street is still listed on the National Register of Historic Places, the town of Park City has become a huge ski resort, housing some of Utah's poshest eateries. In addition to skiing, visitors now can ride a hot-air balloon, go ice skating, ski cross-country on groomed trails, take a snowmobile journey, or play tennis and racquetball. Live theater performances and the Sundance Film Festival add to the town's allure. In the summer, visitors entertain themselves with golf and miniature golf, bicycling, hiking, and an alpine slide that careens riders down a mountainside on a wheeled car. The Park City Arts Festival in August is one of the biggest events of its kind in the state. The landscape of this once quaint mining town is now dotted with hundreds of condominiums, catering to numerous tastes and incomes brackets. Park City is as close as Utah gets to imitating the atmosphere and nightlife of huge ski areas like Vail, Aspen, or Sun Valley.

In 1923, *The Park Record,* Utah's oldest weekly newspaper, published an article predicting that Park City would turn into a mecca for winter sports. It may have taken three-quarters of a century, but that prediction has become a reality—one that the world discovered during the 2002 Winter Olympics, when Deer Valley hosted the slalom and freestyle ski events, Park City Mountain Resort was the site of snowboarding and the giant slalom Alpine races, and the nearby Utah Winter Sports Park was the site of bobsled, luge, and ski jumping.

Park City's appeal to out-of-state skiers is reflected in its prices. Skiing is more costly here than anywhere else in the state, and the exclusive Deer Valley has among the highest lift ticket prices in the United States.

Surveying the slopes at Park City Mountain Resort.

■ **PARK CITY MOUNTAIN RESORT** *map page 268, D-3*

Park City Mountain Resort is one of Utah's largest. With 14 lifts, it can handle 27,200 skiers an hour on its 100 designated runs, 650 acres of wide-open bowl skiing, and more than 3,300 acres of skiable terrain. Nobody has to ski the same run or use the same lift twice in a day. There are runs catering to children and others for powder hounds; a lift connects the resort to the old part of town. This is the home resort for the United States Ski Team, which has its headquarters in town; the resort hosts international ski and snowboarding races nearly every year.

Park City Mountain Resort
P.O. Box 39, Park City, UT 84060; 435-649-8111 or 800-222-7275; www.parkcitymountain.com.
Distance from Salt Lake City airport: 37 miles.
Terrain: 3,300 acres, 100 runs: 18 percent beginner, 44 percent intermediate, 38 percent advanced.
Lifts: Four six-passenger chairs, one quad, five triples, four doubles, and the "Magic Carpet" in the children's area.

Snowmaking: 500 acres.

Vertical drop: 3,100 feet.

Top elevation: 10,000 feet.

Ticket prices: Expensive.

Facilities: Night skiing, child care, summer fun park, summer alpine slide, ice skating rink, rental shops, large base facility, lift connecting resort to town of Park City.

Dining: Because of lift connection to town of Park City, more than 100 restaurants are available.

Accommodations: Major hotels on site, dozens of condominiums in area.

Snowboard facilities: Four terrain parks including 35 rails and 18 jump features, three half-pipes.

Cross-country skiing: Nearby White Pine Touring Center.

■ **DEER VALLEY** *map page 268, D-3*

Just east of Park City, Deer Valley spoils skiers. *Skiing* magazine has called it "the crème de la crème of ski destinations, devoid of most hassles that vacationing mortals are heir to, with uncrowded runs groomed to silky perfection . . . advanced terrain as good as anywhere . . . a cornucopia of slope-side extras, which in the aggregate spell the difference between routine and luxury."

Even the moguls appear groomed at Deer Valley. Expect help unloading the skis from your vehicle and look for attendants clad in elegant green ski suits to help load you onto the lifts. Deer Valley is a place to beat the holiday crowds, because the number of skiers allowed on the mountain at any given time is limited by a reservation system. Lighted signs advise Deer Valley skiers about lines in the restaurants. Lounge chairs even provide places to recline in the snow during skiing breaks. Don't expect paper plates and plasticware, even in the least expensive cafeterias at the resort—everything is served on china. The Glitretind restaurant in the resort's Stein Erikson Lodge is considered one of Utah's most elegant dining spots.

Those who use Deer Valley's 19 lifts notice a feeling of quiet elegance. Each run seems perfectly groomed. Staffers keep the lifts free of snow and the walkways shoveled, and provide tissue boxes at the bottom of the lifts.

Skiing takes place in five areas—with 15 percent of the runs rated as easy, 50 percent as more difficult, and 35 percent as most difficult. Not many locals can afford the stiff lift-ticket prices at Deer Valley, but the few who splurge enjoy being treated like royalty.

Deer Valley Resort
P.O. Box 1525, Park City, UT 84060; 435-649-1000 or 800-424-3337;
www.deervalley.com.
Distance from Salt Lake City airport: 39 miles.
Terrain: 1,750 skiable acres, 88 runs: 15 percent beginner, 50 percent intermediate, 35 percent advanced.
Lifts: One gondola, seven high-speed quads, two fixed-grip quads, seven triple chairs, two double chairs.
Snowmaking: 500 acres.
Vertical drop: 3,000 feet.
Top elevation: 9,570 feet.
Ticket prices: Expensive.
Facilities: Spa, child care, rentals, ski check-in.
Dining: Three evening restaurants featuring fine dining plus on-mountain dining.
Accommodations: Hotels including the Stein Erikson Lodge and the Goldener Hirsch Inn; condominiums; private homes.
Snowboard facilities: Not allowed.
Cross-country skiing: None.

■ THE CANYONS   *map page 268, D-3*
Situated north of Park City near Snyderville (and once known as Park West, and later as Wolf Mountain), The Canyons has been transformed from a sleepy, inexpensive ski area into Utah's newest mega-resort. In terms of acreage, its 3,500 acres make it Utah's largest ski area.

Those who drive by the resort can only see a small part of the mountain. There are actually 146 runs—the most of any Utah ski area. The Canyons is also at the top of the list for many snowboarders.

The Canyons
4000 The Canyons Resort Drive, Park City, UT 84098; information: 435-649-5400; reservations: 800-226-9667; www.thecanyons.com.
Distance from Salt Lake City airport: 33 miles
Terrain: 3,500 acres, 146 runs: 14 percent beginner, 44 percent intermediate, 42 percent advanced.
Lifts: 11 quads, two triples, one double, two surface tows, one cabriolet.
Snowmaking: 400 acres.

Vertical drop: 3,190 feet.
Top elevation: 9,990 feet.
Ticket prices: Expensive.
Facilities: Child care, retail shops, rentals, spa.
Dining: Three on-mountain restaurants, four restaurants within resort village.
Accommodations: 500 slopeside rooms at Sundial Lodge and Grand Summit Resort Hotel.
Snowboard facilities: Large terrain park, seven half-pipes.
Cross-country skiing: No.

■ SUNDANCE   *map page 268, D-4*
Skiers can explore the many nuances of Utah County's only ski resort for years without catching a glimpse of its famous owner, Robert Redford. Yet Redford's spirit seems to live in every part of Sundance, set on a fine ski hill east of Orem.

In 1969, the actor purchased a tiny ski area in the Uinta Forest called Timphaven. He renamed it after the character he played opposite Paul Newman in the movie *Butch Cassidy and the Sundance Kid,* and slowly turned it into a film and arts center, ski resort, and home. Redford also filmed his 1972 Western about a mountain man, *Jeremiah Johnson,* close to his resort; views of Mount Timpanogos dominate the movie setting as they do Sundance.

Sundance is not a flashy resort—one has to search to find the few condominiums located on the site. The base facilities are quiet and tasteful.

Though relatively small even by Wasatch Front standards, the resort's three lifts lead to more than 40 trails on 450 acres. Beginners can find places to fit their abilities at Sundance, but the terrain also challenges good skiers, especially after a heavy snowfall. As a rule, the higher the elevation of the lift at Sundance, the more difficult the runs.

Sundance Resort
R.R. 3, Box A-1, Sundance, UT 84604; information: 801-225-4107; reservations: 800-892-1600; www.sundanceresort.com.
Distance from Salt Lake City airport: 55 miles.
Terrain: 450 skiable acres, 41 runs: 33 percent beginner, 33 percent intermediate, 33 percent advanced.

Lifts: One quad, two triple chairs.
Snowmaking: 112 acres.
Vertical drop: 2,155 feet.
Top elevation: 8,250.
Ticket prices: Inexpensive to moderate.
Facilities: Retail stores, artisan center, rentals, ski school, spa.
Dining: Two restaurants.
Accommodations: Mountain cottages, homes, suites, studios.
Snowboard facilities: Allowed, no terrain parks.
Cross-country skiing: Sundance Cross Country Ski Center.

■ OGDEN VALLEY RESORTS   *map page 268, B/C-1*

Some might question why a skier would want to travel the longer distances from Salt Lake City to ski Ogden Valley's resorts—Snowbasin or Powder Mountain. Variety is one reason, the quality of snow is the other. Some of the highest-quality powder in Utah can be found at tiny Powder Mountain.

■ POWDER MOUNTAIN RESORT   *map page 268, B-1*

The view from Powder Mountain, a resort consisting of three mountains northeast of the tiny community of Eden, is alone worth the price of a lift ticket. One can see the sun setting over the Great Salt Lake, peer into Cache Valley to the north, or see the distant ski runs cut out of the mountainside of Park City to the south.

The resort's facilities are located near the top of the ski area instead of at the base, a rarity in Utah. One actually needs to ski down from the main resort complex to reach a lift. There are 81 runs here, including an excellent night-skiing hill serviced by the aptly named Sundown Lift.

Powder Mountain Resort
P.O. Box 450, Eden, UT 84301; 801-745-3772; www.powdermountain.net.
Distance from Salt Lake City airport: 55 miles.
Terrain: 2,800 skiable acres, 81 runs: 10 percent beginner, 50 percent intermediate, 40 percent advanced.
Lifts: One quad, one triple, two doubles, two surface tows, and a platter lift.
Snowmaking: None.
Vertical drop: 2,400 feet.

Top elevation: 8,900 feet.
Ticket prices: Moderate.
Facilities: Rental shop, ski school.
Dining: Four on-site eateries.
Accommodations: Columbine Inn.
Snowboard facilities: One terrain park, one half-pipe.
Cross-country skiing: No.

■ **SNOWBASIN** *map page 268, C-1*

Though one of the nation's oldest ski resorts, Snowbasin used to be a place known only to a few locals. That all changed in the years leading up to the 2002 Winter Olympics. Earl Holding, who owns Idaho's Sun Valley ski area, purchased the resort with a view to transforming it into the West's new mega-resort. Snowbasin hosted the downhill and super G Alpine events in 2002.

The addition of two high-speed gondolas, a high-speed quad lift, and a small tramway in addition to spectacular new day lodges has transformed Snowbasin into one of Utah's largest resorts. It is still in the process of being discovered, though, making it a great place to beat crowds; on some weekdays you can feel as though you have the entire resort to yourself. Given future development plans—and the spectacular views of the Great Salt Lake and Ogden Valley from the top of the mountain—Snowbasin will be one of the great resorts of the West. The Olympics provided the impetus for expansion of other resort facilities, including a golf course and other amenities.

For an intermediate skier, Snowbasin is ideal. The runs are steep enough to be challenging but well-groomed enough not to contain many surprises.

Snowbasin
3925 East Snowbasin Road, P.O. Box 460, Huntsville, UT 84317; 801-620-1000 or 888-437-5488; www.snowbasin.com.
Distance from Salt Lake City airport: 40 miles.
Terrain: 2,650 skiable acres, 53 runs: 20 percent beginner, 50 percent intermediate, 30 percent advanced.
Lifts: Two gondolas, one tram, one quad, four triples, one double, two surface lifts.
Snowmaking: 600 acres.

(following pages) View from the Olympic Tram at Snowbasin.

Vertical drop: 2,959 feet.
Top elevation: 9,350 feet.
Ticket prices: Expensive.
Facilities: Three day lodges, ski school, rentals.
Dining: Two on-mountain restaurants, one day lodge.
Accommodations: None.
Snowboard facilities: One terrain park.
Cross-country skiing: Available on adjacent national forest land.

■ NORTHERN UTAH

■ BEAVER MOUNTAIN *map page 268, B-1*

At the top of Logan Canyon, on U.S. 89 near the Utah-Idaho border, you'll find Beaver Mountain, a small, family-operated resort that serves the outdoor-oriented students of nearby Utah State University.

In many ways, Beaver Mountain resembles a small-scale Brighton. Its three double chairlifts and one triple serve 30 major runs and provide access to beginner and intermediate hills, with a few expert runs as well.

Beaver Mountain Ski Resort
P.O. Box 3455, Logan, UT 84321; 435-753-0921; www.skithebeav.com.
Distance from Salt Lake City airport: 112 miles.
Terrain: 664 skiable acres, 30 runs: 35 percent beginner, 40 percent intermediate, 25 percent advanced.
Lifts: Three doubles, one triple, one surface tow.
Snowmaking: None.
Vertical drop: 1,600 feet.
Top elevation: 8,800.
Ticket prices: Inexpensive.
Facilities: Rental shop, ski school, gift shop.
Dining: Cafeteria in day lodge.
Accommodations: Beaver Creek Lodge, one mile from the resort; 800-946-4485.
Snowboard facilities: One terrain park.
Cross-country skiing: Available on adjacent national forest land.

■ SOUTHERN UTAH

One might not expect to find places for skiing in the midst of what many picture as red-rock desert, but the Brian Head ski area features high elevations, good powder, uncrowded conditions, and modern facilities.

■ BRIAN HEAD *map page 268, C-7*

South of Parowan on UT 143, Brian Head Resort possesses a bit of the alpine atmosphere of Utah's northern ski areas but looks more like southern Utah. Skiers taking the resort's Giant Steps lift find themselves standing under 11,307-foot Brian Head Peak—an impressive red sandstone mountain some say may have been named (but misspelled) after the famed bald-headed politician William Jennings Bryan. On a clear, cold winter day, skiers look down on a scene of fire and ice, out toward Zion National Park and the red-rock deserts.

The town of Brian Head is large enough to provide for thousands of skiers, while retaining a quaintness that makes it a quiet alternative to the huge California and Colorado resorts. Smaller lodges near Duck Creek and Panguitch Lake offer rustic, out-of-the-way settings to visitors looking to escape the big city. Less expensive lodging can be found in Cedar City and Parowan.

Brian Head Resort
329 South Highway 143, P.O. Box 190008, Brian Head, UT 84719; 435-677-2035; www.brianhead.com.
Distance from Las Vegas airport: 195 miles.
Terrain: 540 skiable acres, 53 runs: 40 percent beginner, 40 percent intermediate, 20 percent advanced.
Lifts: Five triples, one double, two surface tows.
Snowmaking: 180 acres.
Vertical drop: 1,707 feet.
Top elevation: 11,307 feet.
Ticket prices: Moderate.
Facilities: Snow tubing park, day spa, rentals, ski shops, summer mountain biking.
Dining: Two cafeterias, several restaurants in town.
Accommodations: 2,000 lodging units in town.
Snowboard facilities: Four terrain parks, one half-pipe.
Cross-country skiing: Not groomed, but popular outside town.

■ CROSS-COUNTRY SKIING

In many ways, much of Utah could be called a "ski resort." Most of the state receives plentiful snow, and where the white stuff falls, cross-country skiers often find open areas to enjoy their sport. It is not unusual to see the skinny ski tracks on golf courses or parks in the middle of the city.

Most Nordic skiers, however, take to the backcountry. Experts can be seen telemarking down steep powder runs in alpine canyons. Beginners, on the other hand, might take advantage of a road closed to auto traffic in the winter months to see pine trees dusted with snow, quiet canyons in frosty settings, or brooks flowing around magnificently shaped frozen shorelines. On certain days, it is even possible to ski across the slickrock after a snowstorm has covered the red rock with a white coating.

There are also destination resorts catering to Nordic skiers. These cross-country resorts provide a variety of services, including trail grooming, rental services, night skiing, backcountry huts, day and overnight tours, and lessons. In addition, helicopter ski services drop experts at the tops of mountains, where they can ski through the world's best powder on runs untouched by others. Besides Soldier Hollow, the Nordic ski venue of the 2002 Olympic Winter Games, there are developed Nordic centers at Solitude, near Salt Lake City; at Sundance and White Pine in the Park City vicinity; at the Homestead in Midway; at the Sherwood Hills Resort in northern Utah; and at Ruby's Inn in southern Utah.

But don't hesitate to ask about other Nordic ski possibilities—especially at U.S. Forest Service district ranger offices. There are a variety of small, little-known trails in the Wasatch, Uinta, and Manti-La Sal national forests. Particularly appealing are Mill Creek Canyon east of Salt Lake City, the Huntington Canyon area in Emery County, and the Tibble Fork Reservoir area in the north fork of American Fork Canyon. Skiing on the La Sal Mountains allows you to enjoy views of the red-rock country below. A hut-to-hut system is managed by Tag-A-Long Expeditions and affords some of the best backcountry skiing in the West. For additional information about Nordic skiing in Utah, visit the Web site of the Utah Nordic Alliance, www.utahnordic.com.

Snowfall in southern Utah tends to be wetter and less persistent than in the north.

■ NEAR SALT LAKE CITY

The Homestead *map page 268, B-3*
The Homestead holds a special appeal for those who prefer more of a resort atmosphere. This country inn, built near hot springs before 1900 and thus one of Utah's oldest resorts, has been restored to its original elegance and supplemented with newer lodging facilities and a golf course. Skiers can use both the resort's golf course and larger adjacent links at Wasatch Mountain State Park. For special occasions, spend the night and take a romantic moonlit ride on a horse-drawn sleigh. Top it off with a catered dinner for two near the fireplace at the resort's restaurant.
700 North Homestead Drive, Midway, UT 84049; information: 435-654-1102 or 800-327-7220; www.homesteadresort.com.

Soldier Hollow *map page 268, D-4*
The site of biathlon and cross-country ski races during the 2002 Winter Olympic Games, Soldier Hollow is in Wasatch Mountain State Park. With a day lodge, snowmaking, a beautiful view of the Heber Valley, and 31 kilometers of groomed trails for all types of skiers, this ranks among the best Nordic facilities in the country, if not the world.
Wasatch Mountain State Park, Midway, UT; 435-654-2002; www.soldierhollow.com.

Solitude Nordic Center *map page 268, D-3*
The Nordic area closest to Salt Lake City provides excellent skiing for all ability levels on well-groomed trails. In addition, the Solitude center connects the Brighton and Solitude downhill ski areas; because of the proximity of the two alpine resorts, the Solitude Nordic Center is a good place for families who enjoy both cross-country and downhill skiing.
In Big Cottonwood Canyon between Brighton and Solitude Mountain ski resorts, near the top of UT 190; 801-536-5774; www.skisolitude.com.

Sundance Cross Country Ski Center *map page 268, D-4*
The Nordic center at Sundance, located east of Orem at the base of Mount Timpanogos, offers ski and snowshoe trails, some of which are lit at night by gas lanterns.
R.R. 3, Box A-1, Sundance, UT 84604; 801-223-4170; www.sundanceresort.com.

White Pine Touring Cross-Country Ski Area *map page 268, D-3*
The venerable White Pine Touring, with 20 kilometers of groomed trails located mostly on the Park City Golf Course, is Utah's oldest. This is a good place for beginners to get a feel for Nordic skiing before attempting a more difficult canyon run. There is excellent expert instruction here as well.
Corner of Park Avenue and Thaynes Canyon Drive, Park City, UT 84060; 435-649-6249; www.whitepinetouring.com.

■ **NORTHERN UTAH**

Sherwood Hills Resort *map page 268, B-1*
The Best Western Sherwood Hills Resort in Sardine Canyon halfway between Logan and Brigham City serves a primarily northern Utah clientele. Though groomed trails are available on the golf course at the resort, don't be afraid to drive to Logan Canyon to try skiing on U.S. Forest Service trails.
UT 89/91, Wellsville, UT; 435-245-5054 or 800-532-5066; www. sherwoodhills.com.

■ **SOUTHERN UTAH**

Ruby's Inn *map page 268, B-7*
Skiers staying at the Best Western Ruby's Inn, one mile north of the entrance to Bryce Canyon National Park, can glide across groomed trails into the park, where they can ski along the edge of the Bryce amphitheater. If you have the good fortune to arrive in clear weather after a heavy snowfall, the sight of powder snow, blue skies, and bright red rock will reward your skiing efforts. Unlike summer, when crowds of people gather on the edge of Bryce, winter days give you the chance to have the entire park to yourself. Ruby's also grooms trails into nearby national forests.
1000 South Highway 63, Bryce, UT 84764; 435-834-5341; reservations: 866-866-6616; www.rubysinn.com.

■ SNOWMOBILING

Vast expanses of Utah's most scenic forest and red-rock country lie almost untouched in the winter. Thousands of people drive the Mirror Lake Highway between Kamas and Evanston, Wyoming, during summer, but only a few view the snowcapped Uinta Mountains from the road in the winter. Those few ride snow-mobiles—the Mirror Lake Highway is one of several major trail systems estab-lished and groomed by the Utah Division of Parks and Recreation.

Snowmobiles require registration in Utah, where registration fees go toward the grooming and marking of trails by Division of Parks and Recreation rangers. Close to 500 miles of backcountry roads and trails encompassing all sorts of terrain and scenery are groomed. Maps are available from any Division of Parks and Recreation office or any state park.

The **Wasatch Mountain State Park–Mirror Lake Complex,** close to the Wasatch Front, includes 150 miles of groomed trails traversing both the Wasatch and Uinta ranges. In addition to the groomed areas, the complex holds numerous wide open spaces where snowmobilers can play in powder snow. The 50-mile Mirror Lake Highway is covered with snow most years from November until May. Though snowmobiles are not allowed in the adjacent wilderness areas, the road itself offers beautiful views of both the Uintas and the Wasatch Range on crisp, clear winter days. Snowmobiles can be rented at Wasatch Mountain State Park, the state's finest and most complete snowmobiling facility.

Trailheads at **Midway, Park City,** and **American Fork Canyon** offer plowed parking areas, restrooms, designated play areas, warming stations, and 60 miles of groomed trails.

Snowmobilers searching for a chance to view red-rock canyons coated with snow usually head for the **Cedar Mountain Complex,** just east of Cedar City on a high plateau. Trails lead into Cedar Breaks National Monument, which is closed to auto-mobile traffic in winter. Much of the trail leads through the pines and aspens of the Dixie National Forest, but views of the red-rock country are common. Access to the complex is available from the Brian Head, Duck Creek, Strawberry, Navajo, and Midway trailheads, with some package tours offered out of Brian Head.

The **Logan Canyon–Monte Cristo–Hardware Ranch** area in northern Utah is home to 150 miles of groomed trails; these connect with hundreds more miles of trails in neighboring Idaho. Be sure to stop by the **Hardware Ranch Wildlife Management Area** (UT 101, 15 miles east of Hyrum; 435-753-6206) to see the winter feeding grounds of the wild elk. Though snowmobiles are not allowed near the huge animals, visitors can take a horse-drawn sleigh ride near the elk herds. The visitors center provides heated restrooms, a warm fire, vending machines, and information about the elk. The open spaces on Ant Flat between Hardware Ranch and Monte Cristo and in the Sinks area of Logan Canyon give snowmobilers plenty of area to enjoy untouched powder.

In central Utah, you might enjoy a snowmobile ride across a portion of Skyline Drive, where elevations reach nearly 12,000 feet. About 75 miles of trails are groomed in this scenic complex, with trailheads found on both sides of the Manti Range. The ride from Huntington Canyon into Joe's Valley Reservoir is a favorite.

On occasion, the Division of Parks and Recreation also grooms snowmobile trails near Strawberry Reservoir and in the Vernal area—but trail conditions depend on the availability of groomers. If you are in the mood for a bit of adventure and have confidence in your snowmobiling abilities, these are two good areas to try.

■ 2002 WINTER OLYMPIC GAMES

Although a bidding scandal threatened to turn the event into a nightmare, the 2002 Winter Olympic Games not only ranked among the most successful ever but also left the state and U.S. athletes many legacies:

Utah Olympic Park, a year-round winter sports park and training center, is open to the general public near Park City, hosting ski jumpers, bobsledders, lugers, and skeleton racers. Athletes have set Olympic and world records in the **Utah Olympic Oval,** the new speed-skating facility in the west part of the Salt Lake Valley, which is also open to the public and promises to develop future Olympic stars. **Soldier Hollow,** near the town of Midway, remains as a major Nordic skiing and biathlon training center and has been developed as a summer golfing haven as well. And on the University of Utah campus, **Rice-Eccles Stadium,** which was totally renovated and expanded to host the opening and closing ceremonies, is now one of the top college football facilities in the West.

PRACTICAL
INFORMATION

■ AREA CODES AND TIME ZONE

The area code in the metropolitan area of northern Utah is 801; the area code in the rest of the state is 435. Utah is in the Mountain time zone.

■ METRIC CONVERSIONS

1 foot = .305 meters 1 mile = 1.6 kilometers
Centigrade = Fahrenheit temperature minus 32, divided by 1.8
1 pound = .45 kilograms

■ CLIMATE

With at least one notable exception—St. George, in extreme southwestern Utah, which is mild enough in winter for golf—most parts of Utah experience four distinct seasons. And almost everywhere in Utah, including Salt Lake City, winter can be cold.

Summer temperatures throughout most Utah valleys hover between 85°F and 100°F while the nearby mountains might enjoy a cool 60°F. At night, temperatures in the mountains may cool off to between 40°F and 50°F.

Spring and fall are the most comfortable seasons in southern Utah, with daytime temperatures in the 60° to 70° F range. In April and May in northern Utah, it often happens that visitors can spend the morning skiing in the mountains and the afternoon golfing in the valleys.

■ GETTING THERE AND AROUND

■ BY AIR

Salt Lake City International Airport (SLC), the main gateway to Utah, is 5 miles northwest of downtown Salt Lake City. A major hub for Delta Airlines, it is served by more than a dozen carriers, including discount airlines such as Southwest and JetBlue. *776 North Terminal Drive, off I-80; 801-575-2400 or 800-595-2442; www.slcairport.com.*

St. George Municipal Airport (SGU), served by Delta through Salt Lake City and by United from Los Angeles on flights operated by SkyWest Airlines, is 2 miles from St. George in southern Utah, on a plateau overlooking the city. *175 North 200 East; 435-634-5822; www.ci.st-george.ut.us/airport.*

Las Vegas's **McCarran International Airport** (LAS) is also a convenient gateway to southern Utah, particularly to Zion and Bryce Canyon national parks, which are 150 and 270 miles away, respectively. *702-261-5733; www.mccarran.com.*

■ BY BUS

Greyhound Bus Lines provides service to towns and cities throughout the state. *800-231-2222; www.greyhound.com.*

The **Utah Transit Authority** (UTA) provides service throughout the Salt Lake Valley north to Ogden and south to Provo. *801-743-3882 or 888-743-3882 (in-state toll-free); www.utabus.com.*

■ BY CAR

Interstate 15 is the state's major north/south freeway. From Salt Lake City south, UT 89 is slower, but it passes through some of Utah's great small towns. Interstate 80 is the major east/west freeway across the northern part of the state. In the southeast and south-central part of the state, Interstate 70 stretches from Colorado to connect with I-15. Utah 191 serves as the main link to southern destinations. The rugged topography of southern Utah has prevented the building of any major highway in that part of the state, but good state roads link national parks and provide beautiful scenery along the way.

■ FINDING YOUR WAY AROUND UTAH CITIES

Nearly every Utah city was planned in advance by the Mormon pioneers, who laid them out in checkerboard fashion, with wide, square blocks and streets running in true north-south and east-west directions. Finding an address is a relatively easy proposition. Cities have meridian markers from which most main streets are numbered; street addresses increase by increments of 100 every block from that point. Salt Lake City's marker is at the southeast corner of Temple Square. Thus, if you want to find an address at 500 South 700 East Street, you would simply go five blocks south and then seven blocks east from Temple Square. Three of Salt Lake City's main streets—North Temple, South Temple, and West Temple—border the Mormon Temple; Main Street borders its east side.

■ BY TRAIN

Amtrak's ultra-scenic *California Zephyr* stops in Salt Lake City, Provo, Helper, and Green River, Utah, en route between San Francisco and Chicago. *800-872-7245; www.amtrak.com.*

■ ABOUT UTAH RESTAURANTS

The great number and variety of restaurants found throughout the state, especially along the Wasatch Front, prove that eating out is a major Utahn pastime.

In Salt Lake City, for example, it's possible to find a sampling of many different ethnic specialties as well as traditional American meat-and-potatoes fare. The area around the Salt Palace Convention Center and the Delta Center is fast becoming a restaurant center, with many fine establishments setting up in renovated historic buildings. There are also many excellent restaurants in Trolley Square.

One can also find a surprising number of good restaurants in places like Ogden, Provo, Cedar City, Moab, St. George, and Brigham City. Eating in smaller Utah towns can be an adventure. Often, restaurants are operated by colorful characters who not only serve a fine meal but can tell you about local history and attractions. When in doubt at a café or diner in rural Utah, order the chicken-fried steak. You won't be disappointed. In Navajo country in southeastern Utah, pick up a Navajo taco instead of a hamburger. Small-town drive-ins (not franchises) often mix up a fine milkshake or malt—especially when local fruit is ripening. For example, drive-ins around Bear Lake serve great raspberry malts and sundaes in late summer. Try some fresh peach pie in the Willard area in the fall.

■ UTAH'S LIQUOR LAWS

Utah's liquor laws, once difficult for outsiders to figure out, have been liberalized in recent years, so most visitors will find it relatively easy to purchase an alcoholic beverage. The state owns liquor stores in convenient locations throughout the state, including several in Salt Lake City. The stores are open every day of the week except Sundays and holidays, with varying hours. Beer (with up to 3.2 percent alcohol) is available in most grocery stores. There are also a number of microbreweries in Salt Lake, Park City, and Moab. Most fine restaurants and fine hotels in Utah have liquor licenses. Patrons of such restaurants may purchase mixed drinks, wine, and beer with a meal, as long as it's after noon. If in doubt, ask your server about the availability of wine and liquor.

For a nominal fee, visitors can purchase a membership to a private club where liquor is sold by the drink. Many of these clubs can be found inside the larger hotels, some of which offer free club memberships as a courtesy to guests. Alcoholic beverages are sold in private clubs throughout the day. Lounges and taverns sell only 3.2 beer; they do not offer wine or mixed drinks, nor can patrons bring their own liquor or wine into these establishments.

■ ABOUT UTAH HOTELS

Utah's urban areas offer modern, full-service hotels operated by major national chains. Most are listed in the free *Utah! Accommodations Guide,* published annually by the **Utah Hotel & Lodging Association** (801-359-0104; www.uhla.org) and the **Utah Travel Council** (801-538-1030 or 800-200-1160; www.utah.com) and available free from both. You'll get more specific information—and better rates—by calling locally once you arrive in town.

With an increase in tourism in recent years, there has been a building boom of sorts, and some of the older hotels have been razed or converted to office spaces. This means that while the state's hotels and motels tend to be clean and modern, they can also be somewhat sterile. Visitors looking for a spot with more character should try staying at one of Utah's charming bed-and-breakfasts, many of which are colorful old mansions restored to their former glory. Information about them is available from **Bed and Breakfast Inns of Utah** (www.bbiu.org), an association of independently owned properties, some of whose members offer online booking. Some of the major ski areas offer alpine-style lodging; alternatives to lodges are rental condos. For a taste of the Wild West, consult the Utah Travel Council for a list of rustic dude ranches or cabins near fishing areas.

■ HOTEL AND MOTEL CHAINS

Best Western. *800-528-1234; www.bestwestern.com.*
Comfort Inn. *800-228-5150; www.comfortinn.com.*
Days Inn. *800-325-2525; www.daysinn.com.*
Econolodge. *800-446-6900; www.econolodge.com.*
Embassy Suites. *800-362-2779; www.embassysuites.com.*
Hilton. *800-445-8667; www.hilton.com.*
Holiday Inn. *800-465-4329; www.6c.com.*
La Quinta. *800-531-5900; www.lq.com.*

Marriott. *800-228-9290; www.marriott.com.*
Quality Inns. *800-228-5151; www.qualityinn.com.*
Radisson. *800-333-3333; www.radisson.com.*
Ramada Inns. *800-272-6232; www.ramada.com.*
Sheraton. *800-325-3535; www.sheraton.com.*
Shilo Inns. *800-222-2244; www.shiloinns.com.*
Travelodge. *800-255-3050; www.travelodge.com.*
WestCoast and Red Lion. *800-325-4000; www.westcoasthotels.com.*

■ Food and Lodging

Below are some of the authors' favorite places to stay or eat throughout the state.

Room Rates
Prices designations per room, per night, double occupancy, high season

$ = under $75   **$$** = $75–125   **$$$** = $125–175   **$$$$** = over $175

Restaurant Prices
Prices designations per person, excluding tax, tip, and drinks

$ = under $10   **$$** = $10–15   **$$$** = $15–30   **$$$$** = over $30

■ Alta

Alta Lodge
A rustic but elegant throwback to traditional European ski lodges. Though wonderful during ski season, try staying here in July when rates are lower, the pace is quiet, and the canyon wildflowers are blooming. *Little Cottonwood Canyon; 801-742-3500 or 800-707-2582; www.altalodge.com.* **$$$–$$$$**

Cliff Lodge at Snowbird Resort
In addition to world-class skiing at Snowbird, this lodge offers a splendid spa, a climbing wall, fine restaurants, and Rocky Mountain splendor, only a short distance from downtown Salt Lake City. A varied calendar of performances and countless activities keep guests busy all year long. *Little Cottonwood Canyon; 801-933-2222 or 800-453-3000; www.snowbird.com.* **$$$$**

■ BLANDING

Rogers House B&B
Five rooms with Western decor. Private baths and generous breakfasts. *412 South Main Street; 435-678-3932 or 800-355-3932.* **$–$$**

■ BOULDER

Boulder Mountain Lodge
Built in a newer Southwestern style, with pine beams, sandstone bricks, stucco, and weathered metal roof, this is one of southern Utah's true treasures. Rooms have balconies and picture windows overlooking wetlands where there is excellent bird-watching. *UT 12 and Burr Trail; 435-335-7460 or 800-556-3446; www.boulder-utah.com.* **$$–$$$$**

Hell's Backbone Grill
As if a wall of windows showing off the spectacular scenery weren't enough, this restaurant, in the Boulder Mountain Lodge complex, serves up the best of regional fare, featuring organic ingredients. *UT 12 and Burr Trail; 435-335-7464; www. hellsbackbonegrill.com.* **$$–$$$**

■ BRIGHAM CITY

Howard Johnson Inn
Modern rooms; hot tub and swimming pool. This is close, but not too close, to I-15. *1167 South Main Street; 435-723-8511.* **$$**

Idle Isle
In business since 1921, and the soda fountain, café booths, and the adjoining candy factory have changed little. A good place to order turkey steak or pot roast. *24 South Main; 435-734-2468.* **$**

Maddox Ranch House
A northern Utah classic. The beefsteaks, chicken steaks, and especially the turkey steaks are prepared in a traditional American style. Few places in the country serve better basic meat and potatoes. *1900 South U.S. Highway 89, Perry; 435-723-8545.* **$$$**

■ Bryce Canyon National Park

Best Western Ruby's Inn
Operated by the Syrett family for several generations, this sprawling facility is one of the largest full-service hotels in southern Utah. It offers hot tubs, a swimming pool, general store, gift shop, and restaurant. In the summer there are helicopter rides and rodeos; in the winter, ski touring. Nothing fancy, but the hospitality and variety of things to do make it the area's best. *1000 South Highway 63, 1 mile north of the park entrance; 435-834-5341 or 800-468-8660; www.rubysinn.com.* **$$$**

Bryce Canyon Lodge
Built for the Union Pacific Railroad in the 1920s and since refurbished, this lodge nonetheless retains its old charm. It is nestled in pine trees near the rim of the canyon. Open mid-April through October. *Inside the park; 303-297-2757 or 435-834-5361; www.brycecanyonlodge.com.* **$$$–$$$$**

Bryce Canyon Pines
Modern rooms with beautiful views in a relatively secluded setting. The restaurant and swimming pool are open from spring through fall. *UT 12, 6 miles west of the park turnoff; 435-834-5441 or 800-892-7923; www.brycecanyonpines.com.* **$$**

Bryce Canyon Lodge Restaurant
Some of the best dining in the area. Specialties include trout and prime rib. Breakfast and lunch are also served and box lunches can be arranged by calling 12 hours ahead. Be sure to make reservations for dinner. *Inside the park; 435-834-5361; www.brycecanyonlodge.com.* **$$**

■ Capitol Reef National Park

Austin's Chuck Wagon Lodge
Friendly service and immaculate rooms greet you at this shady oasis in a town 5 miles west of the park. You can sleep in a standard room, rent a cabin, or stay in one of the economical rooms above the general store. *12 West Main Street, Torrey; 435-425-3335 or 800-863-3288; www.austinschuckwagonmotel.com.* **$$**

Best Western Capitol Reef Resort
This is a good home base from which to explore the park. The hilltop location gives you excellent views of the colorful cliffs, and the amenities are abundant. A pool is open in the summer. *2600 East Highway 24, 1 mile from the park entrance; 435-425-3761 or 888-610-9600; bestwestern.com/capitolreefresort.* **$$$**

Skyridge Inn Bed and Breakfast
All rooms have views of the canyon country outside Capitol Reef National Park. Several have private decks, some hot tubs. Evening hors d'oeuvres and breakfast are included. *950 East Highway 24, 1 mile east of Torrey; 435-425-3222; www. skyridgeinn.com.* **$$$–$$$$**

Cafe Diablo
Colorfully presented, Santa Fe-style gourmet fare, using fresh herbs grown in the flower garden just outside the restaurant. This is one of southern Utah's best restaurants. *599 West Main Street, Torrey; 435-425-3070; www.cafediablo.net.* **$$$**

Capitol Reef Inn & Cafe
Healthy food dominates the menu here: fresh vegetables and bread, several vegetarian entrées, and juices made on the premises; there's good espresso as well. This is where the locals eat. *360 West Main Street, Torrey; 435-425-3271.* **$–$$**

Sunglow Cafe
This tiny roadside café is known for its unusual pie selection. How does pickle, pinto bean, or oatmeal pie sound? *91 East Main Street, Bicknell, about 10 miles west of the park on UT 24; 435-425-3701.* **$**

■ CEDAR CITY

Abbey Inn
One of southern Utah's modern hotels. The indoor swimming pool and hot tub make it a year-round favorite. *940 West 200 North; 435-586-9966 or 800-325-5411; www.abbeyinncedar.com.* **$$**

Baker House Bed & Breakfast
This elegant, luxurious B&B is a modern replica of a Queen Anne Victorian mansion. Situated on a hill, it has views of nearby mountains. *1800 Royal Hunte Drive; 435-867-5695 or 888-611-8181; www.bbhost.com/bakerhouse.* **$$**

Best Western Town and Country Inn

One of the larger and more centrally located motels in Cedar City, this features a popular gift shop inside an old train station. *189 North Main Street; 435-586-9911 or 800-493-4089; www.bwtowncountry.com.* **$–$$**

Milt's Stage Stop

A charming steak and seafood house in a quiet canyon setting. Steaks and prime rib here are among Utah's best. *In Cedar Canyon, 5 miles east of Cedar City; 435-586-9344.* **$$–$$$**

Pizza Factory

Good pizza, salads, sandwiches, and pasta. An excellent place to take the family. *124 South Main Street; 435-586-3900.* **$**

Sullivan's Cafe

A typical small-town, southern Utah restaurant. Try the potato skins, the prime rib sandwich, or the huge salad bar. *301 South Main Street; 435-586-6761; www.sullivanscafe.com.* **$–$$**

■ FLAMING GORGE NATIONAL RECREATION AREA

Flaming Gorge Lodge

The only lodging in the area, Flaming Gorge Lodge is also the jumping-off point for river trips and fishing expeditions. The rustic surroundings have hiking trails, and there's a good restaurant right in the lodge. *U.S. 191, Dutch John; 435-889-3773; www.fglodge.com.* **$$–$$$**

■ LA SAL

Mt. Peale Resort Inn & Spa

Wonderful food, an outdoor hot tub, and a large stone fireplace add to the charm of this inn at the foot of Mount Peale. A perfect base for exploring the mountain on bicycles in the summer and fall and on cross-country skis or snowshoes in the winter. *Highway 46, Milepost 14, Old La Sal; 435-686-2284 or 888-687-3253; www.mtpeale.com.* **$$–$$$**

■ LOGAN

Anniversary Inn
This B&B comprises a mansion (built over a century ago by Logan's first doctor) as well as four other houses. Theme rooms from the inexpensive to the very expensive include a Grand Bridal Suite and the "King Arthur's Castle" suite; all rooms have two-person jetted tubs. *169 East Center Street; 435-752-3443 or 800-574-7605; www.anniversaryinn.com.* **$$$$**

Comfort Inn
Nice indoor pool and hot tub; a good family hotel. *447 North Main Street; 435-752-9141 or 800-228-5150.* **$$**

Bluebird Restaurant
A Logan institution, founded in 1914 and at its Main Street address since the 1920s. The steak dinners at this café are classic American, and a chocolate factory adds to the ambience. *19 North Main Street; 435-752-3155.* **$–$$**

Gia's
Fine service and a high-quality Italian menu. For a less expensive dining experience, head to the basement "Factory" for an Italian sandwich or pizza. *119 South Main Street; 435-752-8384.* **$–$$**

■ MANTI

Legacy Inn Bed & Breakfast
A newer house designed in Victorian style. A half-block from the Mormon Temple. *337 North 100 East; 435-835-8352; www.legacyinn.com.* **$$$**

Manti House Inn
Built in the 1880s by the builders of the Manti Temple. Besides rooms named after Mormon dignitaries who stayed here in the past, there's a wedding suite with a private balcony. Wedding banquets are a specialty. *401 North Main Street; 435-835-0161 or 800-835-7512; www.mantihouseinn.com.* **$$–$$$**

Yardley Inn & Spa
Indulge in spa treatments while staying at this romantic turn-of-the-century inn. *190 South 200 West; 435-835-1861 or 800-858-6634; www.yardleyinnandspa.com.* **$$–$$$**

■ MARYSVALE

Big Rock Candy Mountain Resort
The rustic cabins here (with TV, telephones, and indoor plumbing) are on a grassy clearing next to a river and across from a hiking area. There's also a nice restaurant, and such activities as river-running and ATV rides. *4479 North Highway 89, 7 miles north of Marysvale; 435-326-2000 or 888-560-7625; www.marysvale.org/brcm.* **$–$$**

Moore's Old Pine Inn
Butch Cassidy and Zane Grey slept in this old hotel, which was built in 1882 and has been carefully renovated by its latter-day owners. Three suites have private baths. Guests in the other four rooms can luxuriate in one of the two large clawfoot tubs down the hall. *60 South State Street; 435-326-4565 or 800-887-4565; www.marysvale.org/pine.* **$$–$$$**

■ MOAB

Castle Valley Inn
One of the state's quietest bed-and-breakfasts, 15 miles northeast of Moab and near Arches National Park. The serene experience includes an adjacent orchard, small cottages with kitchenettes, and a hot tub with views of the sandstone spires of Fisher Towers. *Castle Valley, off UT 128; 435-259-1501 or 888-466-6012; www.castlevalleyinn.com.* **$$$–$$$$**

Dreamkeeper Inn

Tucked away in a quiet neighborhood, this classy B&B is as homespun and friendly as you can get. A gorgeous garden and pool grace the private back yard. *191 South 200 East Street; 435-259-5998; www.dreamkeeperinn.com.* **$$$–$$$$**

Lazy Lizard International Hostel

Choose a private room, dorm room, cabin, or camping at this affordable hostel. *1213 South Highway 191; 435-259-6057; www.lazylizardhostel.com.* **$**

Pack Creek Ranch

A traditional dude ranch offering individual houses and cabins full of interesting decor and books. The food in the dining room is terrific and the views of the nearby La Sal Mountains memorable. Mule deer wander just outside your window. Rate includes three meals a day. One of southern Utah's few first-class lodgings. *Pack Creek Ranch Road, 15 miles southeast of Moab; 435-259-5505; www. packcreekranch.com.* **$$$–$$$$**

Sorrel River Ranch

This luxurious resort sits alongside the Colorado River with a view of Fisher Towers and the La Sal Mountains. A stay here lets you indulge yourself in one of the finest resorts in the West. *Highway 28, Milepost 17, 17 miles northeast of Moab; 435-259-4642 or 877-359-2715; www.sorrelriver.com.* **$$$$**

Sunflower Hill Bed & Breakfast

Rooms, in the old ranch house or the garden cottage, are elegantly and individually furnished, with private baths and television. Homemade pastries grace the breakfast buffet. *185 North 300 East; 435-259-2974; www.sunflowerhill.com.* **$$$$**

Buck's Grill House

In what looks like an old fort with original Western oil paintings on the walls, chef Tim Buckingham serves a good selection of gourmet vegetarian dishes in addition to excellent chicken, steak, and wild game. *1393 North Highway 191; 435-259-5201.* **$$**

Center Café

The kind of dining experience not often found in a small town. With fresh fish, fine vegetarian dishes, gourmet pizzas, and espresso, all served in a simple but elegant atmosphere, this rates among Utah's finest restaurants. *60 North 100 West; 435-259-4295.* **$$–$$$**

Fat City Smoke House
Texas-style barbecue and vegetarian dishes that are both delicious and inexpensive. *2 South 100 West; 435-259-4302.* **$**

Slickrock Cafe
With an eclectic mix of pastas and Mexican food, this restaurant is one of the best eateries in town. It's in a historic sandstone building the middle of Moab. *5 North Main Street; 435-259-8004; www.slickrockcafe.com.* **$–$$$**

Sunset Grill
Built by a colorful old uranium miner, this converted mansion affords views of the red-rock country and the Colorado Plateau. Menu of standard steak, fish, and pasta dishes. *900 North Main Street; 435-259-7146.* **$$$**

■ MONTICELLO

Grist Mill Inn
Built as a flour mill in 1933, this building now houses a unique B&B. The original mill equipment has been restored and left in place, but the six rooms are modern. Hot tub. *64 South 300 East; 435-587-2597 or 800-645-3762; www.thegristmillinn. com.* **$$–$$$**

■ OGDEN

Ogden Marriott
Downtown's major conference hotel, near Union Station. Kids love the indoor pool and hot tub. *247 24th Street; 801-627-1190 or 800-421-7599.* **$$$**

Bistro 258
Fine dining on Ogden's historic 25th Street. Reminiscent of a French bistro, this has outdoor seating in the back. *258 25th Street; 801-394-1595; www.bistro258. com.* **$$$**

Roosters
This microbrewery, across the street from Bistro 258, is the gathering place for Ogdenites. It features special brews and an extensive menu ranging from sandwiches and pizzas to an eclectic mix of fresh nouvelle cuisine entrees. *253 25th Street; 801-627-6171; www.roostersbrewingco.com.* **$$**

Temari

The Japanese owners do all the cooking themselves. Take your time and enjoy their authentic dishes. Closed Mondays. *350 Washington Boulevard; 801-399-9536.* **$–$$$**

Union Grill

In historic Union Station, run by the owners of Roosters. Try the exotic pastas and fresh fish specials. *2501 Wall Avenue; 801-621-2830.* **$$-$$$**

■ OREM

Los Hermanos

Traditional Mexican fare in a pioneer house in nearby Lindon. *395 North State Street, Lindon; 801-785-1715.* **$**

Restaurant Roy

From its setting in the foothills, this old-style restaurant gives diners a view of Utah Lake. The upscale fare features pasta dishes, fresh seafood, and steaks. *2005 South State Street; 801-235-9111.* **$$–$$$**

■ PARK CITY

Best Western Landmark Inn

Just off I-80, near all the factory outlet stores. A nice indoor pool, recreation area, and special group rates make this a nice stopover for families. *6560 North Landmark Drive; 435-649-7300 or 800-548-8824; www.bwlandmarkinn.com.* **$$$–$$$$**

Goldener Hirsch Inn

Located in exclusive Deer Valley and one of Utah's most elegant—and expensive—lodges. Few amenities have been spared at this Austrian-style inn, which has hot tubs, saunas, views, and a wonderful restaurant (see page 308). *7570 Royal Street East; 435-649-7770 or 800-252-3373; www.goldenerhirschinn.com.* **$$$$**

Old Miners' Lodge

Built in 1889 and located in Park City's historic district, this lodge offers a hot tub and complimentary non-alcoholic drinks in the evening. A fun ski vacation spot. *615 Woodside Avenue; 435-645-8068 or 800-648-8068; www.oldminerslodge.com.* **$$$–$$$$**

Stein Eriksen Lodge
Among the best "ski town" lodges in the country, this Deer Valley hostelry spoils its guests with kitchens, pools, and an excellent restaurant (see Glitretind, below). *7700 Stein Way; 435-649-3700 or 800-453-1302; www.steinlodge.com.* **$$$$**

Treasure Mountain Inn
One of the few places to stay on historic Main Street, among the many turn-of-the-century buildings, charming shops, and restaurants. The inn is close to the top of the street, where the Town Lift whisks skiers to the Park City slopes. *255 Main Street; 435-655-4501 or 800-344-2460; www.treasuremountaininn.com.* **$$–$$$$**

Adolph's
A Park City institution where diners can choose among veal, spinach pasta, venison, steak, and roast lamb. *1500 Kearns Boulevard; 435-649-7177.* **$$$–$$$$**

Eating Establishment
A less expensive but not necessarily lower-quality dining experience near the top of Main Street, with a patio that is delightful in summer. Food ranges from full dinners to pasta, burgers, sandwiches, and salads. Try the mud pie. *317 Main Street; 435-649-8284.* **$–$$**

Glitretind
With Austrian country decor, including exposed beams and stone fireplaces, this restaurant in the Stein Eriksen Lodge serves European cuisine, including wonderful seafood and homemade breads and pastries. *7700 Stein Way; 435-649-3700 or 800-453-1302; www.steinlodge.com.* **$$$–$$$$**

Goldener Hirsch Inn
Come to this Alpine retreat for a special occasion: entrées in the dining room include delights such as venison, caribou, and sea bass. *7570 Royal Street East; 435-649-7770 or 800-252-3373; www.goldenerhirschinn.com.* **$$$–$$$$**

Grub Steak Restaurant
A Park City tradition: famous for its steaks, ribs, and prime rib. *2200 Sidewinder Drive at Prospector Square; 435-649-8060.* **$$**

Main Street Pizza and Noodle
Sandwiches, pizzas, calzones, and stir-fries. One of the city's best family restaurants. *530 Main Street; 435-645-8878.* **$**

■ PRICE

Greenwell Inn
A full-service inn with 125 rooms, a convention center, indoor pool and spa, exercise facilities, free continental breakfast, and a good Mexican family-run restaurant (see Ricardo's, below). *655 East Main Street; 435-637-3520 or 800-666-3520; www.greenwellinn.com.* **$**

Holiday Inn Hotel and Suites
A large hotel with an indoor pool and a restaurant open on Sundays. *8388 Westwood Boulevard; 435-637-8880 or 800-465-4329.* **$$–$$$$**

China City
Huge portions of reasonably priced Chinese and American dishes. The Cantonese-style chow mein is excellent; the prime rib's good too. *350 East Main Street; 435-637-8211.* **$–$$**

Cowboy's Kitchen
For a touch of cowboy, drive into Wellington and stop at the Cowboy's Kitchen. A poem by Matt Warner, a local member of Butch Cassidy's gang, graces the back of the menu. Lamb specialties hark back to the days of sheep and cattle ranching. Country-and-western bands and dancing weekend nights. *31 East Main Street, Wellington; 435-637-4223.* **$$**

Grogg's Pinnacle Brewing Company
A local microbrewery that features generous portions of pizza, burgers, and gourmet sandwiches. *1653 North Carbonville Road, Helper; 435-637-2924.* **$**

Ricardo's
Solid Mexican and American dishes are served at this Greenwell Inn eatery; open for breakfast, lunch, and dinner. *655 East Main Street; 435-637-2020.* **$–$$**

■ PROVO

Provo Marriott
The city's best full-service hotel, complete with conference facility, pool, and hot tub. Located downtown, this large hotel is a convenient place to stay. *101 West 100 North; 801-377-4700 or 800-777-7144.* **$$–$$$$**

Bombay House

Brigham Young University's missionary program and its emphasis on foreign countries has given rise to an affinity for foreign food. The popularity of this Indian restaurant, opened in 1993, is evidence. *463 North University Avenue; 801-373-6677; www.bombayhouse.com.* **$$**

Brick Oven

Adjacent to the BYU campus, this café is a popular place for students to pick up pasta, pizza, and sandwiches. *111 East 800 North; 801-374-8800.* **$**

Magleby's Restaurant

This is a popular gathering place for parents of BYU students. Try the pies. The restaurant doubles as an art gallery—the paintings and sculptures displayed, by well-known Utahns, are for sale. *1675 North 200 West; 801-374-6249; www. maglebys.com.* **$$–$$$**

Sundance Tree Room

At Robert Redford's ski resort, and a bit of a drive from downtown: take U.S. 189 north, then UT 92 for 2.5 miles. The atmosphere here is sophisticated, and the food consistently good. The Sunday brunch tops all the competition. *Provo Canyon; 801-225-4107; www.sundanceresort.com.* **$$$–$$$$**

■ ROOSEVELT

Frontier Grill

A family-style restaurant serving traditional American food; breakfast, lunch, and dinner. *75 South 200 East; 435-722-3669.* **$–$$**

■ SALINA

Mom's Cafe

A central Utah classic. Located at the main crossroads in town, Mom's serves pies and meat and potatoes just like Mom used to fix. Large portions and reasonable prices. *Corner of State and Main; 435-529-3921.* **$–$$**

■ St. George

Best Western Abbey Inn
Next to the St. George Convention Center, with a microwave and a fridge in all rooms. Complimentary full breakfast. *1129 South Bluff Street; 435-652-1234 or 888-222-3946; www.bwabbeyinn.com.* **$$$**

Green Gate Village Historic Inn
Nine restored Mormon pioneer homes with modern conveniences surrounding a village green in the historic part of St. George. Swimming pool and hot tub, too. The Bentley House Restaurant serves five-course, excellently prepared dinners to guests and non-guests. *76 West Tabernacle Street; 435-628-6999 or 800-350-6999; www.greenegate.com.* **$$$**

Howard Johnson Express Inn & Suites
A clean, reasonable alternative to the more expensive hotels in town. There's a heated pool and hot tub, and all rooms have microwaves and refrigerators. *1040 South Main; 435-628-8000 or 800-332-0400.* **$–$$$**

Olde Penny Farthing Inn
Built in the 1880s and fully restored. Most of the six rooms have a country pioneer decor and claw-footed tubs, but there are jetted tubs in the Bridal Suite and the Empress Room. *278 North 100 West; 435-673-7755 or 800-943-2920.* **$$–$$$**

Seven Wives Inn
Thirteen rooms in two neighboring houses and a cottage make up this inn, so named because an ancestor of the innkeeper was a polygamist with seven wives. Rooms are decorated with antiques, and one has a jacuzzi in an old car. *217 North 100 West; 435-628-3737 or 800-600-3737; www.sevenwivesinn.com.* **$$$**

Scaldoni's
The great food makes up for the location in a strip mall. This eatery bills itself as an Italian "Gourmet Grocer and Grill," but the menu includes other fare besides Italian. *929 West Sunset Boulevard; 435-674-1300; www.scaldonis.com.* **$$**

■ SALT LAKE CITY

Anniversary Inn Salt City Jail
In a late-19th century brewery, this has been fabulously outfitted with 36 theme suites—the hotel restaurant used to be at the old Salt Lake City jail. *460 South 1000 East; 801-363-4900 or 800-324-4152; www.anniversaryinn.com.* **$$$$**

Anniversary Inn South Temple
Probably the most elegant place to stay in the Salt Lake area. The Kahn Mansion, built in the 1890s, has been remodeled into 14 theme suites, each of which has a large-screen television and VCR and a jetted tub. *678 East South Temple; 801-363-4953 or 800-324-4152; www.anniversaryinn.com.* **$$$$**

Grand America
Built to show off during the 2002 Winter Olympics, this deluxe 775-room hotel has posh fittings, indoor and outdoor pools, and a health club. The food at its restaurant is superb and the Sunday brunch is one of the best in the city. *555 South Main Street; 801-258-6000; www.grandamerica.com.* **$$$$**

Hilton Salt Lake City Center
With 499 rooms, this is one of the larger full-service hotels in Salt Lake City. Its location is convenient to the Salt Palace Convention Center and the city's restaurant and brewpub district. *255 South West Temple; 801-328-2000 or 800-445-8667.* **$$$**

Inn at Temple Square
The answer for those craving quiet elegance but tired of upscale chain hotels. Across the street from Temple Square and the Family History Library, and very close to Abravanel Hall; includes pool and health club privileges. Totally non-smoking. *71 West South Temple; 801-531-1000 or 800-843-4668; www.theinn.com.* **$$–$$$$**

Marriott Salt Lake City Downtown
Across the street from the Salt Palace Convention Center and adjacent to Temple Square, this 515-room hotel has business bustle; it features balconies, an indoor-outdoor pool, exercise room, and large suites. *75 South West Temple; 801-531-0800.* **$$$–$$$$**

Monaco

This sophisticated, modern hotel occupies a bank building dating from the 1920s; it is across from the Capitol Theatre and within walking distance of Temple Square and other downtown sights. The complimentary evening wine tasting in the lobby lets guests get to know each other. *14 West 200 South; 801-595-0000; www. monaco-saltlakecity.com.* **$$$–$$$$**

Peery Hotel

Built in 1910, this boutique hotel of 73 rooms has been handsomely restored to that era. Have a look at the elegant lobby even if you don't stay here—it's within walking distance of downtown sights. *110 West 300 South; 801-521-4300 or 800-331-0073; www.peeryhotel.com.* **$$–$$$$**

Saltair Bed & Breakfast

Utah's oldest continuously operated bed-and-breakfast. Guests sleep in antique brass or oak beds, and there's a hot tub on the redwood deck. Full breakfast. Some rooms include kitchen facilities. *164 South 900 East; 801-533-8184 or 800-733-8184.* **$$**

Wyndham Hotel

Among the city's newer hotels, and very convenient to the Salt Palace Convention Center and the Delta Center. Swimming pool; good restaurant. *215 West South Temple; 801-531-7500 or 800-553-0075.* **$$$–$$$$**

Baba Afghan

Though some meat is served, this is a good place for vegetarians. One of the city's best luncheon buffets and some fine Afghan curry dishes. *55 East 400 South; 801-596-0786* **$–$$**

Baci Trattoria

Gourmet Italian cuisine, outstanding antipasti, lively atmosphere. Sit indoors, in the pleasant dining room, or out on the patio. *134 West Pierpont Avenue; 801-328-1500.* **$$–$$$$**

Bambara

The class of the adjacent Hotel Monaco rubs off on this restaurant. Cuisine that matches the best restaurants in town is priced a little lower here, so diners return. *202 South Main Street; 801-363-5454; www.bambara-slc.com.* **$$$–$$$$**

Cafe Trang

A large menu, and some of Utah's best Vietnamese food. Chinese dishes are available as well. *818 South Main Street; 801-539-1638.* **$–$$**

The Cinegrill

Famous for its salad, a delightful creation heavy on garlic. Good, inexpensive Italian. *344 South 300 East; 801-328-4900.* **$–$$**

Five-Alls

A quiet atmosphere, consistently good service, and sophisticated cuisine. Filet Oscar is a filet mignon with asparagus tips, crabmeat, and bearnaise sauce. *1458 South Foothill Drive; 801-582-1400.* **$$$**

La Caille

This might be Utah's most elegant and expensive dining experience. Lush gardens, a flowing creek. and wonderful service make this the place to visit for a special event. *9565 South Wasatch Boulevard, Little Cottonwood Canyon; 801-942-1751; www.lacaille.com.* **$$$$**

Lamb's Grill Café

The city's oldest restaurant looks much as it did when it opened in the same building in 1939. The town's movers and shakers often meet here for breakfast or lunch. Try the Greek bread for a real treat. *169 South Main Street; 801-364-7166.* **$–$$$**

Log Haven

Enjoy the beautiful canyon setting from a table indoors or on the patio. Some of the best fusion cuisine in Salt Lake is served here, 4 miles up Millcreek Canyon—a 20-minute drive from downtown. *East Millcreek Canyon (3800 South); 801-272-8255; www.log-haven.com.* **$$$–$$$$**

Martine

The food is a work of art, and delicious. Spanish tapas (appetizers) are offered at dinner. *22 East 100 South; 801-363-9328.* **$$–$$$$**

The Metropolitan

Amid modern decor, a menu ranging from Asian-fusion to standard Rocky Mountain dishes is served in small, elegant portions. *173 West Broadway; 801-364-3472; www.themetropolitan.com.* **$$$$**

Red Iguana
Not much on atmosphere, but this place features Utah's best Mexican food. Instead of ordering something like tacos and enchiladas (which *are* good here), be adventurous and savor a mole dish. *736 West North Temple; 801-322-1489.* **$–$$**

Rodizio Grill
Waiters dressed as Argentine gauchos bring skewers of various grilled meats, chicken, vegetables, and sausage. The full meal includes a salad bar with the staples and some great specialties. Bring a big appetite! *600 South 700 East; 801-220-0500.* **$$**

The Roof
At the top of what was once the elegant Hotel Utah, but is today the Joseph Smith Memorial Building, holding Mormon Church offices. The Roof serves a dinner buffet with a variety of soups and salads, meat, seafood, and pasta entrees, cheeses, fresh fruits, and desserts. (No alcohol, coffee, or tea, however.) Nice views of Temple Square, too. *15 East South Temple; 801-539-1911.* **$$$–$$$$**

Ruth's Diner
Though lunch and dinner are also served here, this is a favorite Salt Lake gathering place for breakfast. Dining outside in the spring, summer, and fall is delightful. *2100 Emigration Canyon; 801-582-5807.* **$$**

Wagonmaster Steak House
Sit in a covered wagon and eat expertly prepared cowboy-style steak and chicken. Watch for the occasional gunfight. *5485 South Vine, Murray (south of town); 801-269-1100.* **$$–$$$**

■ VERNAL

Best Western Antlers
Modern hotel with indoor hot tub, exercise room, playground, and pool. *423 West Main Street; 435-789-1202.* **$$$**

Casa Rios
South-of-the-border cooking for lunch and dinner. Try the chicken fajitas. *2015 West U.S. 40; 435-789-0103.* **$–$$**

■ ZION NATIONAL PARK

Flanigan's Inn
A step above the franchise motels and restaurants in the area, and within walking distance of the Zion Canyon Visitor Center. Both modern and older units, a nice pool area, and a very good restaurant (see Spotted Dog Cafe below). *428 Zion Park Boulevard, Springdale; 435-772-3244 or 800-765-7787; www.flanigans.com.* **$$–$$$**

Harvest House Bed & Breakfast
This classic, two-story Western ranch house is just off the main drive through Springdale, a half-mile from the park entrance. Request the rooms with private decks that sit beneath the park's Watchman formation. *29 Canyon View Drive, Springdale; 435-772-3880; www.harvesthouse.net.* **$$$**

Under the Eaves Guest House
Beautiful views of Zion National Park. Besides the main house, built in the 1930s, there are terraced gardens and a garden cottage. *980 Zion Park Boulevard, Springdale; 435-772-3457; www.under-the-eaves.com.* **$$–$$$**

Zion Lodge
The only lodging in the park, this historic lodge is open year-round. The old cabins, with individual fireplaces, are popular, as are the more modern motel suites, so make reservations well in advance. *Zion National Park; 303-297-2757; www.zionlodge.com.* **$$–$$$**

Bit and Spur Restaurant and Saloon
Interesting Mexican dishes put this restaurant among the best south-of-the-border-style spots in the state. Music some weekends. *1212 Zion Park Boulevard, Springdale; 435-772-3498.* **$$–$$$**

Spotted Dog Cafe
The dining room at Flanigan's Inn—there's also a sidewalk café—serves American bistro-style cuisine, including wood-fired pizza, salads, pastas, and regional specialties such as local trout and Black Angus beef. Open for breakfast and dinner. *428 Zion Park Boulevard, Springdale; 435-772-3244 or 800-765-7787; www.flanigans.com.* **$$–$$$**

A spring and grotto in Zion National Park.

Switchback Grille

Large picture windows overlook Zion National Park, and Indian rugs add to the Southwestern decor. The wonderful menu features the freshest ingredients in thoughtfully prepared vegetarian dishes, wood-fired pizzas, and specialty fruit drinks. *1149 Zion Park Boulevard, Springdale; 435-772-3777; www. switchbackgrille.com.* **$$**

Zion Lodge Dining Room

Historic lodge offering traditional fare such as trout and rib eye, as well as good pastas. Great views of the park. Picnics can be ordered in advance. *Zion National Park; 435-722-3213. www.zionlodge.com.* **$$–$$$**

Zion Pizza and Noodle Company

In an old church. Stop in at the photography gallery downstairs before dinner. *868 Zion Park Boulevard, Springdale; 435-772-3815.* **$**

■ Utah's Public Lands

Utah almost literally belongs to the nation. Nearly 80 percent of its land is controlled by government agencies for such public uses as recreation, timber, and wildlife management; mineral leasing; and livestock grazing.

Before venturing into the state's thousands of miles of backcountry roads and trails, check with the administering agency about fire restrictions and other regulations. Permits are required in some BLM primitive areas. Travel maps listing places open to off-highway vehicle use are available from local U.S. Forest Service and BLM offices. Backpackers going into National Park Service–administered lands are required to pick up a free permit from a ranger station or visitors center. Camping in most national forests, national parks, recreation areas, and BLM lands is on a first-come, first-served basis. Large group sites, however, can be reserved in advance.

■ Boating and River Rafting

Although Utah is a dry state, it ranks in the nation's top 10 in surface acres of boatable waters. Powerboats and sail-craft must meet both Utah and Coast Guard regulations on reservoirs, lakes, and rivers. Some areas restrict the use of motors. For information, contact the Division of Parks and Recreation, the agency charged with managing boating in Utah. *801-538-7220; www.stateparks.utah.gov.*

The state also holds more than 400 miles of raftable rivers. Dozens of outfitters are eager to show visitors the state's white-water rapids and calm scenic waters. For more detailed information, contact the Utah Travel Council and request their free *Utah Travel Guide.* (See page 327.)

■ WILDLIFE VIEWING

While Utahns can enjoy watching wildlife in most parts of the state, few places in the world offer the diversity of the marshes that surround the east side of the Great Salt Lake. The huge federal Bear River Migratory Bird Refuge west of Brigham City and state-managed refuges such as Farmington Bay, Ogden Bay, Salt Creek, and Locomotive Springs host thousands of birds each year, including swans, stilts, avocets, waterfowl, eagles, hawks, peregrine falcons, and grebes. In the middle of the winter, for example, visitors to Willard Bay State Park can see dozens of bald eagles in the trees or working the water for fish. Add to this mix Antelope Island State Park, with its herd of 800 bison coupled with large mule deer, antelope, coyote, and bighorn sheep, and it is easy to find large numbers of wildlife to view within an hour's drive of the Wasatch Front.

In Northern Utah, a popular winter activity for many is to visit the Hardware Ranch, near Hyrum, where the Division of Wildlife Resources feeds elk in the winter. Visitors take a sleigh pulled by Clydesdale horses into the midst of the elk.

The federal Fish Springs National Wildlife Refuge on the Pony Express Trail in western Utah and the federal Ouray National Wildlife Refuge in eastern Utah offer excellent bird-watching opportunities. The Beaver Dam Wash area, in the extreme southwestern part of Utah, provides a look at desert bird life, especially in the winter months; the site is operated by Brigham Young University and the Nature Conservancy. This is a zone where the Great Basin, Colorado Plateau, and Mojave Desert meet, creating great diversity.

The state contains an extremely diverse selection of wildflowers. The different ecosystems and microclimates produce showy displays at all times of year, but April and May offer the biggest show. The Great Basin is carpeted with brilliant orange globemallow, and Canyonlands explodes with ephemeral wildflower shows, especially in wet years. Spring comes at different times at different altitudes, however. The Cottonwood canyons of the Wasatch Front host hundreds of wildflower enthusiasts in June and early July, after the snow melts and flowers bloom. The elusive state flower, the sego lily, blooms in the foothills of Utah in early June. Ubiquitous rabbitbrush covers the deserts of the Uinta Basin and Canyonlands with yellow flowers in September. Visit the Red Butte Garden Web site for specific flowering dates in each region: *www.redbuttegarden.org.*

■ FISHING AND HUNTING

Utah's fishing season—with a few exceptions—is year-round. Pick up a free fishing update for details on special regulations, limits, and license fees. Anglers can catch trout, bass, walleye, bluegill, whitefish, Bonneville cisco, yellow perch, crappie, and catfish. Hunting seasons are set for deer, elk, antelope, pheasant, duck, geese, sage grouse, forest grouse, chukar partridge, mourning dove, wild turkey, cottontail rabbit, and snowshoe hare. Special permits may be purchased to hunt bear, mountain lion, and bobcat. Once-in-a-lifetime permits for buffalo, desert bighorn sheep, moose, and Rocky Mountain goat are also available via special lottery drawings. Antelope and some deer and elk hunts are on a lottery basis only. Specific hunting regulations are issued annually by the Utah Division of Wildlife Resources. To hunt or fish in Utah, purchase a license at any Utah Division of Wildlife Resources office (see page 326) or in most sporting goods stores.

■ NATIONAL PARKS, MONUMENTS, HISTORIC SITES, AND RECREATION AREAS

Utah's national parks, monuments, recreation areas, and historic site are all open year-round. The road into Cedar Breaks National Monument does close in the winter months, but the monument can still be seen by skiers and snowmobilers. Some of the most popular parks are crowded in the summer, but there is always lodging and camping available in private facilities nearby. If you want to camp in Arches, Bryce, Capitol Reef, or Zion national parks in summer, arrive early in the day to assure yourself a space or, at Arches, Bryce, or Zion, make reservations ahead of time.

The **National Parks Pass,** valid for one year from the date of its first use, provides free admission to all the national parks. At those charging a per-vehicle fee, it covers the pass holder and accompanying passengers; at those charging a per-visitor fee, it covers the pass holder, spouse, children, and parents. It cost $50 in 2004 and it can be bought online at www.nps.gov. The **Golden Age Passport,** for persons over 62, and the **Golden Access Passport,** for the blind and permanently disabled, provide free or discounted entry to the national parks for a lifetime. These passports can be obtained at the parks or agency offices and provide a discount on campsites and other features where a use fee is charged.

Arches National Park. *P.O. Box 907, Moab, UT 84532; 435-719-2299; www.nps. gov/arch.*

Bryce Canyon National Park. *P.O. Box 17001, Bryce Canyon, UT 84717; 435-834-5322; www.nps.gov/brca.*

Canyonlands National Park. *2282 SW Resource Boulevard, Moab, UT 84532; 435-719-2313; www.nps.gov/cany.*

Capitol Reef National Park. *HC 70, P.O. Box 15, Torrey, UT 84775; 435-425-3791; www.nps.gov/care.*

Cedar Breaks National Monument. *2390 West Highway 56 #11, Cedar City, UT 84720; 435-586-9451; www.nps.gov/cebr.*

Dinosaur National Monument. *4545 East Highway 40, Dinosaur, CO 81610; 970-374-3000; www.nps.gov/dino.*

Flaming Gorge National Recreation Area. *P.O. Box 279, Manila, UT 84046; 435-784-3445; www.fs.fed.us/r4/ashley.*

Glen Canyon National Recreation Area. *P.O. Box 1507, Page, AZ 86040; 928-608-6404; www.nps.gov/glca.*

Golden Spike National Historic Site. *P.O. Box 897, Brigham City, UT 84302; 435-471-2209; www.nps.gov/gosp.*

Grand Staircase-Escalante National Monument. *190 East Center Street, Kanab, UT 84741; 435-644-4300; www.ut.blm.gov/monument.*

Hovenweep National Monument. *McElmo Route, Cortez, CO 81321; 970-562-4282; www.nps.gov/hove.*

Natural Bridges National Monument. *P.O. Box 1, Lake Powell, UT 84533; 435-692-1234; www.nps.gov/nabr.*

Timpanogos Cave National Monument. *RR 3, Box 200, American Fork, UT 84003; 801-756-5238; www.nps.gov/tica.*

Zion National Park. *State Route 9, Springdale, UT 84767; 435-772-3256; www. nps.gov/zion.*

■ NATIONAL FORESTS

Utah's six national forests—all nine-plus million acres of them—range from alpine peaks covered with aspen, pine, and fir to red-rock mountains rich with juniper, piñon, and ponderosa pine. Maps designating roads and areas open to off-highway motorized travel are available at ranger districts and supervisor offices throughout the state. *Campground reservations are available through: National Recreation Reservation Service, 877-444-6777; www.reserveusa.com.*

■ U.S. FOREST SERVICE VISITOR CENTER

Union Station, 2501 Wall Avenue, Ogden, UT 84401; 801-625-5306.

■ ASHLEY NATIONAL FOREST

Duchesne Ranger District. *85 West Main, Duchesne, UT 84021; 435-738-2482.*

Flaming Gorge Ranger District Headquarters. *P.O. Box 279, Manila, UT 84046; 435-784-3445.*

Roosevelt Ranger District. *650 West Highway 40, Box 333-6, Roosevelt, UT 84066; 435-722-5018.*

Vernal Ranger District. *355 North Vernal, Vernal, UT 84078; 435-789-1181.*

■ DIXIE NATIONAL FOREST

Cedar City Ranger District. *1789 Wedgewood Lane, Cedar City, UT 84720; 435-865-3200.*

Escalante Ranger District. *P.O. Box 246, Escalante UT 84726; 435-826-5400.*

Pine Valley Ranger District. *196 East Tabernacle, St.George, UT 84770; 435-688-3246.*

Powell Ranger District. *P.O. Box 80 Panguitch, UT 84759; 435-676-8815.*

Teasdale Ranger District. *P.O. Box 90, Teasdale, UT 84773; 435-425-9500.*

■ FISHLAKE NATIONAL FOREST

Beaver Ranger District. *575 South Main, Beaver, UT 84713; 435-438-2436.*

Fillmore Ranger District. *390 South Main, Fillmore, UT 84631; 435-743-5721.*

Loa Ranger District. *138 South Main, Loa, UT 84747; 435-836-2811.*

Richfield Ranger District. *115 East 900 North, Richfield, UT 84701; 435-896-9233.*

■ MANTI-LASAL NATIONAL FOREST

Ferron Ranger District. *115 West Canyon Road, Ferron, UT 84523; 435-384-2372.*

Moab Ranger District. *62 East 100 North, Moab, UT 84532; 435-259-7155.*

Monticello Ranger District. *496 East Central, Monticello, UT 84535; 435-587-2041.*

Price Ranger District. *599 West Price River Drive, Price, UT 84501; 435-637-2817.*

Sanpete Ranger District. *540 North Main Street, Ephraim, UT 84627; 435-283-4151.*

■ UINTA NATIONAL FOREST

Main Office. *88 West 100 North, Provo, UT 84601; 801-342-5100.*

Heber Ranger District. *2460 South Highway 40, P.O. Box 190, Heber City, UT 84032; 435-654-0470.*

Pleasant Grove Ranger District. *390 North 100 East, Pleasant Grove, UT 84062; 801-342-5240.*

Spanish Fork Ranger District. *44 West 400 North, Spanish Fork, UT 84660; 801-342-5260.*

■ WASATCH-CACHE NATIONAL FOREST

Main Office. *8226 Federal Building, 125 South Street, Salt Lake City, UT 84138; 801-524-3900.*

Kamas Ranger District. *50 East Center Street, P.O. Box 68, Kamas, UT 84036; 435-783-4338.*

Logan Ranger District. *1500 East Highway 89 Logan, UT 84321; 435-755-3620.*

Ogden Ranger District. *507 25th Street, Ogden, UT 84401; 801-625-5112.*

Salt Lake City District. *6944 South 3000 East, Salt Lake City, UT 84121; 801-733-2660.*

■ BUREAU OF LAND MANAGEMENT

The Bureau of Land Management (BLM) administers approximately half the land in Utah, including Grand Staircase–Escalante National Monument. Off-road vehicle use, hiking, and camping are popular in most of these areas. The BLM administers river rafting in both Desolation and Westwater canyons on the Green and Colorado rivers, as well as in a number of primitive areas. Several million acres of BLM land are under consideration for national wilderness area designation. The BLM offices located throughout the state often are a good source for topographical maps and advice on hiking and camping conditions. Popular developed BLM recreation sites, like the Little Sahara Sand Dunes near Delta, the Dixie Red Cliffs near St. George, and the Calf Creek area near Escalante, give campers a chance to get away from the crowds often found in nearby national and state parks. *www.ut.blm.gov.*

Utah State Office. *2370 South 2300 West, Salt Lake City, UT 84119; 801-977-4300.*

Cedar City District Office. *176 East D.L. Sargent Drive, Cedar City, UT 84720; 435-586-2401.*

Fillmore Field Office. *35 East 500 North, Fillmore, UT 84631; 435-743-3100.*

Grand Staircase–Escalante National Monument, Interagency Office. *190 Center Street, Kanab, UT 84741; 435-644-4300. (Also Cannonville Visitor Center: 10 Center Street, Cannonville, UT 84718; 435-679-8980.)*

Kanab Field Office. *318 North First East, Kanab, UT 84741; 435-644-4600.*

Henry Mountains Field Station. *P.O. Box 99, Hanksville, UT 84734; 435-542-3461.*

Moab Field Office. *82 East Dogwood, P.O. Box 970, Moab, UT 84532; 435-259-2100.*

The primrose in bloom in the Henry Mountains, on BLM land near Hanksville.

Monticello Field Office. *435 North Main Street, Monticello, UT 84535; 435-587-1500.*

Price Field Office. *125 South 600 West, Price, UT 84501; 435-636-3600.*

Richfield Field Office. *150 East 900 North, Richfield, UT 84701; 435-896-1500.*

St. George Field Office. *345 East Riverside Drive, St. George, UT 84720; 435-688-3200.*

Salt Lake Field Office. *2370 South 2300 West, Salt Lake City, UT 84119; 801-977-4300.*

Vernal District Office. *170 South 500 East, Vernal, UT 84078; 435-781-4400.*

■ **UTAH DIVISION OF PARKS AND RECREATION**
The Utah Division of Parks and Recreation administers approximately 40 developed state parks. They contain individual or group campsites and facilities for boating, hiking, off-highway vehicle use, and other outdoor sports. In addition, several parks contain cultural and natural history museums. *801-538-7220; or for camping reservations: 800-322-3770; www.stateparks.utah.gov.*

■ **UTAH DIVISION OF WILDLIFE RESOURCES**
Recorded information: 877-592-5169; www.wildlife.utah.gov.

Salt Lake Office. *1594 West North Temple, Salt Lake City, UT 84114; 801-538-4700.*

Central Region. *1115 North Main Street, Springville, UT 84663; 801-491-5678.*

Northeastern Region. *152 East 100 North, Vernal, UT 84078; 435-781-9453.*

Northern Region. *515 East 5300 South, Ogden, UT 84405; 801-476-2740.*

Southeastern Region. *475 West Price River Drive, Suite C, Price, UT 84501; 435-636-0260.*

Southern Region. *Mailing address: P.O. Box 606, Cedar City, UT 84721. Building address: 470 North Airport Road, Cedar City, UT 84720; 435-865-6100.*

■ **PROFESSIONAL SPORTS**

Ogden Raptors
The Pioneer Baseball League's Ogden Raptors play at Lindquist Field in Ogden. *2330 Lincoln Avenue, Ogden; 801-393-2400 or Smith'sTix: 800-888-8499; www. ogden-raptors.com.*

Salt Lake Stingers
Salt Lake City's Franklin Covey Field is the home of the AAA Pacific Coast League's Salt Lake Stingers, a minor-league baseball team affiliated with the Anaheim Angels. *77 West 1300 South, Salt Lake City; 801-485-3800 or Smith'sTix: 800-888-8499; www.stingersbaseball.com.*

Utah Blitzz
This United Soccer League team plays in the Rice-Eccles Stadium at the University of Utah. *451 South 1400 East, Salt Lake City; 801-401-8000 or Smith'sTix: 800-888-8499; www.utahblitzz.com.*

Utah Grizzlies
A professional hockey team in the International Hockey League, the Utah Grizzlies play in the E Center. *3200 South Decker Lake Drive, West Valley City; 801-988-8888 or Smith'sTix: 800-888-8499; www.utahgrizzlies.com.*

Utah Jazz
The NBA's Utah Jazz play in the Delta Center. *301 West South Temple, Salt Lake City; 801-325-7328; www.nba.com/jazz.*

■ OFFICIAL TOURISM INFORMATION

Utah Travel Council. *801-538-1030 or 800-200-1160; www.utah.com.*

Moab Area Travel Council. *435-259-8825 or 800-635-6622; www.discovermoab.com.*

Park City Chamber of Commerce/Convention and Visitors Bureau. *435-649-6100 or 800-453-1360; www.parkcityinfo.com.*

St. George Area Chamber of Commerce. *435-628-1658; www.stgeorgechamber.com.*

Salt Lake Convention and Visitors Bureau. *801-521-2822 or 800-541-4955; www.visitsaltlake.com.*

■ USEFUL WEB SITES

Church of Jesus Christ of Latter-day Saints. An official church site for those who want to learn more about its basic doctrines, history, and organization. *www.mormon.org.*

Church of Jesus Christ of Latter-day Saints. Another official church site, for members. *www.lds.org.*

FamilySearch. The search for your ancestors begins at this LDS genealogy site. *www.familysearch.org.*

Mormon Tabernacle Choir. Choir facts, plus info on its touring schedule. *www.mormontabernaclechoir.org.*

Salt Lake Tribune. Online version of the daily paper (with Pat Bagley's editorial cartoons just a click away). *www.sltrib.com.*

UDOT. Information on road conditions and construction sites, from the Utah Department of Transportation. *www.dot.state.ut.us.*

Utah Arts Council. General information about Utah arts organizations. *www.arts.utah.gov.*

Utah.gov. The official site of the State of Utah. *www.utah.gov.*

Utah Heritage Foundation. Nonprofit organization that offers guided tours of historic buildings and downloadable self-guided tours. *www.utahheritagefoundation.com.*

Utah History To Go. The nitty-gritty on everything, courtesy of the Utah State Historical Society. *historytogo.utah.gov.*

■ FESTIVALS AND EVENTS

■ JANUARY

Bluff International Balloon Festival. Hot air balloonists gather from all over the country to enjoy the amazing scenery from above the Valley of the Gods. *435-672-2446.*

Sundance Film Festival, Park City. Premieres the works of independent filmmakers; takes place mainly in Park City, but also in Salt Lake City and at Sundance. *801-328-3456 or 877-733-9497 for tickets; festival.sundance.org.*

■ FEBRUARY

Utah Special Olympics Games, Ogden. Athletes participate in a variety of events aimed at their skill level. *801-626-6349.*

■ **MARCH**

Canyon Country Western Arts Festival, Cedar City. Cowboy poets, quilters, potters, and other Western artists populate this festival, which celebrates the best of the West. *435-586-5124; www.westernartsfestival.org.*

Easter Jeep Safari, Moab. Join thousands of 4WD enthusiasts on the backcountry trails surrounding Moab. *435-259-7625; www.rr4w.com.*

■ **APRIL**

Rod Benders Car Show, Moab. Classic cars fill the streets. *435-259-5858; www.moab-utah.com/aprilaction.*

■ **MAY**

Living Traditions Festival, Salt Lake City. Celebration of folk and ethnic arts, food, music, and dancing. *801-533-5760.*

Scandinavian Heritage Festival, Ephraim. Celebrates the food, crafts, and dancing of Scandinavian settlers in Utah. *www.scandinavianheritagefestival.com.*

■ **JUNE**

Bear River Bird Festival, Brigham City. Held at the Bear River Migratory Bird Refuge. *435-723-5886.*

Mormon Miracle Pageant, Manti. Utah's biggest outdoor pageant: Mormon history told in musical drama. *435-835-3000 or 888-255-8860; www.mormonmiracle.org.*

Utah Arts Festival, Salt Lake City. Outdoor performances and art exhibits. *801-322-2428.*

Utah Shakespearean Festival, Cedar City. Enjoy plays by the Bard in a replica of the Globe Theatre. June to October. *435-586-7880 or 800-752-9849; www.bard.org.*

■ **JULY**

America's Freedom Festival, Provo. Arts, crafts, food, country music, and fireworks are part of this four-day celebration of America's freedom. *801-370-8052; www.freedomfestival.org.*

Days of '47, Salt Lake City. Month-long celebration honoring the 1847 arrival of the Mormon pioneers in Salt Lake Valley. Rodeo, pops concert, Western heritage art show, and old-fashioned picnics. Also features one of the largest parades in the country. *801-250-3890; www.daysof47.com.*

Northern Ute 4th of July Pow Wow, Fort Duchesne. Authentic Native American arts and crafts, food, dancing, rodeo, and other cultural activities are part of this festival, which has been taking place for nearly 40 years. *435-722-8541.*

Pioneer Days, statewide. On July 24, from Salt Lake City to the tiniest rural communities, Utah celebrates its heritage with parades and wholesome parties. For a complete list of celebrations visit *www.utah.com.*

Utah Festival of the American West, Logan. Re-created Frontier Street and Native American village, crafts fair, cowboy poetry, World Championship Dutch Oven Cook-off, Western-style entertainment. *435-797-1143.*

Utah Symphony Summer Series at Sundance. Some of Utah's best music in a gorgeous mountain setting. *801-223-4272; www.sundanceresort.com.*

■ AUGUST
Park City Kimball Arts Festival. Art exhibits and entertainment on historic Main Street. *435-649-8882; www.kimball-art.org/artsfestival.*

Railroader's Festival, Golden Spike National Historic Site, Promontory. Railroad spike–driving contests are the highlight of this one-of-a-kind festival held the second Saturday in August. *435-471-2209.*

Speed Week, Bonneville Salt Flats. Land speed racing. *801-977-4300; www.roadsters.com/bonneville.*

■ SEPTEMBER
Green River Melon Days. Join the parade and eat some of the best melons in the nation. *435-564-8225.*

Moab Music Festival. Chamber music is performed against a backdrop of Canyonlands red rock. *435-259-7003; www.moabmusicfest.org.*

Swiss Days, Midway. Celebrates the Swiss heritage and customs of Heber Valley. *435-654-1576.*

Utah State Fair, Salt Lake City. Ten-day festival including rodeo. *801-538-3247; www.utah-state-fair.com.*

■ OCTOBER

Moab Fat Tire Festival. Bicycle rides and events for all ages in the town that practically invented mountain biking. *435-260-1182; www.moabfattirefestival.com.*

■ NOVEMBER

America's Opening, Park City. Ski racing and exhibitions. *435-649-8111.*

Festival of Trees, Salt Lake City. *801-588-3684.*

Temple Square Christmas Lighting, Salt Lake City. *801-240-1000.*

■ DECEMBER

Electric Light Parade, Helper. A parade featuring floats adorned with Christmas lights. *435-472-5391.*

Electric Light Parade, Moab. The whole town gets in on the act, building floats or decorating their houses with Christmas lights. *435-259-7814.*

Hof Winter Carnival, Ogden. Ogden celebrates German traditions with its sister city, Hof. *801-399-8491.*

RECOMMENDED READING

■ DESCRIPTION AND TRAVEL

Abbey, Edward. *Desert Solitaire* (1968). One of Abbey's most prized essay collections, much of it describing Arches National Monument. River-runners also like to quote from *Down the River* (1982), in which Abbey describes his travels down the rivers and through the deserts of the West.

Rusho, W. L. *Everett Ruess: A Vagabond for Beauty* (1985). A collection of the young wanderer's letters home, sent before his disappearance in the Utah desert in 1934.

Till, Tom. *In the Land of Moab* (2001). Photographs and essays of the Canyonlands and Arches national parks areas.

Van Cott, John W. *Utah Place Names* (1990). How Utah towns and geographic features got their names.

Zwinger, Ann. *Run, River, Run: A Naturalist's Journey Down One of the Great Rivers of the American West* (1975). The author's experiences along the Green and Colorado rivers mixed with her knowledge of geology, Indian ruins, plants, and wildlife.

■ HISTORY AND ARCHAEOLOGY

Cuch, Forrest S., ed. *A History of Utah's American Indians* (2000). Finally, a history written by representatives of each of the state's six official tribes.

Fradkin, Philip L. *A River No More* (1981). Historical account of water usage in Utah.

Kelner, Alexis. *Skiing in Utah: A History* (1980). Full of anecdotes as well as facts.

LeBlanc, Steven A. *Prehistoric Warfare in the American Southwest* (1999). Controversial new information and theories about the ancient Pueblo Indians.

Morgan, Dale L. *The Great Salt Lake* (1947). History of the lake written before the development of the late 20th century.

Powell, John Wesley. *The Exploration of the Colorado River and Its Canyons* (1895). First published in 1895, Powell's descriptions are still a must for all river lovers.

Reisner, Marc. *Cadillac Desert: The American West and Its Disappearing Water* (1986). A history of water use in the West and, as its title implies, a warning.

Rutter, Michael, *Outlaw Tales of Utah: True Stories of Utah's Most Famous Rustlers, Robbers, and Bandits* (2002). Butch Cassidy is Utah's most famous outlaw. This book introduces you to others.

Schindler, Harold. *In Another Time: Sketches of Utah History* (1998). A series of features first published in the *Salt Lake Tribune.*

Stegner, Wallace. *Beyond the Hundredth Meridian* (1954). A biography of John Wesley Powell, the man who first explored the Colorado River, by the "dean of Western writers."

Wharton, Gayen, and Tom Wharton. *It Happened in Utah.* 1998. Twenty-six events that shaped the state.

■ BICYCLING, CLIMBING, HIKING, SKIING, AND CAMPING

Bjornstad, Eric. *Desert Rock I: Rock Climbing in the National Parks* (1996), *Desert Rock II: Wall Street to the San Rafael Swell* (1997), *Desert Rock III: Moab to Colorado National Monument* (1999), and *Desert Rock IV: The Colorado Plateau Backcountry* (2003). Descriptions of climbing routes.

Bromka, Gregg. *Mountain Biking Utah* (1999). More than 100 rides, from the Wasatch Front to Southern Utah.

Hall, David. *The Hiker's Guide to Utah, Revised* (1995). Day and overnight hikes all over Utah, ranging in difficulty.

Kelner, Alexis, and David Hanscom. *Wasatch Tours* Vols. I (1993), II (1995), and III (1998). First published in 1976, these provide a comprehensive look at ski touring in the Wasatch Mountains, with maps, trails, and avalanche information.

Veranth, John. *Hiking the Wasatch* (1999). Hiking trails of varying difficulty through the Wasatch Mountains east of Salt Lake City.

Wharton, Gayen, and Tom Wharton. *Utah Camping* (2001). Details and reservation information for more than 400 campgrounds.

■ GEOLOGY AND NATURAL HISTORY

Baars, Donald L. *Canyonlands Country: Geology of Canyonlands and Arches National Parks* (1994). An introduction to what makes the area special.

Bagley, Pat, and Gayen Wharton. *Dinosaurs of Utah and Dino Destinations.* (2001). The most recent information on dinosaurs found in Utah, with fanciful illustrations by the *Salt Lake Tribune*'s editorial cartoonist.

Chronic, Halka. *Roadside Geology of Utah* (2003). A road guide to the state's rocks and landforms.

Shaw, Richard J. *Utah Wildflowers* (1995). A guide to the state's wildflowers, complete with color photographs.

Tekiela, Stan. *Birds of Utah: Field Guide* (2003). Photos and other information for identifying the birds you'll see in Utah.

Williams, David. *A Naturalist's Guide to Canyon Country* (2000). A comprehensive guide to plants, birds, mammals, lizards and everything that lives in southeastern Utah. Beautifully illustrated.

■ MISCELLANEOUS

Lyon, Thomas, and Terry Tempest Williams, eds. *A Great and Peculiar Beauty: A Utah Reader* (1995). Essays and excerpts from fiction and nonfiction about Utah by diverse Utahns of every era.

Williams, Terry Tempest. *Refuge: An Unnatural History of Family and Place* (1991). A personal look at the "dying" of the Great Salt Lake waterfowl refuges, told as the narrator's mother dies of cancer (after having been exposed to fallout from atomic testing in the 1950s).

■ MORMONS

Arrington, Leonard. *Brigham Young: American Moses* (1985). The author was a former head of the church's history division, but this bio is objective and readable.

Brodie, Fawn M. *No Man Knows My History: The Life of Joseph Smith* (1945). Published in 1945 and revised in 1970, this biography is controversial and a classic.

Burton, Sir Richard F. *The City of the Saints: Among the Mormons and Across the Rocky Mountains to California.* (1861). The British explorer spent three weeks in Salt Lake City and filed an even-handed, thorough, and entertaining report.

Freeman, Judith. *Red Water* (2002) A historical novel in which the life of polygamist John D. Lee is told—beautifully—from the point of view of three of his wives.

Grey, Zane. *Riders of the Purple Sage* (1912). Considered Grey's best, this novel deals with polygamy in Utah and a natural wonder, Rainbow Bridge.

Krakauer, Jon. *Under the Banner of Heaven* (2003). Krakauer investigates religious fanatics who use Mormon theology as an excuse to kill.

Ostling, Richard, and Joan K. Ostling. *Mormon America: The Power and the Promise* (2000). An outgrowth of a 1997 *Time* magazine article, this overview of the church by outsiders is respectful and enormously informative.

Stegner, Wallace. *Mormon Country* (1942). A good look into the Mormon culture of Utah, which hasn't changed much in the decades since the book was written.

Twain, Mark. *Roughing It* (1872). Twain's travels through Utah occupy only a few chapters of this account of his trip through the West, but that's enough for him to poke fun at the Mormons he meets.

Harry Longbaugh, a.k.a. the Sundance Kid, and Etta Place.

INDEX

COMPASS AMERICAN GUIDES

Alaska	Kentucky	Oregon Wine Country
American Southwest	Las Vegas	Pacific Northwest
Arizona	Maine	Pennsylvania
Boston	Manhattan	San Francisco
California Wine Country	Massachusetts	Santa Fe
Cape Cod	Michigan	South Carolina
Chicago	Minnesota	South Dakota
Coastal California	Montana	Tennessee
Colorado	Montréal	Texas
Connecticut & Rhode Island	Nevada	Utah
Florida	New Hampshire	Vermont
Georgia	New Mexico	Virginia
Gulf South	New Orleans	Washington Wine Country
Hawaii	North Carolina	Wisconsin
Idaho	Oregon	Wyoming

COMPASS AMERICAN GUIDES

Critics, booksellers, and travelers all agree: you're lost without a Compass.

"This splendid series provides exactly the sort of historical and cultural detail about North American destinations that curious-minded travelers need."
—*Washington Post*

"This is a series that constantly stuns us . . . no guide with photos this good should have writing this good. But it does." —*New York Daily News*

"Of the many guidebooks on the market, few are as visually stimulating, as thoroughly researched, or as lively written as the Compass American Guide series."
—*Chicago Tribune*

"Good to read ahead of time, then take along so you don't miss anything."
—*San Diego Magazine*

"Magnificent photography. First rate."—*Money*

"Written by longtime residents of each destination . . . these handsome and literate guides are strong on history and culture, and illustrated with gorgeous photos."
—*San Francisco Chronicle*

"The color photographs sparkle, the archival illustrations illuminate windows to the past, and the writing is usually of the utmost caliber." —*Michigan Tribune*

"Class acts, worth reading and shelving for keeps even if you're not a traveler. "
—*New Orleans Times-Picayune*

"Beautiful photographs and literate writing are the hallmarks of the Compass guides." —*Nashville Tennessean*

"History, geography, and wanderlust converge in these well-conceived books."
—*Raleigh News & Observer*

"Oh, my goodness! What a gorgeous series this is."—*Booklist*

ACKNOWLEDGMENTS

■ **FROM THE AUTHORS**

For the first edition: We would like to thank editor Barry Parr for patiently reviewing and re-reviewing our manuscript. Not only was Barry an editor, he was a friend. Tom Till's fine photographs reveal the diversity of Utah's landscapes. We also wish to thank the following individuals: Bob Donohoe, our expert reader, for invaluable advice; Gary Topping, Manuscripts Curator of the Utah State Historical Society; and the society's Photograph and Map Librarian, Susan Whetstone, who helped us track down the historical photos used in the book. The late Dr. William Lee Stokes, our geology professor at the University of Utah, graciously edited our text for accuracy. Mark Goodwin of U.C. Berkeley, contributed much on the subject of dinosaurs. Other institutions providing invaluable help include: Utah Division of Wildlife Resources, Utah Division of Parks and Recreation, National Park Service, U.S. Forest Service, Bureau of Land Management, Utah Symphony & Opera, Ririe-Woodbury Dance Company, Ballet West, Pioneer Memorial Theatre, Salt Lake Acting Company, Repertory Dance Theater, University of Utah, Brigham Young University, Utah State University, Weber State College, and Southern Utah State College. Tom's long-time employer, the *Salt Lake Tribune,* has given him a chance to explore Utah over the course of decades. For this, he is extremely grateful. Finally, we would like to thank our children—Emma, Jacob, Rawl, and Bryer—for putting up with their parents' book-writing effort, which took precious time away from family activities.

■ From the Publisher

Compass American Guides would like to thank Rachel Elson for copyediting the manuscript, Ellen Klages for proofreading it, and Joan Stout for indexing it.

All photographs in this book are by Tom Till unless noted below. Compass American Guides would also like to thank the following individuals and institutions for the use of their photographs or illustrations:

Overview
Page 9, Kerrick James

The First Utahns
Page 25, Yale Collection of Western Americana, Beinecke Rare Book and Manuscript Library
Page 42, Utah State Historical Society

The Early Explorers
Page 47, Utah State Historical Society
Page 52, Denver Public Library, Western History Collection, Noah H. Rose (Call # X-32269)
Page 56, Utah State Historical Society
Pages 58–59, Utah State Historical Society

The Mormon Pioneers
Page 60, Library of Congress Prints and Photographs Division
Page 65, Utah State Historical Society
Page 66, Church of Jesus Christ of Latter-day Saints Archives
Page 67, North Wind Picture Archives
Page 68, Utah State Historical Society
Page 71, Yale Collection of Western Americana, Beinecke Rare Book and Manuscript Library
Pages 72–73, © Intellectual Reserve, Inc./Museum of Church History and Art
Page 79, Utah State Historical Society
Page 82, Utah State Historical Society
Page 84, Special Collections Dept., J. Willard Marriott Library, University of Utah (Thorne Photo Studio Collection, P0272)

Salt Lake City

Pages 90–91, Kerrick James
Pages 94–95, Library of Congress Geography and Map Division
Page 98, Richard Cummins/The Viesti Collection, Inc.
Page 101, Utah State Historical Society
Page 102, Richard Cummins/The Viesti Collection, Inc.
Page 105 bottom, L. Tom Perry Special Collections/Harold B. Lee Library/Brigham Young University
Page 107, © Intellectual Reserve, Inc.
Page 108, © Intellectual Reserve, Inc.
Page 114, Richard Cummins/The Viesti Collection, Inc.
Page 117, Eric Schramm/Salt Lake Convention and Visitors Bureau
Page 121, Utah Museum of Fine Arts, Gift of Mr. and Mrs. Alan B. Blood, Museum # 1996.54.1
Pages 128–129, Richard Cummins/The Viesti Collection, Inc.

The Wasatch Front

Page 143, James Devaney/WireImage.com
Page 144, Fred Hayes/WireImage.com
Page 151, Utah State Historical Society

Northeastern Utah

Pages 170–171, Kerrick James

Great Basin

Page 185, Utah State Historical Society
Page 187, Utah State Historical Society
Page 199, Utah State Historical Society

Southern Utah

Page 226, Kerrick James
Page 263, Waldo Ruess

Skiing Utah
Page 267, Chris Deaver/Brian Head Resort
Page 270, Special Collections Dept., J. Willard Marriott Library, University of Utah
    (Einer Fredbo Collection, P0686)
Page 278, Eric Schramm/Park City Mountain Resort
Pages 284–285, Kerrick James

Recommended Reading
Page 335, Utah State Historical Society

■ About the Authors

Tom and Gayen Wharton are natives of Utah who have spent much of their lives exploring and enjoying the many cultural and recreational opportunities found in their state. The Whartons both graduated with honors from the University of Utah, where Gayen earned her degree in education and Tom studied journalism.

Tom is now the travel editor of the *Salt Lake Tribune,* where he has worked since 1970. His first book, *Utah! A Family Travel Guide,* appeared in 1987. He is a past president of the Outdoor Writers Association of America and has captured numerous national and local awards for his journalism. Gayen taught elementary school for eight years, and has been active in a number of community service projects. She co-authored the book *Dinosaurs of Utah and Dino Destinations* with Pat Bagley.

Tom and Gayen have four children and two grandchildren.

■ About the Photographer

Tom Till, a resident of Moab, Utah, is one of America's most published photographers. His work has appeared in *National Geographic, Time, Smithsonian,* the *New York Times,* and thousands of other publications. He has been sole photographer for 30 books, including *Plateau Province, In the Land of Moab,* and *Great Ghosts of the West.* Till has won many awards for his photographic work, including a special award for conservation photography from the Nature Conservancy. Though best known for his Southwestern work, Till has photographed landscape, nature, and travel subjects in all 50 states and on every continent. Tom lives with wife, Marcy, and son, Bryce, in Spirit Canyon.